PERSPECTIVES ON
A U.S.-CANADIAN
FREE TRADE AGREEMENT

ROBERT M. STERN
PHILIP H. TREZISE
JOHN WHALLEY
Editors

PERSPECTIVES ON A U.S.-CANADIAN FREE TRADE AGREEMENT

Based on a conference jointly sponsored by
the Institute of Public Policy Studies at
the University of Michigan and the Centre
for the Study of International Economic Relations
at the University of Western Ontario

THE INSTITUTE FOR RESEARCH
ON PUBLIC POLICY
Ottawa, Ontario

THE BROOKINGS INSTITUTION
Washington, D.C.

Library of Congress Cataloging in Publication data

Perspectives on a U.S.-Canadian free trade agreement.
Includes bibliographical references and index.
  1. Tariff—Law and legislation—Canada.   2. Duty-free
importation—Law and legislation—Canada.   3. Tariff—
Law and legislation—United States.   4. Duty-free importa-
tion—Law and legislation—United States.   I. Stern,
Robert Mitchell, 1927–   II. Trezise, Philip H.,
1912–   III. Whalley, John.
KF6668.C3P47   1987   382.9'71073   87-17657
ISBN 0-8157-8132-6
ISBN 0-8157-8131-8 (pbk.)

9 8 7 6 5 4 3 2 1

THE BROOKINGS INSTITUTION is an independent organization devoted to nonpartisan research, education, and publication in economics, government, foreign policy, and the social sciences generally. Its principal purposes are to aid in the development of sound public policies and to promote public understanding of issues of national importance.

The Institution was founded on December 8, 1927, to merge the activities of the Institute for Government Research, founded in 1916, the Institute of Economics, founded in 1922, and the Robert Brookings Graduate School of Economics and Government, founded in 1924.

The Board of Trustees is responsible for the general administration of the Institution, while the immediate direction of the policies, program, and staff is vested in the President, assisted by an advisory committee of the officers and staff. The by-laws of the Institution state: "It is the function of the Trustees to make possible the conduct of scientific research, and publication, under the most favorable conditions, and to safeguard the independence of the research staff in the pursuit of their studies and in the publication of the results of such studies. It is not a part of their function to determine, control, or influence the conduct of particular investigations or the conclusions reached."

The President bears final responsibility for the decision to publish a manuscript as a Brookings book. In reaching his judgment on the competence, accuracy, and objectivity of each study, the President is advised by the director of the appropriate research program and weighs the views of a panel of expert outside readers who report to him in confidence on the quality of the work. Publication of a work signifies that it is deemed a competent treatment worthy of public consideration but does not imply endorsement of conclusions or recommendations.

The Institution maintains its position of neutrality on issues of public policy in order to safeguard the intellectual freedom of the staff. Hence interpretations or conclusions in Brookings publications should be understood to be solely those of the authors and should not be attributed to the Institution, to its trustees, officers, or other staff members, or to the organizations that support its research.

Foreword

WHEN THE General Agreement on Tariffs and Trade was negotiated in 1947, its drafters provided for the possibility that some of the signatories might eventually wish to group themselves in smaller free trade arrangements. The leading examples of such less encompassing agreements have been the European Community's Common Market or customs union and the European Free Trade Association's free trade area.

In 1986 Canada and the United States began negotiations for the comprehensive elimination of their mutual trade barriers, an undertaking that was widely labeled as "historic." Since the founding of the Canadian Confederation in 1867, the two governments have periodically discussed a free trade treaty and each time have backed away out of concern for the possible political consequences. In the meantime, despite a commercial border marked by numerous government-installed obstacles, Canada and the United States have developed the largest bilateral economic relationship in the world. Full-scale free trade between these similar yet disparate countries, if achieved, would warrant the "historic" appellation.

The papers in this volume examine the implications of regional free trade in North America. They were presented by Canadian and American specialists at a conference sponsored by the University of Michigan and the University of Western Ontario held in London, Ontario, in April 1985, as the bilateral free trade talks were about to begin. Questions abound. What gains are to be expected from free trade between countries whose tariffs, on average, are already low? How will the gains be shared? Can a trade agreement accommodate differing ideas about the appropriate role for government in private-sector decisionmaking? What about the impact on third-country trade, especially that of the developing countries? Can barriers to trade in agricultural goods be reduced, let alone eliminated, given the extent to which production is subsidized and otherwise governmentally managed on both sides of the border? These and other difficult issues will have to be addressed in the text of the formal treaty-like agreement that the U.S. Congress and the Canadian Parliament would in due course be asked to consider.

Robert Stern is professor of economics and public policy and head of the international program of the Institute of Public Policy Studies at the University of Michigan; Philip Trezise is a senior fellow in the Foreign Policy Studies program at the Brookings Institution; and John Whalley is William G. Davis Professor of International Trade and director of the Centre for the Study of International Economic Relations at the University of Western Ontario. The editors are indebted to Nancy Davidson for editing a diverse group of essays; to Janet Smith for secretarial assistance; to Eric Stein for verifying factual content; and to Diana Regenthal for preparing the index.

The conference on which this volume was based and the publication itself were funded in part by the Donner Foundation of Canada and the Institute for Research on Public Policy in Ottawa. Brookings is grateful for their support.

The views expressed here are those of the authors and the conference participants and should not be attributed to the supporting foundations, the institutions with which the participants are affiliated, or the trustees, officers, and other staff members of the Brookings Institution.

BRUCE K. MACLAURY
President

June 1987
Washington, D.C.

Contents

PERSPECTIVES ON
A U.S.-CANADIAN
FREE TRADE AGREEMENT

PHILIP H. TREZISE

U.S.-Canadian Free Trade: An Idea Whose Time Has Come?

AS AN IDEA, Canadian-American free trade has had a long life, full of disappointments but surprisingly enduring. In 1854, before confederation in Canada, Great Britain negotiated on behalf of its North American colonies a reciprocity treaty with the United States providing for the mutual elimination of tariffs on a substantial range of tradable goods. The Elgin-Marcy treaty had a short existence, for the United States chose to abrogate it within a dozen years of its signing.

A new version of the reciprocity treaty was soon agreed upon by the recently established confederation of Canada and the United States, only to fail of ratification in the U.S. Senate in 1874. Periodically thereafter one side or the other has revived the idea, never successfully. In 1911 there was a near miss, when the United States proposed and the Ottawa government agreed to remove duties from much of bilateral trade. But an election in Canada intervened, the incumbent Liberals lost, and there the matter ended. After World War II, again at Washington's initiative, an understanding on a far-reaching agreement reportedly was reached at staff level before Prime Minister Mackenzie King decided that the uncertainties in both countries made further action inadvisable.

Even before the war, Washington and Ottawa had begun to edge away from the high tariff policies that in Canada dated from 1879 and in the United States, in their most recent manifestation, from the Republican electoral victory in 1920. Tariff concessions were exchanged in 1935 and

1

1938 under the new U.S. Reciprocal Trade Agreements Act and after the war in a series of negotiations held under the umbrella of the General Agreement on Tariffs and Trade (GATT). The impact of these bargained tariff reductions was powerfully reinforced in 1965, when a bilateral agreement was reached to eliminate tariffs on most automobiles and their component parts. This led to a very large increase in bilateral trade and in the share of that trade moving free of duties. With the additional tariff cuts agreed to during the GATT negotiations in the 1970s, it is estimated that 80 percent of American imports from Canada and 65 percent of Canadian imports from the United States will be duty free once the GATT reductions have been completed in 1987.

Meanwhile, the idea of a more comprehensive free trade arrangement lay seemingly dormant. Sperry Lea recalls in his retrospective essay that in the early 1960s private Canadians and Americans felt obliged to avoid using the word "free" when discussing bilateral trade for fear of arousing opposition in Canada. And the automobile agreement, whatever its originators may have hoped, remained *sui generis*. After a while, even discussion of its trade-hampering "safeguards" was allowed to lapse in the face of Canadian unwillingness to consider any further liberalization of its provisions.

During the 1970s, when Canadian nationalist sentiment ran high, a principal object was to assert the country's independence, economic and otherwise, of the United States. In those years Ottawa created the Foreign Investment Review Agency to screen investments by multinational firms, mostly American, and established the National Energy Policy to reduce foreign ownership, mostly American, of Canadian oil and natural gas resources. Free trade in autos was itself the source of frequent squabbles over relative "gains and losses" from the agreement. A threat to Canadian culture was discovered in American periodicals and border broadcasting stations, to be countered by domestic content rules and by the withdrawal of business tax deductions for advertising placed with foreign-owned magazines and radio or television outlets. On the American side, too, trade policy was drifting toward restrictionism, as the nation's external accounts worsened and as the conviction grew that the U.S. trading partners, Canada not excluded, were playing the game unfairly.

Yet it was in this nominally hostile environment that the concept of a specifically North American trade deal showed signs of renewed vitality. In 1979 a freshman senator from Montana was able to have inserted in that year's Trade Agreements Act an amendment directing the president to study "the desirability of trade agreements" with Canada and, presumably, Mexico. Then in the preliminaries to the 1980 election such disparate political hopefuls as Senator Edward M. Kennedy, Governor Jerry Brown of California, and former Treasury Secretary John Connally were found espousing something called a "North American Economic Community." Putatively more important, candidate Ronald Reagan, in accepting his party's nomination, promised to pursue "economic partnership" with Canada and Mexico.

These underdeveloped phrases no doubt had a variety of origins. One must have been the belief that a response was needed to the widening scope of regional free trade in manufactured goods in Western Europe and to the semiclosed agricultural system in the European Community. It was a time when an offset to OPEC's then frightening power was sought in more secure supplies of energy fuels from Mexico and Canada. There may also have been a belated recognition that Canada's policies toward foreign investment, energy, and cultural imports were those of a sovereign power. Rhetoric alone was unlikely to bring change. Closer economic association might. At another level entirely, Canada is the country whose diplomats aided the hostages in Iran, the country with which the United States shares a continent-spanning undefended border, and the country widely perceived to be most like the United States.

For all that, vague aspirations in 1980 toward "community" or "partnership" proved to have little immediate meaning. Indeed, in 1981 when Reagan as president found himself responsible for the reply to the Senate's 1979 directive, he could offer nothing more than a "consultative mechanism" to explore opportunities for increased trade with Canada.

In Canada, on the other hand, the free trade idea, once revived, was pursued with an evident sense of direction. The first major step, in 1983, was to suggest to Washington a joint examination of further sectoral free trade arrangements. When this turned out to be a nonstarter—the automobile agreement proved to be an inapplicable model for other industries—the next move was toward a comprehensive arrangement. In due course, after extensive consultation and hearings at home, and a summit meeting with President Reagan devoted to bilateral economic issues, in October 1985 Prime Minister Brian Mulroney was able to propose to the United States a full-scale bilateral trade negotiation.

Why the decision to opt now for a particularly ambitious version of a time-honored, never-realized concept? The answer lies in judgments about Canada's economic situation and outlook.

The Canadian economy is small, heavily dependent on exports, and increasingly dependent on exports of manufactures. For many Canadian industries the domestic market cannot provide the economies of scale and the benefits of specialization that are needed to be fully competitive abroad. The one potentially realistic route to the requisite larger market is to have better and—of prime importance—more assured access to the $4 trillion U.S. economy to which the preponderant share of Canadian exports already is directed. At the same time, lower tariffs at home would not only provide direct gains from trade but would also, by promoting domestic competition, tend to increase the scale of output and cut costs. A free trade pact with the United States, arguably, could strengthen the prospects for Canadian growth and prosperity.

In the immediate background, moreover, was the 1981–82 recession, which had hit Canada harder than any other industrial nation, with real gross national expenditure falling over a period of six quarters by no less than 6.5 percent.[1] That experience could not fail to call into question some of the premises of existing economic policy. When recovery came, it was spurred by exports to the United States. But, as the American propensity to import soared, so did the pressure for protectionism. The implications for Canada were that jobs and incomes would be gravely at risk if new trade barriers were to seal off any important part of the American market. Negotiated free trade could be a way to minimize that risk.

The American response to the Canadian initiative was affirmative. It could hardly have been otherwise, for Reagan had in effect already made the commitment at his summit meeting with Mulroney. A factor in his administration's thinking, as reflected in public statements, was the expectation that a free trade negotiation with Canada, coming on the heels of a bilateral agreement with Israel, would help to convince other trading partners that the United States had practical alternatives to the multilateral GATT approach to reducing trade barriers. The failed GATT ministerial meeting in 1982 had shown that few of the contracting parties were ready for the wide-ranging multilateral negotiation that Washington desired. These attitudes, it was suggested, might change if the United States were seen to be occupied in serious negotiation for bilateral free trade with its principal trading partner, Canada.

1. Canadian Department of Finance, *Economic Review* (Ottawa: Minister of Supply and Services Canada, 1984), table 1.2, p. 4.

This apart, the prospect of an American-Canadian free trade area has its own attractions. Important groups in the United States have a proximate interest in widened trade and economic relations with Canada. Multinationals with large investments in Canada, exporters to the Canadian market, industries that rely on materials imported from Canada, communities where Canadians have made investments—in all, these make up a considerable force in American economic and political life. It was from these sectors that support was rallied when the Senate Finance Committee threatened to block the free trade negotiation. By comparison, opposition within the business world, while not negligible, was much less impressive.

Economists, Canadian and American, have tried to estimate more specifically the benefits that could accrue to Canada from trade liberalization, whether it be unilateral, bilateral, or multilateral. Since the assumptions and the techniques in these studies have been various, the results have varied, with some researchers finding potentially large positive welfare gains for Canada.

In this volume Drusilla K. Brown and Robert M. Stern report on a model that assumes, among other things, constant returns to scale and gives no weight to greater security of access for Canada. It suggests that in the short run bilateral removal of tariffs (but not nontariff barriers) would slightly worsen Canadian terms of trade and welfare and slightly improve them on the American side. Peter Petri, commenting, observes that, as Brown and Stern have recognized, if Canada is modeled as a small country and if scale economies are introduced, the outcome will be positive for Canada. Richard Harris notes that the Brown-Stern model points up the important issue of the terms-of-trade consequences of trade liberalization. He believes, however, that because of its strong qualifying assumptions the results need to be treated with caution.

David Burgess approaches the subject in terms of capital flows between Canada and the United States. He assumes that an agreement would modify nontariff barriers and liberalize foreign investment, as well as provide for the elimination of conventional tariffs. He thus concludes that Canada would probably gain from net new inflows of foreign direct investment and that wages and incomes in Canada would increase with free trade. Randy Wigle would qualify Burgess's arguments, noting that in some cases the dominant incentive might be to relocate plants from Canada to the United States.

Judgments of possible gains and losses clearly are affected by what a free trade agreement is expected to encompass. The standard expectation is that all or most customs tariffs will be eliminated on a time schedule, which may differ among products or conceivably between Canada and the United States on the ground that Canadian tariffs are higher and potential adjustment problems thus more severe. Although American tariffs on dutiable goods are modest on average, Canada's are relatively high (9–10 percent after the Tokyo round cuts have been completed in 1987), and both nations have genuinely burdensome duties on some goods. It is right, therefore, to put initial emphasis on this traditional form of protection even though much of Canadian-American trade already moves free of duty. Thereafter, however, a large number of subjects are open for consideration and possible negotiation.

The United States, for its part, will wish to have included in the discussion trade in services, a subject that is also being pursued in GATT. Some services can be best provided or can be provided only in the recipient country. This leads to the question of rules governing foreign direct investment, which would be introduced into the negotiation anyway because of the American interest in dealing with the imposition of domestic content or export requirements on foreign-owned firms and in obtaining assurances about the right of establishment and national treatment for would-be foreign investors. Since Canadians have invested far more heavily in the United States than Americans have in Canada, the right of establishment or national treatment objectives might be thought to be of mutual concern, but that is far from certain. However, as has been discussed, the scale of benefits from a free trade area will likely depend in considerable part on the movement of capital, notably direct investment. That proposition accepted, a formula to make capital flows easier ought not to be beyond the skill of the negotiators.

In both countries, federal and state or provincial governments engage in costly buy-local purchasing practices. Each side doubtless would wish to negotiate away the other side's restrictions, which may argue that a bargain could be struck. But the federal writ does not extend fully to the provinces in Canada or, as a practical matter, to the states in the United States, and this makes public purchasing an inherently complex and difficult issue.

Virtually all Canadian participants and observers put a high premium on negotiating about the problem of American "contingent protection." This term, evidently coined by Rodney Grey,[2] refers to a range of import

2. In *Trade Policies in the 1980s: An Agenda for Canadian-U.S. Relations,* Policy Commentary no. 3 (Montreal: C. D. Howe Institute, 1981).

restrictions aside from "classic" tariffs and quotas—antidumping penalties, countervailing duties against export subsidies, other legislative provisions aimed widely at "unfairness" in international trade, and the clause that allows an escape from earlier trade concessions. As seen from Canada, these amount to a battery of ways to justify restrictions that could nullify the gains from ostensible free trade. As Simon Reisman once put the case, "the actual imposition of trade restrictions is not necessarily the most serious aspect of the problem. The threat posed by an investigation under, say, the countervailing duty law . . . may be sufficient to serve as an effective deterrent to investment in Canada. The dog need not bite. He need only bark now and then to do the damage."[3]

Murray Smith covers the nontariff issues from a Canadian perspective. His judgment is sobering but doubtless accurate: A Canadian-American free trade area "will have to go further than previous bilateral and multilateral agreements . . . if it is to address the concerns and meet the objectives of both countries. . . . A truly comprehensive agreement that covers a broad range of issues and sectors is likely to be easier to negotiate than a narrower deal."

Larry Butcher's response centers on U.S. trade remedy laws. In his view, the relevance of these laws to investment decisions and to the potential gains from free trade is exaggerated in Canada. Their existence should not be a major obstacle to an agreement.

An important but hardly adequate precedent for a Canadian-American free trade area is the European Free Trade Association (EFTA). In the 1959 Stockholm Convention seven EFTA countries contracted to eliminate tariffs and import quotas on one another's products but to leave agricultural trade essentially in the status quo. A "comprehensive" Canadian-American free trade area might need to identify other sectors in which trade would be governed, at least temporarily, by special arrangements.

Andrew Schmitz and Colin Carter observe in their joint essay that to achieve any marked degree of free (or freer) trade in agricultural products between Canada and the United States will require hard political choices, especially in Canada, where provincial as well as national farm policies would have to be revised or scrapped. A limited sectoral agreement, with an open-ended commitment to negotiate further liberalization in the future, might be a practical answer to that bilateral trade problem.

3. "The Issue of Free Trade," in Edward R. Fried and Philip H. Trezise, eds., *U.S.-Canadian Economic Relations: Next Steps?* (Brookings, 1984), p. 49.

Melvyn Fuss and Leonard Waverman raise what could be a still more sensitive issue: should the 1965 auto agreement be scrapped, rather than subsumed within the eventual agreement? The association of the pact with a massive increase in bilateral automobile trade has made it a point of major interest to the two governments and to the automobile companies and the Canadian auto workers' union. They argue, however, that the pact's positive results for Canada have been much oversold—the gains from rationalization have been smaller than expected, and the built-in bias toward assembly rather than parts production in Canada was wrongheaded to begin with. Their prescription, presumably, would be to start over.

Steel is a troubled sector in the United States, so much so that the White House has undertaken to construct an elaborate regime of import quotas to give the industry relief from foreign competition. The Canadian industry is healthy by comparison and has enjoyed a sizable market for its products in the United States. Robert Crandall notes that tariff rates on most carbon steel items are roughly the same in Canada and the United States, so that the removal of duties probably would have little effect on net trade. More important, he thinks, will be relative costs, as determined by wage settlements and exchange rates, and the location decisions made by Japanese and Korean automobile companies planning to invest in North American production facilities. Both countries, as he points out, have raised protectionist fences around government purchases of structural steel products. With depressed markets in both countries for these products, those nontariff barriers promise to be an exceedingly stubborn problem for the negotiators.

In the United States a free trade agreement with Canada is sometimes discussed as a companion piece to the free trade area negotiated with Israel in 1984–85. The link is there, of course, in the sense that in both cases the aim is to remove barriers to bilateral trade. From a third-party or international point of view, the implications of the two cases are wildly different. American-Israeli trade is small and the implicit discrimination resulting from a free trade area is of marginal concern to others. Trade between the United States and Canada, on the other hand, is larger than between any other two nations. A preferential agreement between two such important commercial partners inevitably will tend to divert trade, in some instances significant amounts, away from otherwise competitive suppliers. Beyond that, a bilateral trade accord between two of the heretofore most steadfast supporters of GATT could further weaken the already frayed fabric of multilateralism in international trade.

Margaret Biggs views the possible consequences of a North American bilateral free trade area with some apprehension. Its trade diversion effects, she suggests, may be greatest for products of the developing countries, but would extend elsewhere as well. Nor does she consider it likely that bilateral liberalization of trade in "sensitive" goods—for example, clothing—will open the way to multilateral liberalization; an equally or more probable result would be to enhance protectionist pressures as more labor and capital are drawn into industries that nevertheless will remain vulnerable to third-country competition. Further, she sees no assurance that the proposed free trade area will lead to broader international cooperation rather than to the formation of additional trade blocs. For it to complement the new round of GATT bargaining in a positive way, the bilateral negotiation will need to be carefully managed to promote multilateral outcomes; among other conditions, she would leave open the possibility of third-country accession to the eventual agreement.

John Whalley, responding, points to the extensive bilateral component already present in Canadian-American trade relations, represented especially by the auto pact and the 1941 Defense Production Sharing Agreement. He thinks trade diversion is likely to be modest and the influence on the multilateral negotiation affirmative, as was the experience when the Dillon and Kennedy rounds were decided upon in order to ease the accommodation to the newly created West European customs union and free trade area. And if the free trade arrangements in Europe and North America were to lead to a trade grouping centered on Japan in the Far East, the benefits to the developing-country participants in that region might be substantial. On a similar but more general note, David Richardson prefers to see the U.S.-Canadian negotiation as a way to stimulate "renewed multilateralism" rather than as a threat to the GATT system or its developing-country members.

Harold Koh surveys a range of legal issues, both domestic and international, related to a U.S.-Canadian free trade agreement. Domestic law presents no really critical problems in the United States—although political problems may well do so—but in Canada the provincial-federal jurisdictional issue doubtless will need to be resolved by an internal negotiation before the bilateral pact has been concluded. Looking at the international legal aspects of the bilateral pact, Koh expects that a comprehensive agreement almost surely would be accepted by the contracting parties as conforming to the letter of article 24 of GATT. Like Whalley, he inclines to the position that the bilateral negotiation could favorably influence the multilateral scene: in fact, it has already been used as a threat to move reluctant GATT members toward a full-scale multilateral session. And by showing the way to understandings on a number of contentious matters—trade in services, for example— the Canadian-American negotiation could "invigorate and spur" the multilateral process. In the case of a deadlocked GATT round, a North American agreement still could produce results applicable to a later, resumed multilateral negotiation.

The focus of Michael Hart's comments on the Koh paper was the subsidy issue, in both its legal and its political and economic dimensions. While GATT is silent on the treatment of subsidies in a free trade area, Hart says that it cannot be avoided in the U.S.-Canadian negotiation. He cites official data that show government subsidies to be widespread and costly in the United States—which suggests, although he does not press the point, at least a partial basis for an eventual bilateral compromise.

Martin Wolf is the Jeremiah of this volume. His paper offers a generally gloomy perspective on the worldwide persistence of mercantilist ways of thinking and the erosion of the principles—most notably nondiscrimination—that made the postwar international trading system as successful as it proved to be. To strengthen and extend liberal and stable trade policies, an attempt could be made to have a group of like-minded countries agree to tighter obligations and more liberal practices than GATT now requires. With that as an objective, a North American free trade area could be viewed as a starting point for wider trade liberalization, along the lines, for example, of the once widely discussed North Atlantic free trade area. The challenge to policymakers, especially those in the United States, is to "make the simultaneous discussion of a free trade area in North America and a GATT round . . . the beginning of something that works still better" than does the present trading system.

SPERRY LEA

A Historical Perspective

ONE might expect a historical view of the current negotiations for a bilateral trade agreement to draw on the many previous attempts to accomplish some such arrangement. These have extended from the Reciprocity Treaty of 1854–66 through numerous frustrated projects since then to the last such attempt, the short-lived preliminary negotiations for a free trade area carried out in great secrecy over several months in 1947–48.

The point of reference for this paper is a single, quite different, previous project, but one that best enables me to trace the striking change in Canadian attitudes signaled by its current initiative. This is *A Possible Plan for a Canadian-U.S. Free Trade Area*, an outline treaty I helped to prepare, which was published in 1965 by the Canadian-American Committee.[1]

What most distinguishes the 1965 exercise from the many previous projects is, of course, its sponsors—a group of private-sector leaders in the two countries. In no way did it reflect the official views of either government. Both governments were then dedicated exclusively to the multilateral approach to trade liberalization and fully occupied with the challenge of carrying out this commitment in the Kennedy round, which had been launched in 1962.

One fact alone justifies using this unofficial exercise to serve as a useful reference point for the present effort: it occurred recently enough so that the arguments that animated its existence are basically similar to

1. *A Possible Plan for a Canada-U.S. Free Trade Area*, a Staff Report of the Canadian-American Committee prepared by Sperry Lea and Arthur J. R. Smith (Washington, D.C., and Montreal: CAC, February 1965).

11

those responsible for the present attempt. Specifically, both projects grew from the conviction by certain Canadians—a few private-sector leaders and academics then, and the federal government and business community now—that emerging circumstances compelled them to ask a bold question: might some sort of bilateral approach to trade liberalization be a desirable supplement to the postwar system of multilateral bargaining under GATT? In the mid-1960s the preponderant Canadian response to the "possible plan" was clearly "no"; since 1983 it appears to have become "yes."

This paper will note a series of sudden events and gradual developments, mainly between 1973 and 1983, that appear to have been responsible for this shift in Canadians' answer to that question. But first I will review the origins of the Canadian-American Committee's interest in exploring bilateral free trade in the early 1960s and three publications on this subject that it published in 1963, 1965, and 1966.

Activity of the Canadian-American Committee: 1958–66

The Canadian-American Committee (CAC) was patterned after the National Planning Association, which had been established in Washington during the 1930s to provide an appropriate setting for frank discussions among leaders from the major segments of the U.S. private sector—business, organized labor, agriculture, and the professions. The NPA's animating belief was that these leaders' experiences and insights could serve the national interest in guiding practical studies of current issues or, better yet, if brought into some measure of consensus and put before policymakers and the public.

The Americans and Canadians who founded the CAC in 1957 considered that the active attention of just such a group could throw useful light on the many diverse problems then troubling relations between the two countries.[2] Accordingly, the committee's initial attention focused largely on such irritants, many of which involved bilateral trade.

2. The initial American and Canadian cochairmen of the committee were R. Douglas Stuart, chairman of Quaker Oats Company and former U.S. ambassador to Canada, and Robert M. Fowler, president of the Pulp and Paper Association of Canada. John F. Miller, assistant chairman of the National Planning Association, served as secretary of the committee, and Arthur J. R. Smith, secretary of the Private Planning Association

Origins of Interest in a Bilateral Trade Area

During the CAC's first full year, 1958, the Treaty of Rome was signed, establishing the original six-member European Common Market. The commitment to form this customs union provoked other European countries to consider a second, less ambitious trade bloc in the form of a free trade area involving Great Britain and several other countries, eventually to emerge as the seven-member European Free Trade Association (EFTA). These developments widened the CAC's initial concern about trade problems from merely the numerous ones that Canada and the United States were causing each other to those that the sudden rush toward European integration threatened to cause for both of them, especially Canada.

For most U.S. business members of the CAC, the prospect of European discrimination against American exports appeared manageable since many of them were already serving these markets from their European plants or were planning to do so. In addition, European economic integration was the first step of the "Grand Design," a policy goal enthusiastically supported by the Kennedy administration in 1961.[3] Finally, U.S. goods did not stand to lose privileged access to the British market.

Canadian members of the committee saw European developments from a different perspective. They were predominantly heads of corporations or associated trade unions that were exporting to Europe the products of Canadian forests and mines. Thus they felt more vulnerable to prospective discrimination in their important European markets. Still more threatening to them than the Common Market was the likelihood of British participation in a free trade area, which would force Canadians to share their privileged export position in Britain's market with its free trade partners. They would face the even worse prospect of "reverse preferences" were Britain to join the Common Market.

A second concern was beginning to trouble some Canadian members of the committee: Canadian's inefficient industrial structure, character-

---

of Canada (later to become the C. D. Howe Institute), served as director of research. The CAC continues to operate, sponsored by the NPA in the United States and the C. D. Howe Institute in Canada.

3. The "Grand Design" envisioned creating a new political structure in Europe, built upon the plan of Jean Monnet. The European Coal-Steel Community and the Common Market customs union were to be its foundations.

ized by short production runs by many producers. Some Canadian economists saw their country's industrial future frustrated by tariffs. High foreign duties impeded Canadian producers' access to those larger external markets that could provide the opportunity for added economies of scale. Meanwhile, Canada's own tariffs often had the effect of supporting too many producers in one product line, thus further reducing the efficiency of domestic manufacturing.[4]

These twin challenges to Canada—the prospect of increasingly impaired access to Western European countries, most especially Britain, coinciding with a growing need for larger foreign markets—led some Canadian members of the CAC to see enhanced access to the large, affluent, and contiguous U.S. market as more than ever the indispensable requisite to becoming a successful industrial society. Meanwhile, the apparent ease in forming a free trade area under GATT rules (EFTA's Convention of Stockholm was negotiated in only six months) suggested that a counterpart in North America would be easy to establish—once it was generally considered desirable.

But was it? The minutes of committee meetings from 1958 through 1961 expose strong and contrasting feelings. On the one hand, Canadian members showed clear interest in the possibility of some form of "bilateral trade area" (the word "free" never appears in the record), especially following reports of the latest progress in European trade blocs and their implications. On the other, the Canadians were reluctant to be party to any action that would appear to repudiate their country's basic commitment to separateness from the United States.

Early in 1960 the committee staff arranged an informal meeting of ten recognized trade experts from the two countries to exchange views on some form of bilateral trade area and to suggest how the committee might provide a better factual basis for public discussion of this topic. The U.S. contingent included William Diebold of the Council on Foreign Relations. Among the Canadians were John Deutsch, one of the officials who had negotiated secretly with Washington in 1947–48 for what would have been a free trade area, and Simon Reisman, who was soon to lead Canada's negotiations of the automotive agreement and is its chief negotiator for the present attempt to form a bilateral agreement.

The experts proved to hold the same diversity of strongly held views

4. This was a major point in H. Edward English, *Industrial Structure in Canada's International Competitive Position* (Montreal: Canadian Trade Committee of the Private Planning Association of Canada, 1964), especially chap. 4.

as did the committee that had convened them. A central question was whether the minimalist approach to free trade then being initiated by EFTA—avoiding policy coordination or economic integration—could stay so limited. Or would such a scheme inevitably, though inadvertently, evolve into an economic union in which Canada would lose many of the attributes of sovereignty? The group remained divided on this key question. Upon receiving a report to this effect, CAC members decided to drop the subject of a trade area per se. For the next eighteen months they concentrated instead on a series of factual studies of various problems in the existing state of bilateral trade.

By late 1961, however, rapid developments in Europe again provoked the committee to attempt some kind of study of a bilateral trade agreement. The problem was how to throw useful public light on such a possibility without seeming to advocate it. Addressing the ultimate question, "Is it desirable?" was certainly not a starter. In any event, that question required some credible conclusions to a prior one: "What would be its impact?"—especially on Canada. The committee deferred attention to this question while it sought to clarify an even more basic one: "What are we really talking about?" That is, given the current realities, which characteristics of a bilateral trade area would probably be adopted if one were to be negotiated? Nowadays, the answers to this question are for the most part obvious. But in the early 1960s virtually no serious thought had been given to this matter, at least not publicly.[5] Indeed, early talk within the committee, and even among the trade experts it had consulted, revealed no common image of a trade area's characteristics.

The Reconnaissance Study of 1963

Accordingly, when the committee's initial trade area project was designed in 1962, its focus was strictly limited to clarifying what such a scheme might look like. This approach was also most likely to protect the committee's determinedly neutral position on a bilateral trade area by providing a model helpful to both those for and those against the idea.

The first of what turned out to be three committee publications on

5. Attention had, of course, been given to this question during the intense but short-lived negotiation in 1947–48 for what would have amounted to a Canadian-U.S. free trade area. But such details were a closely held secret and not available publicly during the 1960s.

bilateral free trade assessed its possible characteristics by laying out a wide diversity of choices within six decision areas: its basic form, the degree of commodity coverage, its geographic scope, the sensitive question of economic integration, its institutional structure, and the timing of the arrangement's coming into force. The committee published this study in October 1963 as *A Canada-U.S. Free Trade Arrangement: A Survey of Possible Characteristics*.[6]

The "Possible Plan" of 1965

Even before the initial reconnaissance study was finished, the CAC decided to apply its findings to the design of a practical model. This parallel project, begun in late 1962, resulted in *A Possible Plan for a Canada-U.S. Free Trade Area*. Its gestation was prolonged by on-site evaluation of the EFTA and interrupted when the initial draft was put out of sight to avoid possible involvement in a hastily called Canadian election.[7]

To select the best choice from within each decision area, a wide range of possible options was confronted by two types of underlying considerations. One was experience gained from the formative periods of various European free trade projects—including the stillborn Nordic Customs Union project as well as the successful Common Market and EFTA. In addition, the committee postulated agreement by the two countries on the following principles:

—The basic purpose of the free trade area would be to provide meaningful trade under conditions maximizing its benefits.

—It would not attempt to create a closer economic union for its own sake.

—It should be developed in a pragmatic manner, specifying at the outset obviously needed rules and agreeing on further provisions if these prove necessary or desirable.

6. Sperry Lea, *A Canada-U.S. Free Trade Arrangement: A Survey of Possible Characteristics* (Washington, D.C., and Montreal: Canadian-American Committee, November 1963).

7. When Prime Minister John Diefenbaker called the election of April 1963, the first draft was in the mail to a small group of CAC members guiding the project. Upon receiving their copies, Canadian members of the group, several of whom were also advisers to challenger Lester Pearson, hid them without prompting until after the election lest Diefenbaker, then headed for defeat and desperate for issues to dramatize, get wind of what could be interpreted as a free trade initiative that could be identified with his opponent's party.

—It should be outward looking, contributing to expanding rather than diverting international trade.

The committee also took into account certain "facts of life":

—The great difference in size between the partners.

—The fact that there would be only two members.

—Canada's fear of possible political absorption by the United States.

—The loyal participation of both countries in GATT.

—The extraction in both countries of fuels and industrial raw materials.

—Differences in commercial policies of the two countries.

—The prerogatives of Congress in setting U.S. trade policy.

—The federal nature of both countries.

—The status of Puerto Rico within the U.S. customs territory.

The publication stated a fundamental assumption underlying the "possible plan": creating any bilateral trade agreement, even a presumably nonpolitical one, is a political act that must enjoy popular support that is strong and fairly distributed among the populations of the two countries. Without widespread determination to carry on, "inevitable conflicts with particular interests or sacred traditions" could quench initial enthusiasm.

In presenting a hypothetical treaty in nonlegal language, the 1965 publication discussed in detail the particular choices made within the six decision areas:

—The *basic form* would be a free trade area as strictly defined by GATT rules, rather than a customs union.

—*Commodity coverage* would permit no exceptions for nonagricultural products, but special measures would be available to ease certain serious adjustment problems anticipated for Canada. By contrast, coverage of agricultural products would be limited, at least at the outset.

—*Geographic scope* would include Canada, the United States, and Puerto Rico but be open-ended for additional members or for linking in time with other regional arrangements.

—*Economic integration* would be minimized, shunning all steps not proven necessary in practice to assure the intended benefits of meaningful free trade. The plan would include, however, certain "rules of competition" to control nontariff practices that distort trade.

—*Institutions* would be simple and not supranational, patterned after those proving effective in EFTA.

—*Timing arrangements* would recognize the larger adjustment problems facing Canada by granting it a longer period than the United States to remove its barriers to bilateral trade.

The publication aroused considerable press coverage, mainly of course in Canada. But those who had expected lively public discussion were disappointed. To the Americans interested in trade matters and preoccupied with maintaining momentum in the Kennedy round, a bilateral scheme was a solution in search of a problem. The activists among them who were looking for future bold steps were meanwhile focusing on closer eventual trading links between a presumably united Europe and the United States—Act II of the Grand Design. To them, bilateral free trade within North America was a sideshow that could only divert attention from the principal future agenda.

For their part, Canadians were understandably more interested than Americans in the "possible plan," which presented in specific terms a possibility they had previously considered only in the abstract. The publication contributed to the discussion at numerous Canadian conferences at the time. Within a few months, however, new uncertainties in Europe incubated new thoughts. President Charles de Gaulle, who had previously vetoed British entry into the Common Market, began a boycott of both the Kennedy round negotiations and discussions necessary for further progress in forming the Common Market. With the multilateral approach to trade negotiations paralyzed, a stronger case could be made for considering bilateral approaches. More important, those Canadians interested in this path saw the outside possibility of extending an arrangement such as described in the "possible plan" across the Atlantic to include the United Kingdom and perhaps other EFTA countries in a North Atlantic Free Trade Area (NAFTA).

The "New Trade Strategy" Statement of 1966

For generally different reasons, the Canadian and U.S. members of the CAC were early supporters of just such an idea. They began preparation of a policy statement in which the committee, while still not advocating bilateral free trade, did argue for serious consideration of this possibility with the door left open for British membership.[8] Issued

8. Understandably, Canadian members were motivated by the opportunity for Canada to enjoy the benefits of free trade with the United States in a broader context, with Britain also at the table. American members tended to support the NAFTA idea as offering Britain an Atlantic option it might wish to accept.

in early 1966 as the third and last original committee publication on bilateral free trade, *A New Trade Strategy for Canada and the United States* noted political and economic benefits to both countries that might come from an arrangement along the lines of the "Possible Plan."[9] It concluded with the following specific recommendations:

1. That, as a first step, the governments of the United States and Canada initiate discussions with the United Kingdom and its partners in EFTA to explore their interest in establishing, under GATT rules, a broad free trade association of developed nations, recognizing that special consideration must be given to less developed countries.

2. That the two governments and interested private groups in Canada and the United States encourage the study and discussion of the economic and political implications of such an arrangement for our two countries.

This publication had a more immediate and visible impact than the previous two issued by the CAC. In Canada it was an important addition to numerous reports supporting the NAFTA concept and was used in conferences on this subject. In the United States it was similarly used by a far smaller group of those who felt that extending a hand to Britain would express their concern for the special Anglo-American relationship.[10] The most enthusiastic response to the statement emerged in Britain among the "Atlanticists," a group of British leaders who remained convinced that their country's destiny lay in closer ties with the United States rather than with Europe. They extolled the CAC's initiative editorially and organized a conference that brought the committee's most active members together with British leaders.

None of this activity among "interested private groups" was duplicated by any of the three governments, each of which had national agendas with which the NAFTA concept was clearly incompatible. Canada refused to consider free trade with the United States, with or without Britain; the latter was increasingly determined to enter the Common Market (which it finally did in 1973); and the United States, still hoping for a unified Europe, strongly supported British entry.

---

9. *A New Trade Strategy for Canada and the United States,* Statement by the Canadian-American Committee (Washington, D.C., and Montreal: CAC, May 1966), p. 17. The committee's second recommendation was implemented in Canada by the Atlantic Economic Studies Program, directed by H. Edward English at the Private Planning Association of Canada.

10. An account of U.S. and Canadian reactions to the three CAC publications is given in Sperry Lea, "Americans for Free Trade," *The Round Table* (London), no. 225, January 1967.

In addition, the general mood in Canada toward the United States changed in about 1967–68 to one less comfortable with any form of partnership. This had been encouraged by events that had slackened Canadians' esteem for the United States and heightened their self-esteem. In 1972 the Canadian government officially announced a clearly more independent course through a paper that considered three possible policy options with the United States. It rejected Canada's seeking "to maintain more or less its present relationship with a minimum of policy adjustments" (the first option) and likewise the choice to "move deliberately toward closer integration with the United States" (the second option). Rather, Canada should henceforth pursue the third option, "a comprehensive long-term strategy to develop and strengthen the Canadian economy and other aspects of its national life and in the process to reduce the present Canadian vulnerability." The accompanying text of what became known as "the third option" paper made it clear that Canada's vulnerability was mainly to the influence of the United States.[11]

After this period, the Canadian-American Committee, whose work in bilateral free trade occupied only a small portion of its program (three of twenty-six publications by 1966), undertook no more original work on this subject until 1985, when the Canadian government was actively seeking to negotiate a broad bilateral trade area with the United States.

An Appraisal

Before leaving the 1960s, I would like to consider briefly why the arguments for serious consideration of bilateral free trade that had prompted the CAC's activity neither resonated widely among Canadians nor received any positive response from Canadian governments at the time.

This outcome signaled the uneven contest between two policy goals that many Canadians regard as imperative for their country, yet are often considered to be incompatible. The first, which might be called Canada's "political imperative," was a founding principle for the nation: maintaining "distinctness from the United States." This phrase was used in the official third option's rationale for what came to be called the

11. "Canada-U.S. Relations: Options for the Future," by Mitchell Sharp, secretary of state for external affairs, published in a special edition of *International Perspectives* (Ottawa), Autumn 1972. The quotations are taken from summary definitions of the three options given at the outset of the paper.

"nationalist" stance on bilateral relations. The second, Canada's "economic imperative," was the growing belief that, regardless of how well multilateral trade negotiations progressed, open access to the U.S. market was essential to attaining Canadians' desired standard of living. The incompatibility lay in the conviction of many believers in the political imperative that it would be compromised by following the economic one. The activity of the CAC during the 1960s gave witness to the fact that the economic imperative was beginning to matter among Canadians, but the political imperative clearly mattered more. As for the government, it gave no support whatsoever to comprehensive free trade along the lines of the "possible plan" and officially rejected it in the "third option" statement of 1972.

Canada Changes Her Mind: 1973–83

Between 1972 and the equally official Trade Policy Review in 1983 lies a fascinating intermezzo. The Canadian government's commitment to more nationalist policies did not stop with advocating the third option.[12] Yet by the end of that period the government was recommending cautious exploration of closer bilateral trade relations. The full story of those eleven years deserves serious study. I merely note here certain developments that appear to have influenced—or, more accurately, forced—Canada's change of mind. Some are sudden events, others gradual trends, while still others represent not so much a change in realities as in how Canadians perceived them.

Crucial Developments

Most of these developments occurred or were perceived after the "third option" paper of 1972. But one previous event deserves mention— the Automotive Agreement of 1965. Providing bilateral free trade for new vehicles and associated parts, the auto pact appeared to demonstrate a practical way for Canada to gain access to the U.S. market in a few important sectors without the risks that were feared to follow a compre-

12. The major examples include establishing the Foreign Investment Review Agency in 1973; discouragement of Canadian advertising on U.S. TV stations in 1976; numerous steps to construct an "industrial policy" during the decade; and the National Energy Policy of 1980.

hensive free trade arrangement. Numerous sequels to the auto pact were suggested. However, what had appeared to be a model turned out to be a mirage when the two governments first attempted in 1984 to negotiate free trade in other sectors. But the agreement did serve to beckon the Canadian government on to its first serious open consideration of bilateral free trade since 1911.

Anticipating present events, it is worth noting that though popularly classified as a "sectoral free trade agreement," the auto pact's purpose for Canada was to assure a high level of domestic production. The free trade aspect was the inducement it offered the four U.S. manufacturers to maintain sufficient investment in their Canadian facilities to achieve a permanent "fair share" of total North American production there. If named solely for its animating purpose for Canadians, therefore, the auto pact is a "sectoral investment agreement." [13]

The second development was the British entry into the European Common Market on the first day of 1973. This restricted Canada's trading prospect in two respects. As long feared, it reversed, vis-à-vis a growing group of other European countries, Canada's traditionally preferential position in the British market. Its "free access market" of about 70 million (Canada plus Britain) would now shrink to Canada's domestic population, then a bit over 20 million, while that of virtually all European countries, including several far smaller than Canada, would expand to well over ten times that figure. It became a cliché, and also an important argument for the "economic imperative," to state that among the industrial nations, Canada alone had free access to a market of less than 100 million.

Britain's membership in the Common Market also quenched any hope among Canadians of having free trade with the United States in the NAFTA format, with the United Kingdom a welcome third party. This left only two ways by which Canada could gain access to large foreign markets: outstanding success in a long series of multilateral trade negotiations, for which the Tokyo round was just being launched, or a bilateral arrangement with the United States.

13. Canada's propensity to link transborder trade and investment also showed up in the Foreign Investment Review Agency in 1973. But here the *quid* and *quo* of the deal were reversed. The auto agreement permitted the U.S. vehicle makers to benefit from free trade provided they agreed to increase their production, and therefore investment, in Canada. The FIRA rules permitted foreign firms to increase their investment positions in Canada provided they undertook certain commitments, which could include increasing their exports from that country.

In the third development, also in 1973, the U.S. government applied countervailing duties on imports of radial tires manufactured in Nova Scotia (the *Michelin* case). An official U.S. investigation had found that production there, three-quarters of which went to the U.S. market, had benefited from an export subsidy in the form of regional assistance programs offered by the federal and provincial governments. This celebrated case called attention to a dilemma for Canada that had not been so starkly evident heretofore: given the increasingly high percentage of Canadian production exported to the United States, governmental policies to assist output, even if undertaken mainly to benefit local employment or regional growth or for social reasons, could easily be interpreted by U.S. law as export subsidies and be countervailed as such. "Michelin" thus became a metaphor for the apparently increasing vulnerability of Canadian efforts to make its industry more competitive. This was all the more serious since the Canadian political culture regarded governmental support for industry, especially in less developed regions, as a traditional obligation.

Contributing most to developments that have changed Canada's mind on bilateral free trade was the gradually emerging end of the postwar era, generally thought to have been reached by 1973. In retrospect, this period was distinguished by reasonably stable world economic growth under orderly regimes for trade and finance established just after World War II. The more volatile new era came to be identified with the abandonment of traditional ground rules and practices, sometimes by sudden destruction. It was heralded in 1971 by the U.S. decision to devalue the dollar and the subsequent move to floating exchange rates. It began unequivocally with the first oil price shock of late 1973. By then trading countries were feeling the growing effects of Kennedy round tariff cuts, phased in since 1967. Meanwhile, technological advances were changing the nature of many products, their manufacturing processes, and who could make them most competitively. The latter point was illustrated by the increasingly competitive prowess of Japan and the newly industrializing countries, who were combining state-of-the-art technology, low wages, and emphasis on quality to challenge seriously the traditional industrial countries of Europe and North America.

Sequels in 1979 to two of these developments were the conclusion of the Tokyo round of trade negotiations, which initiated further trade liberalization, and the second oil price shock, which contributed to the severe world recession of the early 1980s. Meanwhile, trade flows were being distorted and reduced by exchange rate misalignment and volatility and by the need of some severely indebted nations to constrain imports.

One consequence of this constellation of circumstances deserves individual mention: declining respect for the international trading system under GATT rules. The most obvious evidence was rising protectionism and trade management being practiced by virtually all countries. In this regard, the United States was by no means the foremost practitioner. However, the sensitivity of U.S. trade law in detecting and counteracting foreign dumping and what it considered subsidies on exported products (the *Michelin* case) was particularly troubling to Canadians, who called such practices "contingent protection."[14] This development broadened the goal of Canada's economic imperative from merely gaining better access to the U.S. market to gaining more assured access to it.

As such practices came to affect an increasing share of world trade, confidence eroded in the ability of further multilateral negotiations in GATT to accomplish the next group of tasks. Countries felt themselves increasingly free to resolve their trade problems through plurilateral arrangements or by bilateral deals or even unilateral actions. In short, the world trading system was becoming more existential, that is, more accurately described by the existing behavior of trading nations than by the traditional framework of GATT rules. While the United States and Canada certainly remained among the countries most supportive of GATT, whatever inhibitions their governments had previously felt against forming free trade arrangements, even under GATT's special rules for such schemes, were shown to have disappeared by the early 1980s.

In looking at the statistical record of major bilateral transactions, one can see a significant shift in the composition of Canadian exports to the United States between the mid-1950s and the current period from mainly forest products and industrial raw materials to manufactured items (see table 1). This trend was well under way before the 1955 auto agreement raised this sector's performance from insignificance in 1960 to the largest single category by as early as 1967. Meanwhile, nonautomotive manufactures grew steadily in importance, attaining the second largest role by 1985.

14. According to the person credited with coining the phrase and warning Canadians of the increasing propensity of Americans to use it, contingent protection "is a system in which producers obtain protection when they can make a political or legal case for it." Rodney de C. Grey, *Trade Policy in the 1980s: An Agenda for Canadian-U.S. Relations,* Policy Commentary no. 3 (Montreal: C. D. Howe Institute, 1981), pp. 13–14.

Table 1. *The Composition of Canadian Exports to the United States, 1955–85*
Percent

Sector	1955	1960	1965	1970	1975	1980	1985
Farm and fish	11	10	8	5	3	3	4
Forest products	48	43	33	19	16	17	14
Metals and minerals	29	32	32	24	32	31	20
Petroleum[a]	2	4	8	8	20	15	11
Other	27	29	25	16	12	17	9
Chemicals[b]	3	3	4	3	4	5	4
Manufactures	9	12	23	49	46	44	57
Automotive	*	*	5	32	28	22	36
Other	9	12	18	18	17	22	21
Total excluding automotive	100	100	95	68	72	78	64
Total	100	100	100	100	100	100	100

Source: Developed from Bank of Canada statistical summaries.
* Less than 0.5 percent.
a. Includes natural gas.
b. Includes fertilizer.

This trend reflects the gradual reduction of trade barriers following the Kennedy and Tokyo rounds, as well as the growing role (unfortunately unmeasurable) of intracompany transfers by multinational corporations between the two countries. It also records the decline in markets for Canada's basic materials, on which it had traditionally depended.

Also notable is the rising share of Canada's total merchandise exports to the United States, especially since 1980, despite Canada's aspiration to limit dependence on that country. In 1960 and 1965, this share was about 55 percent; it grew to about 65 percent by 1970, remained at that level through 1980, and jumped to 75 percent in 1984.[15]

Likewise, flows of direct investment funds to and from Canada have shifted direction significantly. Table 2 shows a reversal from net inflows to larger net outflows, beginning in the second half of the 1970s. This reflects both a shift by foreign investors from large net investment in Canada to larger net divestment (column A) and a sharp increase in annual outflows of Canadian capital (column B). To a considerable extent, the more recent figures in column B represent investments by Canadians in manufacturing facilities south of the border. This raises concern in Canada that there has been a migration to what is now the safer production site by firms that under a free trade agreement might serve the U.S. market from Canada.

15. *Bank of Canada Review*, various issues.

Table 2. *Annual Direct Investment Flows Involving Canada,*
1960–85[a]
Millions of Canadian dollars

Period	Foreign direct investment in Canada (A)	Canadian direct investment abroad (B)	Net flows (A + B)
1960–64	+457	−93	+364
1965–69	+665	−170	+495
1970–74	+825	−505	+320
1975–79	+357	−1,424	−1,067
1980–84	−540	−3,530	−4,070
1985	−2,950	−5,100	−7,850

Source: Alan M. Rugman, *Outward Bound: Canadian Direct Investment in the United States* (Washington, D.C., and Toronto: Canadian-American Committee, 1987).
a. A minus sign in column A indicates a reduction in liabilities to nonresidents, and in column B an outflow of capital from Canada.

The Great Reappraisal of 1983

Issued in what was to prove the twilight of the postwar era, the "third option" paper argued its case in terms of aspirations that were perhaps realistic for the recent past, but certainly not for the new era about to start. After 1973, even the largest countries found their ability to determine their own futures increasingly curtailed by unprecedented events. Planned actions often had to be replaced by improvised reactions. For Canada, several of the developments described above frustrated major policy initiatives designed to further its strategies to develop and strengthen the Canadian economy. For example, the Foreign Investment Review Agency, established in 1973 to screen incoming direct investment, eventually recognized the more serious threat arising from its recent tendency to leave. The National Energy Policy of 1980 was forced to retreat in the face of the world recession and more especially the fall in oil prices. During the early 1980s, Canada found itself particularly vulnerable. Markets for its basic commodities had declined sharply; the world trading system had become a Darwinian jungle; and the U.S. market had grown in importance for Canadian exports, but also in the unpredictability of their access to it.

In 1982 a serious rethinking of Canadian trade policy was initiated that faced these new and often threatening facts of life. Its product was the historic Trade Policy Review of 1983. The Canadian government now recognized the "economic imperative": Canadian prosperity depends on assured access to the U.S. market.[16] Canada's traditional insistence on maintaining distinctness from the United States was not abandoned; the compromise was the policy recommendation that "careful consideration will be given to the advantages and disadvantages of limited free trade arrangements with the USA in particular sectors."[17] After a joint examination proved this approach to be unfeasible, the Canadian government took the bolder step at the beginning of 1985 of suggesting that a more comprehensive approach be examined as well. This would presumably take the form of a broad free trade area that would be along the general lines of the "possible plan" but designed to deal with contemporary issues such as U.S. contingency protection—an even greater Canadian concern following U.S. restrictions on lumber in 1986—and including services as well as goods. In September 1985 the Macdonald Royal Commission also recommended negotiating a comprehensive free trade agreement with the United States.[18]

The Canadian rationale for such a project can be summarized in a series of related propositions:

—Canadians aspire to a prosperous society with full employment benefiting citizens from all regions.

—Lacking confidence that natural resources can ever again furnish the economic base for such a society, Canadians will rely instead on a modernized industrial base to play this role in the future.

—But, given the increasingly competitive world for industrial production, this sector cannot prosper in Canada unless it approaches world-class efficiency.

—Achieving this will require a significant investment in Canada of new capital, accompanied by top-level entrepreneurship and management.

—Such resources, Canadian and foreign alike, have been increasingly

16. External Affairs Canada, *Canadian Trade Policy for the 1980s: A Discussion Paper*, and *A Review of Canadian Trade Policy: A Background Document to Canadian Trade Policy for the 1980s* (Ottawa: Minister of Supply and Services Canada, 1983).

17. The quotation is from "Canada Trade Policy Review: Highlights," a brief summary issued by External Affairs Canada to accompany the report. The sectors investigated by the two governments were urban mass transport equipment, steel, agricultural equipment and inputs, and computer services. Free trade by sector was abandoned when it proved impossible to balance gains and losses for each country within each industry. Unlike the auto pact, where all the vehicle manufacturers were American, no attempt could be made to exchange their investment commitments for the benefits of free trade.

18. *Report of the Royal Commission on the Economic Union and Development Prospects for Canada*, vol. 1 (Ottawa: Minister of Supply and Services Canada, 1985).

flowing out of Canada in recent years. To induce them to remain there or enter there, Canadian manufacturing production must have secure, unrestricted access to a far larger market than its 25 million population.

—Given the present prospects for the world trading system, the only such market is that of the United States.

—To gain free access on a secure basis will require a comprehensive bilateral agreement established by treaty.

Two related points about this formulation of Canada's rationale deserve mention. First, as noted in the case of the automotive agreement, the objective of increasing investment in Canada serves its ultimate goal more directly than does the free trade agreement, which is considered an indispensable means to attracting that investment. Otherwise put, Canada's historic initiative is more basically a plan to enhance investment in Canadian manufacturing than it is one to assure bilateral free trade.

In this connection, the series of related propositions presented above include what has been called a "leap of faith." This refers to the assumption that once Canadian products have gained assured free access to the U.S. market, sufficient Canadian and foreign investment will indeed be forthcoming to build a competitive industrial base both large and successful enough to play its expected role in supporting future Canadian prosperity.

A Final Comment on Motivation

This paper has focused on the dramatic shift in the Canadian government's position on bilateral free trade, from unequivocal rejection in 1972 to determined advocacy today. I will end by briefly comparing this present Canadian commitment with the arguments supporting the current negotiations being presented in the United States. The contrasts are striking.

For Canadians, bilateral free trade has been aptly called "the issue that will not die," kept alive by agreement on its historic importance but subject to spirited dispute over whether it represented a major threat or a major promise.[19] As discussed, Canada's present decision rests on the

19. Bruce Macdonald, *The Issue That Will Not Die* (Toronto: Canadian Institute for International Affairs, 1967).

belief that secure access to the U.S. market is indispensable to its future prosperity. Accordingly, the intensity of Canadian advocacy among the prevailing majority is great.

For Americans, by contrast, bilateral free trade has never lived as a national issue. On widely separated occasions it has attracted passing interest, but has never been perceived as a major threat or opportunity. Thus reasons for responding positively to the present Canadian initiative have emerged slowly among Americans as a collection of separate purposes of only modest importance by comparison with other current U.S. international objectives. The elimination of relatively high Canadian trade barriers naturally interests certain U.S. producers, especially if national treatment is accorded U.S. investment fairly widely. For its part, the administration now appears to welcome a successful negotiation with Canada as potentially its major achievement on foreign trade. Some U.S. trade officials also consider bilateral negotiations with Canada as the most promising way to develop solutions to challenging new tasks facing the next GATT round of multilateral negotiations.

Whether such contrasting differences in the nature and intensity of the two countries' motivations will prove a weakness in the eventual agreement—as is suggested by an underlying assumption for the "possible plan"—is a question that remains to be answered but deserves to be asked.

A more immediate question provoked by these striking asymmetries in motivation should be addressed to the Americans: will they supplement their present diverse reasons for supporting the bilateral negotiations with a broader and longer-term sense of purpose, one related to enlightened self-interest? It is significant that Americans do not appear to be seeking such a rationale based on what Canada's present rationale, if correct, would mean for the United States. If the Canadians responsible for the "great reappraisal" are right in concluding that a bilateral free trade agreement will contribute decisively to their country's future prosperity, then Americans should ask what difference this outcome for Canada would make for the full range of their own national interests—economic, political, and strategic.

MURRAY G. SMITH

A Canadian Perspective

CANADA and the United States are engaged in a historic set of negotiations aimed at developing new rules for the world's largest bilateral trade and investment relationship. Major issues will arise in negotiating and implementing a comprehensive bilateral free trade agreement between the two countries. The outcome could have implications far beyond the effects on the two countries' bilateral relations and economic prospects because of potential linkages with the new round of multilateral negotiations.

My paper first focuses on negotiating the permanent elements of the agreement.[1] In part the Canadian-U.S. negotiations can build on the experience of previous free trade area agreements among industrial countries. Yet there are major issues in these negotiations that are without adequate precedents in previous bilateral or multilateral trade agreements and require innovative approaches to dealing with them. I next examine the issues that would arise in implementing such an agreement; successful resolution of these issues also is critical to the success of the negotiations. Finally, I examine possible interactions between bilateral and multilateral negotiations and some strategic implications of a bilateral agreement.

I wish to acknowledge helpful comments from Michael Aho, Wendy Dobson, Sperry Lea, Richard Lipsey, and Peter Morici, but they bear no responsibility for the final text.
1. This discussion builds on the broad outline of a Canadian-American free trade area proposed in Richard G. Lipsey and Murray G. Smith, *Taking the Initiative: Canada's Trade Options in a Turbulent World* (Toronto: C. D. Howe Institute, 1985).

31

Negotiating a Bilateral Agreement

Following the March 1985 "Shamrock" summit between Prime Minister Brian Mulroney and President Ronald Reagan, both countries prepared reports that provided a preliminary indication of their negotiating objectives.

Canada's objectives were outlined by James Kelleher, minister for international trade, in a report tabled in the House of Commons on September 26, 1985. They were reducing the potential of U.S. trade laws to frustrate or prevent market access to the United States; eliminating U.S. tariffs that inhibit the further processing of Canadian resource products and the development of Canadian world-scale manufacturing industries; removing "Buy America" procurement practices that inhibit Canadian exports; and improving mechanisms that deal with trade disputes and the interpretation of international agreements.

U.S. Trade Representative Clayton Yeutter's report to the president in 1985 summarized the U.S. preliminary objectives: eliminating high Canadian tariffs that act as major impediments to U.S. exports of a wide variety of products; removing Canadian nontariff barriers to trade at both the federal and provincial levels of government; eliminating or reducing bilateral barriers to U.S. exports of services; and obtaining clarification and liberalization of Canadian policies toward U.S. direct investment.

Undoubtedly the negotiating objectives of both countries will be refined through interaction among, and lobbying by, domestic interest groups as the negotiations proceed. The immediate focus of these domestic lobbying pressures is likely to be on the sectoral coverage of the negotiations. In more conventional parlance, what is on the negotiating table?

Sectoral Coverage

The proposed agreement is likely to be a comprehensive trade agreement or free trade area (FTA) consistent with article 24 of the General Agreement on Tariffs and Trade (GATT).[2] The precise nature

2. In principle, at least, the possibility also exists that the bilateral arrangement could be a series of narrow sectoral deals analogous to the U.S.-Canadian auto pact.

of the arrangement that might be negotiated is less clear. At a minimum, it could be a conventional free trade area analogous to that of the European Free Trade Association (EFTA), which eliminated tariffs and other border impediments to trade in industrial products among its member countries.[3] But a number of issues not negotiated in forming EFTA—such as trade remedy laws, trade in services, and investment policies—also have to be addressed. The outcome of negotiations on these issues is more uncertain.

Previous FTA agreements—such as EFTA and agreements between EFTA and the European Community (EC)—could provide precedents for exempting certain sectors from the scope of the Canadian-U.S. trade negotiations. These earlier agreements eliminated virtually all tariffs and quotas on industrial products, but maintained them selectively on agricultural, fish, and food products. The United States and Canada may wish to follow a similar pattern and make it clear from the outset that there will be no exemptions in the industrial sector. If they do not, and allow the exemptions-seeking process to get started, there is a risk that the overall trade deal could unravel.

Both countries could follow the EFTA pattern and choose to exempt certain agricultural products from the agreement. GATT article 24, in conjunction with article 11, permits the retention of import quotas that are part of a system of supply management or domestic price supports for agricultural producers. That being the case, neither Canada nor the United States is likely to be interested in opening up trade in, say, their dairy products industries. The United States might want to include commodity segments, such as eggs or broiler chickens, where Canadian marketing boards and import quotas create significant cross-border price

---

Negotiation of such arrangements, however, is a very difficult undertaking. For example, when Canada and the United States attempted sectoral trade negotiations in 1983, they found it very difficult to identify sectors in which both countries had a mutual interest in freeing bilateral trade. Moreover, such arrangements require a waiver under article 25 of GATT, whereby two-thirds of the GATT members approve and endorse the proposed bilateral trade arrangement, and obtaining such approval is likely to be difficult.

3. The European Free Trade Association came into existence in November 1959. The seven original member countries were Austria, Denmark, Norway, Portugal, Sweden, Switzerland, and the United Kingdom. In 1961 Finland signed an association arrangement with EFTA, as did Iceland subsequently. The character of EFTA changed significantly when the United Kingdom and Denmark joined the European Community. With the exception of Portugal, which embarked on a tortuous process toward full membership in the European Community, all of the remaining EFTA countries have concluded free trade association agreements with the EC.

discrepancies. At the same time, however, there are likely to be strong domestic pressures to retain the highly protectionist U.S. sugar regime. On balance, therefore, neither country is likely to press for inclusion of all agricultural commodities.

Precedents also exist for the elimination of such nontariff barriers as preferential government procurement practices. Here, Canada and the United States could look at the example of the Tokyo round nontariff barrier codes. A complication in the bilateral talks, however, could be the issue of the participation of subnational governments, particularly on the Canadian side, since the provincial share of government purchases in Canada is much larger than the state share in the United States.

The more difficult negotiating issue will concern the nontariff barriers to trade, investment, and trade in services that have not been dealt with effectively in previous FTAs or multilateral negotiations. The recently concluded U.S.-Israeli FTA agreement touched on some of these issues, but it did not address the application of U.S. trade remedy laws against unfair trade. It is not, therefore, a satisfactory precedent from a Canadian perspective. The uncertainty created by such laws has significant implications for Canadian economic activity and investment. Furthermore, trade actions by the United States against trade practices of foreign governments also have an indirect influence on Canadian economic policy. At the same time, if Canadian commitments on trade in services and investment policies of interest to the United States are analogous to the loose arrangements in the U.S.-Israeli agreement, these are unlikely to satisfy U.S. firms that deal with Canada.

Will Common External Barriers Be Required?

In his initial announcement of the bilateral trade initiative to the House of Commons on September 26, 1985, Prime Minister Mulroney stated that Canada would seek "the broadest possible package of mutually beneficial reductions in tariff and nontariff barriers between our two countries." He indicated that the proposed negotiations would be consistent with GATT rules and that it would not be Canada's intention to negotiate "a customs union, a common market or any other economic arrangement which would affect our own independence or our relations with the rest of the world."

Even so, the concern is sometimes expressed that common external barriers may be required, either immediately at the conclusion of the agreement or eventually because of subtle forces set in motion by the agreement. The source of this concern is that when two countries in an FTA have different external trade barriers, an incentive exists to route a product through the country with the lower external barrier and then reexport it duty free to the country with the higher external barrier. This problem is known as "trade deflection."

To prevent trade deflection, virtually all FTAs impose "rules-of-origin" criteria before products can qualify for duty-free access. These criteria set minimum levels of value added by member countries according to the type of product involved. For example, primary products such as fresh fruit or coal simply would have to be produced in one of the member countries in order to qualify for duty-free access to the other member countries, while manufactured end products might require that 30, 40, or 50 percent of the value added in processing and manufacturing occur in the member countries in order to qualify. Thus rules-of-origin criteria are intended to avoid the need to harmonize external import restrictions.

Rules-of-origin criteria can be more or less restrictive, depending on the amount of value added required to qualify for duty-free trade. When there are small discrepancies between the two countries in the levels of effective protection for particular activities, relatively modest value-added requirements are usually sufficient to prevent significant deflections of trade or production. But when discrepancies are large, strict rules of origin with higher North American content requirements are likely to be necessary. For most commodities, Canada and the United States have a very similar structure of external barriers, but significant differences exist or can arise, particularly in sectors characterized by managed trade. One option could be to design different rules-of-origin criteria for different sectors.[4]

A special issue is raised by the existing provisions of the Canadian-U.S. auto pact. On the U.S. side, the auto pact requires 50 percent North American value added. On the Canadian side, the auto pact involves a duty remission scheme, available to third-country producers as well as to indigenous North American auto companies. Canada will be reluctant to harmonize its duty remission scheme with the U.S. requirement,

4. Murray G. Smith, "Implications for Canadian Commercial Policy of Negotiating a Free Trade Area with the United States," in Richard G. Lipsey and Murray G. Smith, eds., *Policy Harmonization: The Effects of a Canadian-American Free Trade Area* (Toronto: C. D. Howe Institute, 1986), pp. 101–22.

because that could allow duty-free entry into Canada of Japanese automobiles assembled in the United States. From a Canadian perspective, this outcome is undesirable because the decisions of Japanese automobile companies to invest in the United States were influenced by the U.S.-Japan bilateral restraint arrangements and the threat of U.S. domestic-content requirements.

Yet U.S. observers view Canada's long-standing duty remission scheme as an export subsidy and express concern about plans by offshore firms to assemble automobiles in Canada. Canada is likely to resist any alteration in the existing auto pact arrangements, but the provisions could come under political pressure in the United States as auto production capacity expands in North America. Thus rules of origin for automotive trade are likely to be a contentious negotiating issue, but the trade talks also provide the opportunity to avoid and resolve a potential major bilateral dispute on automotive trade.

Beyond the application of rules of origin to determine which goods move duty free are more general concerns about regulating imports from third countries. Since each country would retain its own customs agents at customs points between the two countries, the same administrative arrangements involving rules of origin for goods subject to tariffs could be applied to goods subject to antidumping and countervailing duties or other trade remedies. Even if each country exempted the other from the application of trade remedies, both could still retain separate external systems. It is not necessary for them to merge their trade regulatory apparatus for dealing with third countries, and it is very unlikely that either would want to do so.

The assertion that an FTA will inevitably lead to a customs union seems implausible. Technical difficulties alone make the harmonization of external trade barriers and trade regulatory procedures a very complex task. Because it would also require considerable political will to harmonize external barriers, an FTA agreement is more feasible to negotiate than a customs union. This general proposition applies with particular force to an agreement between the United States and Canada, because of the discrepancy between the size of the two economies.

The experience with FTAs among industrial countries indicates that rules of origin can be administered effectively. As Victoria Curzon says about the EFTA experience:

> It was an amazing technical success, in that the various administrative problems associated with operating a free trade area worked smoothly and

did not impede the growth of trade. Visible distortions in the pattern of production and investment due to variegated national tariffs did not occur. The EFTA experience therefore confounded the critics . . . , who had predicted dire consequences if no harmonization of external tariffs took place.[5]

The EFTA experience does not support the hypothesis that a free trade area will tend to evolve into a customs union. If appropriate rules of origin are negotiated, each country can retain considerable independence in relations with third countries.

Issues outside the Agreement

The purpose of a free trade agreement is to provide a more stable framework for economic relations between the two countries. Some economic policy areas will not be incorporated into the agreement, either because the policies in those areas do not affect bilateral trade and investment flows substantially or because the particular policies do affect bilateral trade but the policy issues are not amenable to bilateral solutions. Into the first category fall broad-based policies such as income redistribution measures or public funding of education, while macroeconomic and exchange rate policies fall into the latter category.

Although broad-based tax or spending measures are unlikely to have enduring effects on trade and investment flows, macroeconomic policies and exchange rates clearly can have significant implications for trade in the short term. Much of the recent concern about bilateral exchange rates has involved perceptions that the Canadian dollar has been undervalued as a matter of policy. However, the high level of integration of Canadian and U.S. financial markets and the mobility of short-term capital flows prevent Canada from pursuing an exchange rate policy independent from domestic monetary and fiscal policies so long as there are no restrictions on capital flows.[6] I would suggest that the gradual decline of valuation of the Canadian dollar relative to the U.S. dollar in the 1980s can be explained by higher domestic inflation in Canada, the appreciation of the U.S. dollar against all currencies in the first half of the 1980s, and persistent weakness in Canada's terms of trade, reflecting low real prices for resource commodities.

5. Victoria P. Curzon, *The Essentials of Economic Integration: Lessons of EFTA Experience* (London: Macmillan for the Trade Policy Research Centre, 1974), p. 18.

6. Paul Boothe and others, "International Asset Substitutability: Theory and Evidence for Canada," *Bank of Canada Review* (February 1985), pp. 9–10.

Many of the pressures on exchange rates, and the associated pressures on trade and investment flows, stem from the underlying monetary and fiscal policies of the countries involved. In the context of divergent national macroeconomic policies, efforts to peg exchange rates will simply deflect, but not prevent, the international transmission of macroeconomic disturbances. The 1986 Tokyo summit communiqué on policy coordination quite properly focused on the underlying macroeconomic policies of the major industrial countries, since in the short term exchange rates are influenced heavily by capital flows arising from shifts in national monetary and fiscal policies.

Efforts to manage the bilateral exchange rate between Canada and the United States to promote a desired pattern of trade are unlikely to yield satisfactory results because exchange rates influence a country's aggregate trade performance. Thus bilateral trade flows that may be viewed as inappropriate by either country arise as a by-product of overall external trade and current account imbalances of one or both countries.

These factors suggest that a bilateral agreement can only deal with exchange rates indirectly by affirming and strengthening the two countries' international obligations to ensure that exchange rates cannot be used as a separate policy instrument to promote exports and inhibit imports. Canada should resist any proposal to manage exchange rates as part of a bilateral trade agreement, but both countries could enter into commitments not to manipulate rates. In particular, commitments to refrain from applying controls or taxes on short-term capital flows would help ensure that the exchange rate could not be manipulated in a sustained effort to influence trade.

Having discussed a controversial issue that in my view is peripheral to a bilateral accord, I now turn to a controversial issue that could be the stumbling block in the negotiations.

Negotiating Import-Relief Laws

Import-relief laws—a country's system of laws and regulatory procedures that allow domestic industries to seek redress from what they regard as unfair or disruptive import competition—are a contentious bilateral issue and are likely to require major attention in negotiations. As tariffs have been lowered through multilateral negotiations, industries threatened by imports have tended to resort to antidumping and countervailing duties and emergency import quotas, particularly since the conclusion of the Tokyo round. Rodney Grey coined the term "contingent protection" to refer to these trade remedies and procedures.[7]

Negotiations are likely to be difficult because of differing perceptions in the two countries of how each other's system operates. For example, it is likely to be particularly difficult to agree on what constitutes fair trade. In addition, competitive imbalances in particular sectors create pressures for protective measures on goods that are acknowledged to be fairly traded.

The U.S. and Canadian Systems

From the U.S. perspective, U.S. trade legislation provides a transparent, nonpolitical system of dealing with disputes about allegedly unfair trade and with import disruption caused by fair trade. To Canadian exporters, however, the U.S. system seems to provide opportunities for import-competing interests to harass foreign firms and to provide a potential outlet for surreptitious protectionism that can lead to highly arbitrary barriers to Canadian exports.

U.S exporters often express concerns about Canada's contingent-protection system as well. Antidumping duties are the most frequently applied remedy in Canadian trade legislation. Reflecting the influence of GATT negotiations, in particular the Tokyo round, Canadian trade legislation has evolved along lines similar to U.S. trade laws. Important procedural differences remain, however, between the two systems. For example, the Canadian government screens cases more severely, making it harder to bring spurious actions.

The trade legislation of both countries is two-pronged. One prong consists of remedies that are intended to limit unfair trade practices. In this category fall antidumping and countervailing duties as well as other remedies against unfair foreign trade practices. Both countries require that an independent tribunal make a determination that an industry is experiencing "material injury"—or the threat of such injury—before antidumping or countervailing duties are imposed.

The other prong, sometimes referred to as the "escape clause" or "safeguards," is intended to provide temporary relief to domestic

7. Rodney de C. Grey, *Trade Policies in the 1980s: An Agenda for Canadian-U.S. Relations,* Policy Commentary no. 3 (Montreal: C. D. Howe Institute, 1981).

industries suffering from surges in imports. If industries can demonstrate "serious" injury from imports—a stricter test and more difficult to prove than material injury—then quotas or additional tariffs may be imposed.

Although the two countries have broadly similar trade regulation systems, the asymmetries between them in trade and production mean that Canada has a greater interest in restricting application of contingent-protection systems than does the United States. In the smaller Canadian economy, exports frequently account for a larger proportion of production, and most of those exports go to the United States. The risk of U.S. import restrictions significantly increases the risk to investment in new production facilities in Canada.

The potential application of U.S. countervailing duties is of particular concern to Canadians because it impinges on Canada's choice of domestic economic policies. This was first illustrated by the 1973 Michelin tire decision, in which the United States found Canadian regional development subsidies to be a countervailable subsidy. Before that decision, the U.S. Treasury had applied countervailing duties only in cases involving explicit export subsidies.

Subsidies and countervailing duties were a key issue in the Tokyo round. The United States sought to discipline other countries' subsidies, while other countries sought to limit the application of U.S. countervailing duties. A compromise was achieved whereby the United States introduced the injury test for countries signing the GATT subsidies code, while the definition of countervailable subsidies was broadened. Under present U.S. practice, countervailing duties potentially can be imposed on any domestic subsidies that are not widely available, although recent decisions by the U.S. Court of International Trade cast some doubt on even this latter qualification.[8] The trend toward a broadening of the U.S. definition of a countervailable subsidy operates as an increasing constraint on the domestic policies of Canadian governments.

Two bills introduced into the Ninety-ninth Congress represent a continuation of the trend to redefine unfair trade.[9] Both bills were intended to overturn the U.S. International Trade Administration's

8. *Bethlehem Steel Corp.* v. *United States and Highveld Steel and Vanadium Corp.* (Court of International Trade, 1984); and *Cabot Corp.* v. *United States* (Court of International Trade, 1985).

9. H.R. 1648, Wood Products Trade Act of 1985, and H.R. 2451, which would "amend title VII of the Tariff Act of 1930 in order to apply countervailing duties with respect to resource input subsidies."

softwood products decision of 1983, which found Canadian stumpage policies not to be countervailable subsidies under U.S. law. Neither of these bills found its way into law. Nevertheless, the result desired by some U.S. lumber interests was achieved in October 1986 when the International Trade Administration reversed its previous ruling and in a preliminary determination found that the stumpage practices of provincial governments were countervailable subsidies. This redefinition of subsidy serves to underline the ambiguity of the statutory criteria for imposing countervailing duties.

Options for Negotiating Import-Relief Laws

Various analysts have suggested a number of ways to treat trade remedy laws in negotiating a Canadian-U.S. FTA agreement. These options include (1) complete bilateral exemption in the application of trade remedies and applying national treatment under domestic remedies against unfair competition; (2) binational administration of bilateral trade remedy systems; (3) exclusion of imports from third countries in determining injury; (4) negotiation of stricter criteria for applying antidumping and countervailing duties and other unfair-trade laws; and (5) negotiation of very tight restrictions on the bilateral application of escape clause measures.[10]

Option 1. The possibility of negotiating complete bilateral exemption from antidumping and countervailing duties and other unfair-trade laws raises a number of issues. In the case of antidumping duties, bilateral exemption might make sense once tariff barriers, which segment national markets, were removed, because the potential for harassment of exporters from the other country would be greatly reduced. But if antidumping duties were likely to be applied only rarely once tariffs were eliminated, then retaining such mechanisms for bilateral trade could be

---

10. The first three options were suggested in the *Report of the Royal Commission on the Economic Union and Development Prospects for Canada,* vol. 1 (Ottawa: Minister of Supply and Services Canada, 1985); and the third option is elaborated upon in Debra P. Steger, "The Impact of U.S. Trade Laws on Canadian Economic Policies," in Lipsey and Smith, eds., *Policy Harmonization,* pp. 73–100. The fourth and fifth options are essentially the ones outlined in Lipsey and Smith, *Taking the Initiative,* and also discussed in Steger. A fuller discussion of these options is contained in Murray G. Smith, C. Michael Aho, and Gary N. Horlick, *Bridging the Gap: Trade Laws in the Canadian-U.S. Negotiations* (Toronto and Washington, D.C.: Canadian-American Committee, 1987).

a relatively costless way to reassure domestic firms that fear being overwhelmed when bilateral barriers are reduced.

Complete exemption of bilateral trade from antidumping duties and procedures could be feasible, at least in principle, because each country has domestic laws directed against unfair pricing. Each country would afford national treatment in the application of price discrimination laws. For example, if a company in Cleveland sells a product in its local market at a higher price than it sells it in Hamilton, the company would be subject to Canadian price discrimination laws. If the Cleveland company sells at a lower price in the Buffalo market, it would be subject to U.S. price discrimination laws. If antidumping duties were eliminated, domestic price discrimination laws would then apply with somewhat similar effects.

Domestic price discrimination laws have been criticized in recent years because they can limit price competition that is beneficial to society. In Canada, price discrimination laws have not been applied stringently. In the United States, recent trends in antitrust policy and enforcement have permitted firms greater flexibility in pricing strategies.

The trends in administration of antidumping and domestic price discrimination laws have been diverging, however: the trend in antidumping laws has been toward more zealous enforcement of laws against unfair foreign trade practices. A commitment to national treatment— which means that dumping of imported goods would be treated the same as price discounting of domestically produced goods—would prevent the potential for future discrimination between domestic and foreign firms. Although a commitment to national treatment in price discrimination laws would not necessarily require that each country apply the same criteria, this approach could reinforce the perception that harmonization of competition law and policy in both countries was a consequence of freer bilateral trade.

The issue of bilateral exemption from the application of countervailing duty laws raises particularly difficult problems, in large part because there are no domestic mechanisms in either country to limit the extent and effects of subsidies by various levels of government. In principle, one could argue that subsidies are constrained by government budgets and that governments should be free to engage in domestic subsidies. In practice, however, neither U.S. business interests nor Congress is likely to accept this position, because the prospect of U.S. firms competing with foreign treasuries seems to them to be inherently unfair.

Obtaining a bilateral exemption from the application of countervailing duties would seem to require that governments in both countries make specific commitments to limit their subsidy practices in order to be exempted by the other government from the application of countervailing duties. The issue of how these commitments are to be enforced also would need to be resolved. The European Community, for example, does not permit application of countervailing duties to trade among member countries. Instead, it has a complex supranational regulatory and legal system intended to control members' subsidy practices.

Option 2. The Macdonald Royal Commission's proposal to administer countervailing and antidumping laws on a binational basis provides an administrative process to deal with bilateral trade disputes. Some important questions still need to be resolved, however, such as the criteria for the application of these laws.

In light of existing U.S. sensitivities about subsidies and countervailing duties, there is likely to be considerable reluctance to surrender the administration of such unfair trade laws to a binational agency. Legislators will be particularly reluctant to transfer the injury determination process to a binational agency. Such an agency—or an arbitral tribunal of the type discussed below—might, however, be appropriate to deal with disputes about unfair trade that are now dealt with under section 301 of the U.S. Trade Act of 1974.

Option 3. The proposal to separate Canadian imports into the United States (or U.S. exports to Canada) from those of third countries in the application of antidumping and countervailing duties would reduce the likelihood that such duties would be applied to bilateral trade. It would also remove the present incentives to include Canadian (or U.S.) imports in complaints about unfair trade from third countries in order to improve the likelihood of an injury determination. This option could be difficult to negotiate, however, since segregation of imports in this manner runs contrary to recent developments in U.S. trade law. Also, the injury test itself is sufficiently subjective and fluid that there might be a spate of antidumping and countervailing duties, even under this segregated approach, if the administrative criteria for injury determination were relaxed.

Option 4. Negotiating the criteria by which antidumping and countervailing duties should apply could provide greater certainty for producers in one country exporting to the other. The approach I have suggested elsewhere is to take seriously the metaphor of the "level playing field," in the sense of focusing on practices that significantly affect the pattern of trade. Specifically, the proposed points include calculating the net differential subsidy available to a specific industry in Canada and the United States; calculating either cost offsets for regional development subsidies or permitting a threshold level of such subsidies that does not significantly affect international trade flows; exempting subsidies to facilitate pollution control and occupational health; giving greater legislative precision and certainty to the specificity (or general availability) test in determining whether domestic subsidies are subject to countervailing duties; developing agreed-upon procedures and methods for the calculation of subsidies; and eliminating for bilateral trade the constructed-value method of calculating antidumping duties, because under this method companies may not be dumping at all, but may simply be losing money in the domestic and foreign market.[11]

Other proposals along these lines have also been made. One would involve the elimination of countervailing duties if the exporting country can demonstrate that the alleged subsidy does not alter trade patterns.[12] A related proposal would involve a stricter standard of causation in the domestic trade regulation systems of both countries.[13] If adopted, the proposals to define the criteria for application of trade laws would limit some of the potential abuses of fair-trade laws, although import-competing firms taking spurious actions could still harass exporters.

This kind of fine-tuning might be achieved through multilateral negotiations, but this appears to be a very uncertain prospect. Even so, Canadian and U.S. negotiators probably should take the views of third countries into account. For example, other countries might regard Canadian-U.S. criteria for contingent protection as discriminatory if such criteria differ significantly from what is applied to them. Such third-country objections might be defused by making the stricter criteria conditional on trade being free in both directions. Thus, when other countries removed their own trade barriers, they could qualify for a more precise application of fair-trade laws.

Option 5. Conflicting considerations must be weighed in assessing the options for dealing with disruptive import surges of goods that are recognized to be fairly traded. The Macdonald Royal Commission expressed the following views on escape clause or safeguard measures:

11. Lipsey and Smith, *Taking the Initiative*, pp. 148–59.
12. See John J. Barcelo, "Subsidies and Countervailing Duties—Analysis and Proposal," *Law and Policy in International Business*, vol. 9, no. 3 (1977), p. 851.
13. Steger, "The Impact of U.S. Trade Laws on Canadian Economic Policies."

One can argue that the preferred solution would be the complete dismantling of safeguard protection applicable to goods originating in either country. The main purpose of a free-trade arrangement's guarantee of market access may well be to create positive incentives for the parties to undertake industrial restructuring. In this instance, the continued availability of safeguard protection to firms injured by imports would substantially undermine the economic goal of the signatories. On the other hand, a free-trade agreement which offered no prospect of escape for injured domestic industries would probably attract substantial political opposition in both nations. An alternative to a complete dismantling of protection is to draft a rule providing that only if Canadian exports were found to be the primary cause of serious injury to U.S. competitors would the safeguard action apply to Canadian producers. Another possibility would be to retain safeguard measures, but to transfer the responsibility for their enforcement . . . to a transnational panel or tribunal created by the free-trade agreement.[14]

I have proposed that Canada and the United States exempt each other from the application of escape clause measures when the other country is not the principal supplier of a product that disrupts domestic industry. If either country is the principal supplier, the only remedy permitted should be to raise the bilateral tariff to the most-favored-nation level— the tariff applied to other GATT members. This proposal would limit severely the discretion of either country to apply safeguard measures and could be difficult to negotiate.

Proposals for strict limitations on the bilateral application of escape clause measures would have to permit special provisions for the transition period when bilateral trade barriers were being reduced. Ultimately, the issue comes down to one of balancing the interests of exporting firms against those of import-competing firms. Although pressures from import-competing industries are frequently strong, limitations on safeguard actions could prove to be negotiable, because such measures are not imbued with the rhetoric of unfair trade. Indeed, the U.S.-Israeli agreement provides for special procedures for bilateral safeguards and permits exemption of bilateral trade from measures directed at third countries.

Negotiating New Rules

Canadian interest in constraining the application of U.S. legal remedies to bilateral trade will have to be balanced against the elimination of

14. *Report of the Royal Commission*, p. 315.

the higher Canadian tariffs and the negotiation of rules regarding trade
in services and investment policies, which are of primary interest to the
United States. U.S. concerns about investment issues and trade in
services are likely to be addressed by developing broader application of
concepts, such as national treatment, that currently apply to trade in
goods under GATT.

Investment Policies

Two very distinct sets of issues arise in negotiations about policies
affecting direct investment. The first set of issues pertains to policies
that influence business decisions about procurement, production, and
trade. These are often referred to as trade-related investment issues.
The second set of issues involves the effects of policies on direct
investment by firms.[15]

The Canadian government has used, and continues to use, its screening of foreign firms investing in Canada to oblige those firms to meet
broadly defined criteria for economic performance in such areas as job
creation, research and development, procurement, investment, and
international trade. A GATT panel finding on the practices of the Foreign
Investment Review Agency, now known as Investment Canada, established that Canada could not require foreign firms to reduce their imports
of goods. Since neither services nor export performance requirements
fall within GATT's purview, however, Canada continues to ask for
commitments from foreign investors in those activities. A key objective
for the United States in the bilateral negotiations is to obtain a Canadian
commitment to refrain entirely from imposing import or export performance requirements on either goods or services of foreign firms with
investments in Canada.

Beyond those trade-related investment issues are the issues associated
with the policy treatment of direct investment. Different levels of
international obligation regarding direct investment policies could be
embodied in a bilateral agreement, and indeed different sectors could be
subject to different types of obligations.

15. See Harvey E. Bale, "Trade Policy Aspects of International Direct Investment
Policies," in R. E. Baldwin, ed., *Recent Issues and Initiatives in U.S. Trade Policy*
(Cambridge, Mass.: National Bureau of Economic Research, 1984), pp. 67–100; and
A. E. Safarian, "Trade-Related Investment Issues," in William R. Cline, ed., *Trade
Policy in the 1980s* (Washington, D.C.: Institute for International Economics, 1983),
pp. 611–37.

The first level of obligation about investment policies involves a commitment to national treatment; both domestic and foreign firms would be treated the same under tax and regulatory systems. This commitment would not preclude continuation of a policy of screening new investments or acquisitions by foreign firms, but it would rule out discriminatory treatment of foreign firms once established.

A second level of obligation involves a commitment to "right of establishment," allowing foreign individuals and firms to establish a new business in a country. Such a commitment does not prevent the screening, or indeed prohibition, of acquisitions of existing business operations by foreign firms. Canada's Investment Canada legislation, which came into effect in 1985, facilitates the establishment of new businesses except in the case of culturally sensitive areas, but there are no formal international commitments by Canada that this practice will continue.

Of course, both countries could continue to designate sectors where right of establishment is denied. For example, in Canada foreigners cannot own radio or television stations or newspapers; similarly, in the United States aliens are denied the right to own radio stations under the Broadcasting Act of 1934. In Canada these restrictions are rationalized on the basis of cultural considerations, while in the United States they are justified on the grounds of national security. Both countries probably will wish to retain these types of exclusions.

A third level of obligation involves permitting foreign firms to dispose of their operations without being subject to review by a special screening agency such as Investment Canada. (The United States has a monitoring agency—the Committee on Foreign Investment in the United States—but it does not screen foreign investments.) If foreign firms had a right to sell or "right of exit," then domestic firms would seek equivalent treatment, since foreign firms would have better than national treatment. The result of permitting right of establishment *and* right to sell could be that Canadian regulation of direct investment would shift from discretionary screening of foreign acquisitions across all sectors to screening of only key sectors. The only review of mergers and acquisitions in open sectors would be under Canada's new competition legislation.

Many Canadians are reluctant to agree to liberalization of direct investment because of concerns that the high level of U.S. ownership of Canadian industry adversely affects Canada's economic performance and the level of foreign control might increase further if the screening mechanism is dismantled. Yet screening of foreign investment by the

Canadian government creates an "incumbency effect" for foreign multinationals presently operating there; that is, it encourages foreign firms to maintain existing operations which they might otherwise be inclined to sell and discourages establishment of new operations by foreign multinationals not already operating in Canada.[16] This perverse effect is not widely understood, however. Politically, Canada may be just as reluctant to liberalize policies toward direct investment as the United States is reluctant to limit the application of trade remedy laws.

Trade in Services

Services trade among most countries presently takes place largely outside a framework of international rules and agreements.[17] In Canadian-U.S. trade this situation is remarkable, since the value of bilateral traded services, as distinct from investment income in the current account, amounts to about one-sixth of the value of bilateral merchandise trade (and services trade may be systematically underreported). To the extent that services trade is restricted by the policies of either government, its relative significance could increase if barriers are reduced as part of a bilateral agreement. The significance of barriers to trade in services extends beyond the effects upon service transactions, because such barriers can often restrict trade in goods as well.

Extension of GATT rules to cover services trade has been identified as a high priority in the new round of multilateral trade negotiations, notably by the United States, but also by the other industrialized countries, including Canada. The issues raised by efforts to extend

16. Murray G. Smith, "Canadian-U.S. Trade and Direct Investment: Substitutes or Complements?" paper prepared for the North American Economics and Finance Association meeting, December 30, 1985.

17. There are a few limited exceptions to the general proposition that there are no international agreements governing trade in services between Canada and the United States. Coverage of services issues under multilateral arrangements is tenuous and limited. There are consultative arrangements under the voluntary OECD guidelines, and the Tokyo round agreement on trade in civil aircraft also deals with services related to aircraft repair. Although there are bilateral agreements such as that pertaining to civil aviation services, Canada is not a signatory to a friendship, commerce, and navigation treaty with the United States. The United States does have such treaties with a number of countries, including West Germany and Japan, and the provisions of these treaties do apply to services trade.

GATT rules to services trade have been considered by a number of analysts.[18]

The most explicit barrier to services trade consists of laws or regulations that discriminate against or prohibit service transactions with foreign firms. Extending the GATT obligation of national treatment to services would help to reduce or prevent such barriers. Allowing firms to establish subsidiaries, giving them right of establishment, is also necessary in order to liberalize trade in some service sectors, since the sale or provision of services frequently requires a local presence.

Although commitments to national treatment and right of establishment in service industries would remove most explicit barriers to trade in services, differences in domestic regulatory regimes can create actual or perceived barriers. Negotiations about such regulatory issues will inevitably be sectoral and are likely to be protracted.

Intellectual property issues are one example of problems that arise from differences in national regulatory regimes that are consistent with national treatment. In one controversial case, the Canadian policy of compulsory licensing of pharmaceutical patents does not discriminate between domestic and foreign holders of patents and thus is consistent with national treatment. But since almost all drug patents are held by foreign firms, compulsory licensing creates international frictions.

Another related issue pertains to business travel and employee mobility. Although immigration as such is not an issue in the negotiation of a free trade area, impediments to business travel and the temporary assignment of employees to work in the other country can serve as a significant barrier to trade in services and also in some cases as a barrier to merchandise trade. For example, the services of a firm's technicians may be essential to install or to service a specialized piece of machinery. Thus an FTA should facilitate business travel and the granting of temporary work permits to each country's nationals.

The form of a bilateral agreement on services is likely to parallel the approach taken in the U.S.-Israeli agreement, but one might expect U.S. services firms and some Canadian firms to seek an agreement that binds government policies to a greater extent. This could be achieved by negotiating a framework agreement embodying the principles of national treatment and right of establishment, which could be implemented by

18. See, for example, William Diebold, Jr., and Helena Stalson, "Negotiating Issues in International Services Transactions," in Cline, ed., *Trade Policy in the 1980s,* pp. 581–609; and Grey, *Trade Policies in the 1980s.*

subjecting specific service industries to these obligations. Progress in this regard has been limited to the U.S.-Israeli agreement. Some service industries could be designated for inclusion in the FTA immediately, while others could be designated for continuing discussion and eventual inclusion. Still other service industries, such as cultural industries in Canada and those subject to national security considerations in the United States, could be excluded from the services agreement, at least with respect to right of establishment.

Implementing the Agreement

Negotiations about implementation of a Canadian-U.S. bilateral agreement are likely to be at least as intense as those about the key elements of the agreement itself. One set of issues involves transition arrangements for reducing bilateral trade barriers. The rate of transition will affect significantly the magnitude of adjustment costs borne by more vulnerable firms and workers. A second set of issues concerns the implementation of the agreement through changes in domestic laws and procedures in the two countries and in the practices of U.S. states and Canadian provinces. A third issue has to do with the durability and effectiveness of the agreement, which will depend on the development of effective procedures and mechanisms to deal with future bilateral disputes about trade and investment matters.

Transition Arrangements

Transition arrangements will be critical to implementing an effective agreement. These arrangements need to be sensitive to the differences among sectors in the amount and speed of adjustment costs firms and workers will incur. At the same time, an established schedule for the phase-in of the trade agreement will provide certainty and help businesses to make the investment decisions that will facilitate adjustment.

One way to ensure smooth transition is to agree to a norm—such as five years at a flat rate of 20 percent a year—for the phase-in of reductions of tariffs. Such a timetable was utilized to implement the agreements between the remaining EFTA countries and the EC. The advantage of such a fixed formula and short time frame is that it will provide an impetus for firms to restructure their operations. Too slow and protracted a phase-in period could lead firms to discount the significance of freer trade in formulating their present business plans. Past experiences with regional trade liberalization, such as within the EC, among the EFTA countries, or in the recently concluded Australia-New Zealand arrangement, indicate that the adjustments to trade liberalization are relatively painless among similar economies.

Some argue that a longer phase-in should be negotiated. If this is the case, flexibility is required so that if cumulative experience indicates adjustments are less disruptive than anticipated, the schedule for reduction of trade barriers could be accelerated. The problem with this more discretionary approach is that it is counterproductive to the objectives of providing certainty for planning purposes and encouraging economic adjustment.

A strong case can be made for slower reduction in trade barriers in sectors likely to experience large adjustments, such as the textile and clothing industries, in which bilateral trade barriers are high. Similarly, in commodities subject to quantitative restrictions, such as agricultural products that are governed by supply management or price support schemes in either country, quotas might be phased out quite slowly. I suggested above that there might be considerable lobbying pressures to leave these agricultural commodities outside the bilateral agreement. From the economist's perspective, a preferable alternative would be to bring them into the agreement, but to reduce the bilateral trade barriers over a ten- or fifteen-year period.

Another important issue in the negotiations will be whether the reduction of trade barriers is to be symmetric between Canada and the United States or asymmetric, with slower reductions on one side or the other. For example, Canadians are likely to be attracted by the analogy of the FTA agreement between the United Kingdom and Ireland, in which the United Kingdom eliminated all its tariffs in six months while Ireland took ten years. This example may appeal to Canadians, but it is unlikely to be very attractive to U.S. negotiators.

Implementation by Legislatures, States, and Provinces

Differences in the constitutional systems of Canada and the United States create additional complexities for the negotiations and could create difficulties in balancing the interests of the two countries. In the United States, the division of powers between Congress and the president has created difficulties in the past in the implementation of international agreements. After the Kennedy round, Congress failed to implement some of the concessions agreed to by U.S. negotiators. This was not well received by U.S. trading partners who had made reciprocal concessions. In response to these concerns, new procedures for implementation of trade agreements were embodied in the Trade Act of 1974, which included the "fast-track" process (see the paper by Harold Koh in this volume).

The U.S. government is in a stronger constitutional position than the Canadian government when it comes to implementation of international agreements that constrain the practices of subnational governments. Although any constitutional issue is likely to be subject to some legal ambiguity, the U.S. government has a strong presumption of preeminent jurisdiction in international negotiations and the implementation of those agreements. The obstacles to negotiating and implementing international economic agreements involving state legislation and practices are predominantly political rather than constitutional, but difficulty with commitments about U.S. state practices can be expected if Canada cannot make similar commitments on behalf of its provinces.

Constitutionally, the Canadian government has the power to negotiate, sign, and conclude international agreements, but it lacks the constitutional authority of the U.S. federal government. Treaty-making power belongs exclusively to the Crown,[19] and the implementation of an international agreement by Parliament will not pose any difficulties so long as the governing party, which negotiated the international agreement, has a working majority in the House of Commons. Complications will arise because jurisdiction in the Canadian federal system is split between the federal government and the provinces. While the federal government can negotiate, it lacks exclusive power to implement international agreements in such areas as government procurement practices or resource policies. The provinces also have exclusive jurisdiction over "property and civil rights," which means they control many of the regulatory policies that can create nontariff barriers to trade in services or direct investment. Short of amendment of the Canadian constitution, provincial implementation of international agreements will probably

19. See Murray G. Smith and Debra P. Steger, "Canada's Constitutional Quandary: The Federal/Provincial Dimension in International Economic Agreements," in David W. Conklin and Thomas J. Courchene, eds., *Canadian Trade at a Crossroads: Options for New International Agreements* (Toronto: Ontario Economic Council, 1985), pp. 362–84.

require a series of federal-provincial agreements on the Canadian side. Following a conference between the prime minister and provincial premiers in November 1985, federal and provincial governments in Canada began a process to involve the provinces in the negotiation of agreements. In June 1986 they agreed to a consultative process for the negotiations and to a joint exploration of mechanisms for implementation. But specific mechanisms for provincial implementation have not been established.[20]

Managing Future Disputes

A bilateral agreement can affect the management of the inevitable disputes over trade between Canada and the United States and between either country and third countries. Existing multilateral obligations under GATT will, of course, still be relevant, and both countries would continue to manage their relations with third countries through GATT. GATT rules would also still apply to bilateral trade. The U.S.-Israeli agreement, for example, incorporates the common GATT obligations of the two countries. From a Canadian perspective, a bilateral agreement is attractive only in terms of what U.S. Secretary of State George P. Shultz refers to as "tighter trade disciplines" within the GATT framework. Where existing GATT rules are considered to be satisfactory to both countries on particular issues, the bilateral agreement could incorporate those rules. Either country could have recourse to existing dispute settlement procedures under GATT.

Neither country, however, would have recourse to GATT for the settlement of disputes on issues where the bilateral obligations go beyond GATT rules, as is the case with the auto pact. For example, Canada would be unable to lodge a GATT complaint if U.S. policies derogated from the auto pact provisions but did not contravene GATT rules. Although the United States has not introduced measures that directly undermine the auto pact, there is considerable risk that future U.S. actions could erode the benefits obtained from a bilateral agreement.

The first step in dealing with bilateral issues will almost certainly take the form of a process of conciliation and renegotiation between the trading partners. The U.S.-Israeli agreement, for example, set up a joint committee to deal with issues as they arise. Although voluntary resolution of differences through consultation is to be encouraged, such a

20. For a discussion of possible approaches, see Murray G. Smith, "Closing a Trade Deal: The Provinces' Role" (Toronto: C. D. Howe Institute, August 1986).

discretionary approach is unlikely to be sufficient from the point of view of the smaller economic partner. Elsewhere I have recommended a formal bilateral dispute settlement process and the creation of a binational arbitral tribunal.[21] If either party has recourse to the tribunal and a pattern of precedent is established, this will foster trust in the agreement, particularly by the smaller partner.[22] Such a tribunal could investigate the facts on particular disputes and interpret the terms of the agreement. While its findings, like those of GATT panels, would not be formally binding on the two countries, they might be persuasive in most cases. If one country was intransigent in the face of a tribunal ruling, the agreement could provide for a reciprocal withdrawal of concessions, as does GATT. In the event of a severe breakdown in the bilateral agreement, both countries could revert to their common obligations under GATT.

The possibility of such a breakdown in the bilateral agreement raises serious concerns in Canada. The fear is that once Canadian industry has retooled for the North American market, Canada will be more vulnerable to U.S. abrogation of an agreement or to threats of abrogation. Although a comprehensive FTA agreement is much less likely to be abrogated than a narrow sectoral arrangement like the auto pact, the question of abrogation needs to be considered. One possible solution would be to permit termination by mutual consent, with special procedures for unilateral action. If one country wishes to terminate the agreement unilaterally, it would be required to give two years' notice of its intent to do so. In response, the partner country would be permitted to suspend immediately its bilateral reduction of trade barriers.

Bilateral Negotiations in a Multilateral Context

There are divergent views about the longer-term effects of a Canadian-U.S. agreement on the multilateral trading system. One view asserts

21. Smith and Steger, "Canada's Constitutional Quandary"; see also Frank Stone, "Institutional Provisions and Form of a Future Canada-United States Trade Agreement" (Ottawa: Institute for Research on Public Policy, 1985).

22. John H. Jackson, "Dispute Settlement Techniques between Nations Concerning Economic Relations—With Special Emphasis on GATT," in Thomas E. Carbonneau, ed., *Resolving Transnational Disputes through International Arbitration* (University Press of Virginia, 1984); and Louis B. Sohn, "The Role of Arbitration in Recent International Multilateral Treaties," in Carbonneau, ed., *Resolving Transnational Disputes*.

that a bilateral arrangement would contribute to greater fragmentation of an already splintered global trading system. Another view, however, makes the case that a free trade area agreement, consistent with GATT article 24, creates tighter disciplines that serve to reinforce the global trading system.

Although they are seldom distinguished, two quite different concerns appear to be at issue between these two contrasting views. One is a well-established concern about whether a bilateral trading arrangement creates trade and thus enhances world welfare, or whether the arrangement diverts trade and thus may benefit the trading partners, but at the expense of the economic interests of third countries. The second concern has to do with the longer-term effects on the trading system—such as the impact of the bilateral arrangement on the behavior of the trading partners in subsequent multilateral trade negotiations, or the effects on the management of trade relations and disputes in the broader multilateral system.

The extensive literature on the question of trade creation and diversion makes clear that there is no a priori answer to the question. Instead, the impact is determined by the economic structure of the trading partners, the preferences of consumers in the member countries, the height and structure of their respective external trade barriers before the agreement, and, most important, the external structure of tariffs and other trade barriers facing third countries when the regional trade agreement is implemented. If there are opportunities for economies of scale under the trade agreement, the likelihood that the regional arrangement will be trade creating is increased greatly.

An additional, but tangential, question I would like to address here is, which is more likely to be trade creating—an FTA or a customs union? Under most circumstances, one could design a customs union that was more trade creating than an FTA, given two countries' preexisting tariff structures. Yet one practical advantage of an FTA is that it is possible to monitor changes in the external trade barriers of the member countries. A customs union requires the harmonization of external trade barriers, and it is difficult to discern whether the new common structure of protection is more or less open to trade with third countries.

A much clearer case can be made that a customs union or common market is likely to be, over the longer term, more corrosive to the multilateral trading system than an FTA. One reason is that once a common external structure of protection has been erected, the process of reaching a supranational consensus on external trade policy with third countries seems likely to create a bias favoring the retention of preferences among the members of the trading bloc and breeds a least-common-denominator approach to trade liberalization. That is, the degree of trade liberalization is constrained to the level permitted by the major member country that is least willing to accept the discipline of particular trade barriers or nontariff distortions. Certainly, the experience of the European Community is consistent with the hypothesis that a common market creates a protectionist bias in the decisionmaking process of the common institutions.[23]

Although an FTA creates preferences among its member countries, these preferences are unlikely to erode the multilateral system in the longer term. Indeed, proponents of free trade negotiations argue that the creation of such preferences in turn creates incentives for other countries to engage in trade liberalization, just as the innovation of plurilateral negotiations reduces the "free-rider problem" that occurs in most-favored-nation tariff negotiations.[24] Plurilateral negotiations, however, may not solve the least-common-denominator problem among the major industrial trade partners.

The free trade area provision of the U.S. Trade and Tariff Act of 1984 represents a significant innovation intended to alter the incentives for countries to engage in international trade negotiations. It grants the U.S. administration authority to enter into negotiations with other countries to establish an FTA. The rationale for the new approach of negotiating bilateral FTAs was explained by Secretary Shultz:

> From a global perspective, a splintering of the multilateral trading system into a multitude of bilateral arrangements would be a backward step. Bilateral free trade agreements, however, such as we have negotiated with Israel . . . , need not have this result; they can stimulate trade and strengthen the multilateral system. Free trade agreements are sanctioned by the international rules and involve a tighter trade discipline; they can promote freer trade than the multilateral system is currently prepared to accommodate. Our hope, nonetheless, is that the example of greater liberalization—and the recognition that the United States can pursue another course—will help motivate a larger group of nations to tackle the job of expanding trade on a global basis.[25]

23. Gardner Patterson, "The European Community as a Threat to the System," in Cline, ed., *Trade Policy in the 1980s*, pp. 223–42.

24. Richard N. Cooper, "The Future of the International Trading System," in Conklin and Courchene, eds., *Canadian Trade at a Crossroads*.

25. George P. Shultz, "National Policies and Global Prosperity," address to the

Elaborating on this theme, the 1985 report of the U.S. Council of Economic Advisers argues that "the possibility of FTA negotiations . . . offers the United States and others the option of using a free-trade instrument, rather than protectionism, as a lever against protectionist countries. . . ."[26] Thus the preferred access available to members of an FTA provides an incentive for other countries to engage in trade negotiations. This strategy of liberalizing trade on a bilateral or plurilateral basis is preferable to the use of threats of trade restrictions to induce other countries to negotiate. Threatened protectionist measures would impose costs on the home country if implemented, and thus the threats lack credibility. Furthermore, to implement the threats would invite retaliation.

In its 1986 report, the CEA echoed this theme:

> The United States now faces a historic opportunity in the possibility of establishing a free trade agreement with Canada. In September 1985 the Canadian Government proposed that both countries consider bilateral negotiations on the broadest possible package of mutually beneficial reductions in trade barriers. In 1935 Canada and the United States took bilateral steps to reverse the protectionism of that era, steps that became a catalyst for broader international cooperation then. The new Canadian-U.S. initiative offers similar prospects now.[27]

The crucial difference between a free trade area and a customs union is that in a free trade area each member maintains control over commercial policy for, and trade negotiations with, third countries. From the point of view of each member country, the preferential access created by the regional trading arrangement has the character of a public good. It is the external trade barrier of one country that creates the preference for suppliers in the other country relative to third countries. For example, Canada's post–Tokyo round tariff on machinery is 9.2 percent. In the absence of a Canadian-American FTA, under GATT rules Canada would negotiate most machinery tariffs bilaterally with the United States because the United States is the principal supplier of the products. Tariff elimination between Canada and the United States would give U.S. machinery suppliers an advantage relative to producers in third countries such as Japan. In subsequent GATT tariff negotiations Canada could

---

Woodrow Wilson School of Public and International Affairs, Princeton University, April 11, 1985.
26. *Economic Report of the President, February 1985*, p. 126.
27. Ibid., *February 1986*, p. 123.

offer to reduce its machinery tariff in order to obtain reductions in Japanese trade barriers.

A bilateral agreement can be expected to shift the focus of multilateral tariff negotiations, promote restructuring of domestic industry, and improve the industry's capability to meet third-country competition. In general, an FTA member country has an incentive to negotiate reductions in its external trade barriers in multilateral negotiations in order to obtain improved access to third-country markets, whereas in a customs union the maintenance of external barriers becomes the raison d'être of the organization. Thus the preferences created by a free trade area are more likely to be reduced over time through multilateral negotiations than is the case with a customs union.

Similarly, the members of a free trade area have a continuing interest in the international trade rules that provide the framework for managing trade relations and trade disputes. Each member will continue to have separate trade relations with third countries, and important elements of the multilateral trade rules will continue to govern trade among member countries.

Questions do arise about the availability to other countries of the terms of an arrangement between Canada and the United States. Although third countries are unlikely to want to join in the near future, some—such as Australia or Japan—might well seek to do so eventually. If that happens, there could well be problems in making a North American agreement, tailored to bilateral concerns, suitable for membership by third countries. A much more likely alternative is that either or both Canada and the United States might negotiate FTA arrangements with third countries.

If either, or both, countries conclude a bilateral agreement with a major third country, it could create problems in the administration of rules of origin as well as incentives for trade deflection. Since stated U.S. policy is to promote such bilateral agreements, the possible implications need to be examined when negotiating and designing one between Canada and the United States.

It is also possible that components of the bilateral agreement could become part of plurilateral agreements among the industrial countries. Indeed, the bilateral agreement could pioneer approaches to, and provide a model for, dealing with new trade issues, such as barriers to trade in services and investment policies. Other countries, however, might be unwilling simply to accede to an agreement negotiated between Canada and the United States, while those two countries might be reluctant to renegotiate the bilateral agreement in the broader multilateral context.

At a minimum, potential third-country reluctance suggests that if Canada and the United States are genuine in wanting bilateral agreements to serve as a model for plurilateral agreements, the bilateral negotiations should be closely coordinated with multilateral talks. Since the bilateral negotiations must proceed much more quickly if they are to succeed, Canada and the United States could consult with the representatives of third countries when drafting the bilateral arrangement. It is certainly in Canada's interest to take account of the position other major trading partners are likely to take during subsequent multilateral negotiations on trade in services and investment issues.

Conclusion

If the negotiations are to succeed, the bilateral agreement between Canada and the United States must be forged to accommodate the complexity and uniqueness of the world's largest two-way trade and investment relationship. In important respects, the agreement will build on previous experience with free trade agreements among industrial countries. It will have to go further than previous bilateral or multilateral agreements, however, if it is to address the concerns and meet the objectives of both countries.

There appears to be no panacea to the issue of increasing use of trade remedy laws and procedures. The stakes are high, however. Unless each country agrees to clarify and limit the use of trade remedies, there will be no significant improvement in the security of their access to each other's markets.

While both countries probably would accept the same formal obligations regarding trade laws, Canada has the greater interest in obtaining more secure access to U.S. markets. U.S. resistance to negotiation of trade laws is likely to be particularly intense, because the specter of unfair foreign competition touches a deep chord in the American psyche. It is in the long-term interests of the United States to take a selective approach to sanctions against unfair foreign trade, but this point is not widely understood and hardly provides a basis for building a constituency to support an agreement. Consequently, the Canadian interest in negotiating limitations on the application of trade remedy laws would have to be balanced against particular U.S. interests, including elimination of the higher Canadian tariffs and negotiation of new rules for trade in services and investment.

In light of the significant differences in the two countries' negotiating objectives, a truly comprehensive agreement that covers a broad range of issues and sectors is likely to be easier to negotiate than a narrower deal. At the same time, however, negotiations on trade in services and investment policies are likely to proceed on a sectoral, rather than across-the-board, basis. As a result, it will probably be more difficult to resist pressures to keep particular sectors out of the negotiations.

Only a comprehensive agreement offers the opportunity to build a broad coalition favoring the agreement in both countries. Yet there is pressure on the negotiators to try to reach a deal before the current authority for the fast-track process in the U.S. Congress expires on January 3, 1988. This makes it more difficult to negotiate such a comprehensive agreement. If the agreement cannot be concluded within this time frame, then the bilateral negotiations will become entwined with the issue of obtaining congressional extension of negotiating authority for the GATT round.

A bilateral agreement serves the strategic trade policy objectives of both countries. In addition, successful conclusion of bilateral talks could provide needed impetus to the multilateral negotiating process. Indeed, components of the bilateral agreement, such as agreements on trade in services and investment policies, could provide a model for GATT-type agreements. Failure to reach bilateral agreement would not augur well for the multilateral process. Thus the two countries' conduct of the bilateral negotiations will have important implications for both bilateral economic relations and for the global trading system. Yet the strategic implications of the bilateral negotiations seem little understood in the United States.

For the first time in seventy-five years a Canadian government has been prepared to enter into negotiations for free trade with the United States. In light of Canadian sensitivities, U.S. recalcitrance to negotiate could damage its economic relationship with its largest trading partner and risk alienating its strategically important northern neighbor. If U.S. protectionism thwarts the bilateral negotiations, the result could be to undermine the ability of the United States to continue to play a leadership role in the global trading system.

Comments by Larry G. Butcher

Having this opportunity to comment on the perspective offered by Murray Smith on the upcoming negotiation of a U.S.-Canadian free trade area is a pleasure. As he did when coauthoring *Taking the Initiative*, Smith has provided a thoughtful approach to key issues, and, so important at this formative stage of the process, he has not been bound by conventional wisdoms. This is the time to think creatively.

Smith offers a wealth of evenhanded ideas for improving the predictability of market access, transition arrangements, dispute management, and other key issues for the negotiations. For focus and brevity, I would like to comment principally on the first of these issues.

At their Quebec summit meeting, Prime Minister Mulroney and President Reagan agreed that greater predictability of market access was important. International Trade Minister James Kelleher identified this as one of the four principal Canadian objectives in the negotiations. We obviously believe these Canadian concerns can be constructively addressed, and U.S. objectives advanced, in the negotiations.

Smith's treatment of the issue of the predictability of market access and trade remedy laws permeates his paper. His analysis is productive in several ways. First, the distinction between provisions of law aimed at unfair trade practices and "escape clause" or "safeguard" provisions is useful. Second, he has underscored how widely Canadian and U.S. perceptions of the role of trade remedy laws differ, in spite of the fact that legislation of both countries has evolved along basically similar lines. Third, he has shown that there is a spectrum or array of possible approaches to this question. Fourth, the present lack of a mechanism to restrain government subsidies is recognized as a problem. Indeed, as is implicit in this paper, an agreement defining more precisely what constitutes a trade-distorting subsidy and how such practices can be restrained could be the single most important step toward more predictable market access. Fifth, with bilateral application of fair trade laws, the role of antidumping laws could fade in importance in a free trade area. Lastly, the paper implicitly recognizes that solutions to the question of market access are interrelated with whatever approach is eventually adopted on dispute settlement. For example, if a dispute settlement mechanism could reach quick and clear judgments as to whether new government programs should or should not be considered trade distorting, it could reduce the number of cases brought under countervailing duty laws.

I would like to add a few additional thoughts to Smith's treatment of the trade remedy laws. If the perspective is different, it helps to confirm part of his hypothesis. Since diplomats are known to quibble over wording, it should be no surprise that I object to labeling trade remedy laws as "contingent protection." This seems to be a term coined in Canada, and it can be very misleading. Antidumping and countervailing duty laws are clearly aimed at trying to achieve fair trade, or a level playing field, in the face of illegal pricing practices or trade-distorting subsidies. They have no relationship to "protectionism," or acts taken to insulate domestic industry from foreign firms that enjoy a genuine competitive advantage.

We should also recognize that the U.S. approach to trade remedy law is not static, nor is it unique. Several recent court decisions bear on the question of how industry-specific a subsidy must be in order to be considered countervailable. Congress may consider legislation to limit the president's discretion in administration of "safeguard" provisions of section 201 of the trade act, in addition to the bills mentioned by Smith that are aimed at making certain natural resource pricing practices countervailable. The administration is committed to consulting with Congress fully at each stage of the negotiations. How we propose to handle trade remedy laws in the agreement would have a very important influence on its reception in Congress. To consider any significant changes in this area, we would no doubt have to be assured of reciprocal treatment and of a comprehensive final agreement. In the words of Secretary Shultz, the agreement should address "the full range of barriers to the flow of goods, services, and direct investment between our two countries."

Lastly, as a spur to lively discussion, we should remember that it is possible to exaggerate the importance of changing trade remedy laws. An economist would point out that business decisions on where to locate new plants are based on many factors. Being subject to U.S. trade remedy laws might at the margin make some firms lean toward locating in the United States rather than Canada under a free trade area, but it is not clear that this would be a significant factor in the vast majority of cases. After looking at basic economic factors bearing on site selection (for example, proximity to market, relative wage rates, quality of the work force), a rational investor would assess the probability of ever being subject to, say, a countervailing duty petition, the probability of losing the case, and the potential damage to profitability if the case were lost. I would argue that the probability of being subject to a countervailing duty case in the United States, while not zero, is still low, and could be lower still with further understandings on subsidies. Moreover, we can expect that a comprehensive trade agreement would result in more intra-industry specialization, with more trade taking place on the basis of intracompany transfers, where it is hard to imagine cases being filed under the trade remedy laws. Lastly, judging from the large number of antidumping suits brought in Canada, it seems safe to say that neither country would want to deny its citizens ultimate access to laws designed to assure fair competition.

In short, while more predictable market access is important, the benefits from a comprehensive trade agreement would not necessarily rise or fall on how, or whether, trade remedy laws are dealt with.

MARTIN WOLF

A European Perspective

MY ASSIGNED TASK is to provide "a European perspective" on the proposal for a free trade agreement between Canada and the United States. I am delighted that the indefinite article has been used. The views to be expressed are definitely those of *a* European and one often regarded as something of a traitor to the cause of European unity. Before I express those views, however, something needs to be said about other possible European perspectives, not only because they are of relevance in their own right but because they will reveal much about the problems of the trading system as a whole.

General European Views

What might Western Europeans feel about the proposal for a free trade agreement between the United States and Canada? There is no official position of which I am aware. Judging from opinions expressed on the arrangement between the United States and the countries of the Caribbean, however, the general reaction might be one of smug satisfaction over the spectacle of the Americans being forced yet again off their "high horse" on nondiscrimination. As the main progenitors of the principle of discrimination in the postwar world (rather than of its somewhat shamefaced practice, as was the case for the United States until the early 1980s), many observers in the European Community are likely to feel a pleasure at the propagation of the principle of discrimination far outweighing any chagrin over the realization that discrimination can work against them.

Those in the European Community who see a "Fortress Europe"

65

strategy as the solution to the political and economic problems of the member countries may well take a special delight in this arrangement. Whatever the economic merits of their ideas—and they are few—their political force is undeniable.[1] The reason is not far to seek, but it is also central to the theme of my remarks.

Mercantilism and Nationalism

For the mercantilist, trade is war. War is what binds people into nations. It is in war that common purposes override individual purposes and the machinery of the state grows large and civil society small. It is for the purpose of waging war that what divides a people from the enemy is emphasized; such an emphasis is also war's natural consequence. Because the birth of a United States of Europe in an actual war is impossible, some who wish to strengthen Europe politically may declare that a trade war is being waged and thus justify protectionism and centralized industrial interventionism as weapons of defense.

According to the great Swedish economist Eli Heckscher, the mercantilists of the seventeenth and eighteenth centuries were also trying to create strong centralized states by breaking down the internal barriers to state control, which were incidentally also barriers to the free play of the market. Two quotations from his classic work on mercantilism are apposite. "Mercantilism is primarily an agent of [national] unification. Its adversary was the medieval combination of universalism and particularism." He later remarks that there are "two aspects of mercantilism, unification and power."[2]

In short, the aim of mercantilism was to exalt and strengthen the wealth and power of the unitary state, usually the nation-state. Among other things, citizens were to feel part of a corporate body superseding all previous loyalties, and, conversely, all foreigners were to be regarded as part of an alien body. International commerce would then always have a flavor of "trading with the enemy."

Mercantilism was, therefore, more than merely an economic theory.

1. On the economic arguments, see Joan Pearce and John Sutton with Roy Batchelor, *Protection and Industrial Policy in Europe* (London: Routledge and Kegan Paul, 1986).
2. See Eli F. Heckscher, *Mercantilism*, rev. 2d. ed., E. F. Söderlund, ed.; Mendel Shapiro, trans. (London: Allen and Unwin, 1955), pp. 22, 24. A view of the economic function of nationalism similar to the one advanced here is elaborated in an important book by Ernest Gellner, *Nations and Nationalism* (Oxford: Basil Blackwell, 1983).

It was a political tactic, both fruitful and dangerous, aimed at creating and reinforcing the national consciousness that would, *among other things*, support the state's efforts to break down internal obstacles. This kind of national consciousness is of great value to protectionist interests, who have generally succeeded in persuading fellow citizens that any importer really is trading with the enemy. Free choice of where to spend one's income is thus often thought of as unpatriotic. The flavor of this argument is captured in the constant references to a liberal policy as "unilateral disarmament."[3]

Intellectual Achievement of Liberalism

Perhaps the most important and by now most dissipated intellectual achievement of early economics was to turn mercantilism on its head. Adam Smith agreed with the mercantilists on the end of national wealth, thus the title *Wealth of Nations*, but he argued that trade is mutually enriching or, quite simply, that trade is not war, but its obverse. Furthermore, Smith argued, the wealth of the community is gained in spite of government's intervention in foreign commerce, rather than as its result. In practice, therefore, liberal economics subverted both the ends and the means of mercantilism with its two revolutionary propositions that wealth is to be gained neither by plundering foreigners nor by expanding the power of the state.

The construction of the intellectual coffin for this benign liberal view of trade began with the "optimal tariff" argument. The new concept of "strategic trade policy" may prove to be the final nail. In the perspective of strategic trade policy, trade is again at least potentially a war. This view has disturbing resonances for the relation between economic thought, international politics, and the role of the state. A remark on the optimal tariff by the late nineteenth century British international trade theorist, Francis Edgeworth, is both apt and elegant. "Protection," he argued, "might procure economic advantage in certain cases, if there was a government wise enough to discriminate those cases, and strong

---

3. In the United Kingdom unilateral liberalism and unilateral disarmament are constantly equated. See, for example, a comment from the representative of the British Footwear Manufacturers' Federation in a letter to the *Financial Times*, January 22, 1986, attacking a study published by the Trade Policy Research Centre. He remarks that "those who advocate unilateral disarmament on the trade front really do need better arguments than those in this study."

enough to confine itself to them; but this condition is very unlikely to be fulfilled."[4] The passage of a century has not done much to still those concerns among observers of modern bureaucratic machines.

The Strength of Reciprocity

Unfortunately, even when economists labored to support rather than subvert Adam Smith's benign view of international commerce, it was never universally shared, and it had ceased to be very influential in the practical world by the end of the nineteenth century. The growing strength of the notion of reciprocity, fundamental to the General Agreement on Tariff and Trade (GATT) as it is, provides the most important example, for reciprocity is a deeply mercantilist idea.

It is accepted that reciprocity is automatically present in any voluntary transaction between citizens of one state, there being the reciprocal provision of goods and means of payment (ultimately the reciprocal exchange of goods). Only in international trade is a voluntary transaction not regarded as inherently reciprocal. Other members of the collectivity, it is assumed, must be given opportunities to sell if any citizen is to be entitled to buy. What is implicit in the concept of reciprocity is the figment of a corporate economic transactor, the state, which must be allowed to export if it is to import. This implicit emphasis on the state as an economic agent shows reciprocity to be profoundly mercantilist.

Because it is based on the mercantilist notion of reciprocity, the trade policy of the period after World War II is also based on the view that trade is inherently a war.[5] Thus GATT is the peace treaty. Peace is, however, not a satisfactory solution for all. Some participants want trade to be a war that is still being waged and for the very same reason that the original mercantilists did: they want to build states.

This unalloyed, predisarmament, and mercantilist view is held by the intellectual and political leaders of the majority of developing countries,

4. F. Y. Edgeworth, *Papers Relating to Political Economy*, vol. 2 (London: Published on behalf of the Royal Economic Society by Macmillan, 1925), p. 18 (first published in *The Economic Journal* in 1894).

5. This should not be taken to suggest that there is no economic argument for reciprocity. However mistaken the reasons for the emphasis on reciprocity, it can be valuable in practice, to the extent that it secures a far wider spread of liberalization than could ever be achieved by separate, unilateral action. Furthermore, at least in theory the reciprocal approach could encourage avoidance of optimal tariff wars, though in practice this is probably the least common reason for protection.

but it is also shared by at least some enthusiasts for the European ideal. The European Community's trade policy is aimed in part at nation building, or rather Europe building. In the community's case, particularism is represented by the power of the member states and universalism by GATT, and both can be seen as enemies by the committed European. Discrimination against the community by others can, therefore, be attractive to such people since they can argue: "We were right. Trade is war and the rest of the world is conspiring against us. We must retaliate by pursuing a Fortress Europe policy and so defend ourselves against our enemies." In short, indifference or approval is the reaction to be expected of many observers in Western Europe toward the proposed free trade agreement between the United States and Canada. My own reaction, however, is rather one of sadness mixed with understanding. But it is sadness, nonetheless, for the policies now being discussed in North America and especially the United States appear to be proof of the perceived decline of the GATT system in this part of the world, and, what is more, they are likely to further that decline. It is the purpose of the balance of these remarks to justify this reaction.

Principles of the Liberal International Economic Order

GATT is a peace treaty among mercantilist states, but it is more, just as the nineteenth century treaty system was more.[6] GATT is also based on a liberal conception of the relation between the state and the economy, on the one hand, and among the various participating states, on the other hand. An underlying assumption was that the sphere of autonomous individual action needed to be protected from the state and in this way states would be protected from one another. The aim was to end the laissez faire for individual governments that had been the main characteristic of the interwar period and replace it with a system of internationally agreed rules, at whose heart were certain fundamental norms. Those norms were the use of a transparent and market-conforming instrument of protection, the tariff; the binding of protection; the exchange of tariff concessions on a reciprocal basis; and their generalization to trade

6. The arguments in this section are elaborated in Martin Wolf, "An Unholy Alliance: The European Community and Developing Countries in the International Trading System," in L. B. M. Mennes and Jacob Kol, eds., *European Trade Policies and the Developing World* (London: Croom Helm, 1987).

among all contracting parties by means of the principle of unconditional nondiscrimination.

Rationale of the System

The rationale of the GATT system is liberal in two respects. First, it assumes that economic activity would be organized in a spontaneous, competitive manner. Secondly, it attempts to remove international economic relations from politics. The view is that discretionary political interference, especially discrimination among suppliers, can only lead to damaging international conflicts, and that these conflicts are almost always over policies that are damaging to all parties. Thus the system represents an effort to take trade policy from the weaponry of the sovereign state. The attempt may look naive, but given that the major participants are allies, on what other basis should they organize their mutual economic relations?

What justifies the underlying rules for the economist? Over the past decade or so the implications of the system were spelled out in the work of the late Jan Tumlir, formerly director of research at GATT. His thumbnail sketch is as follows:

> In the period since World War II, national economic policies were made compatible, both internally and between countries, by the adherence of governments to international rules articulated in Bretton Woods, Havana and Geneva. On the monetary side, these rules ensured relative stability of national price levels, and thus also of exchange rates, and on the trade side they secured stable and non-discriminatory access of all exporters to at least the large markets of the developed countries.[7]

What would be achieved by the adherence of major countries to the fundamental norms of the international trading system? The answer is stability in change. The price mechanisms of each participating economy would be tied together in a global system, thus facilitating coordination of economic activity throughout the global economy, signaling of chang-

---

7. Jan Tumlir, "International Economic Order—Can the Trend Be Reversed?" *World Economy,* vol. 5 (March 1982), pp. 33–34. See also Tumlir, *Protectionism: Trade Policy in Democratic Societies,* AEI Studies no. 436 (Washington, D.C.: American Enterprise Institute, 1985). A little known earlier work of great importance is Lionel Robbins, *Economic Planning and International Order* (London: Macmillan, 1937), especially chap. 9.

ing opportunities, and autonomous adjustment by private decisionmakers to those changes.[8]

Economists can object to these norms as not ensuring optimality, but this is a misconceived objection. If the world economy is to function at all, the most important information—about relevant changes—must be disseminated and adjustment to those changes must occur. Within a system of bound tariffs there is, indeed, a deadweight efficiency loss. Nevertheless, information about economic change is distributed throughout all the linked markets, and the normal reactions of profit-seeking firms ensure coordination of supplies. Furthermore, in the absence of particularly perverse distortions in national economies, adjustment can also be expected to occur in each economy in the direction required by economic developments elsewhere. Bound tariffs stabilize the conditions for the global market process, while quantitative restrictions terminate it.

One aspect of such a liberal international trading system needs to be noted. It is particularly valuable to small, economically dynamic countries. It is valuable to small countries because they are likely to be dependent on trade yet incapable of independently securing satisfactory access for the goods and products of their citizens. It is valuable to dynamic countries because it is they who most need the automatic accommodation to their growing exports that would result from the pursuit of profit by buyers and sellers in the market. What is new is almost always viewed as disruptive. If change has to be negotiated between gainers and losers, political forces usually ensure that it will be slowed. It is for this reason that, as managed trade has come to the fore, it has been seen as a way of preserving traditional patterns both of trade and international relations while curbing the impact of disruptive newcomers. That, in a nutshell, is what makes the idea of selective safeguards so seductive.

Reciprocity and Nondiscrimination

The principal economic function of the norms of the international trading system is to ensure the existence of an international market economy. The objective is modest because of the limited restraints over

8. See Jan Tumlir, "Can the International Economic Order Be Saved?" *World Economy*, vol. 1 (October 1977), pp. 3–20.

sovereign discretion that can be achieved. But is even that objective achievable? Can such an agreement be enforced?

A liberal international trading order is a collective good in two senses. First, countries that do not contribute cannot be excluded entirely from the benefits, and, second, provision of full measure of the good requires a cooperative effort among several governments. Theory suggests that provision of a public good will be inadequate unless there is coercion or, as Mancur Olson has put it, "selective incentives."[9]

There is, however, one situation in which an international trading order would be supplied both voluntarily and adequately. If a sufficiently large number of countries were to act on a view that free trade is *unilaterally* optimal, provision of the collective good would create no problem because the providers would not see it as imposing a cost on themselves. This idea was at its strongest in the nineteenth century. In the almost ninety years after the repeal of the Corn Laws there was little difficulty in this regard with respect to the United Kingdom. But this was never true in all major countries, such as France and the United States. Liberalization was also spread through international bargaining on the basis of reciprocity starting with the Cobden-Chevalier Treaty of 1860.

Reciprocity has, therefore, always played a major part in the trading system, but in the postwar era, when no major power has believed in unilateral liberalism, it has been just about the only incentive for provision of a liberal order. The essence of the postwar trading system, therefore, is the attempt to achieve a policy limited to the use of tariffs and to liberalize and stabilize those tariffs by exploiting the mercantilism of its participants, revealed in the demand for reciprocity.

Reciprocity alone does not make for an international trading order. Since small countries have little power to retaliate, there is a danger of discrimination in which large powers permit liberal exchange only where one another's citizens are concerned. There is also the danger of purely unilateral determinations of reciprocal fairness, with resulting bitter disputes.

Nondiscrimination is, accordingly, central to a system whose principal technique of liberalization is reciprocity and whose principal sanction is retaliation. It is nondiscrimination that creates a global order out of an

---

9. Mancur Olson, *The Logic of Collective Action: Public Goods and the Theory of Groups* (Harvard University Press, 1977), p. 51.

essentially mercantilist system.[10] By virtue of nondiscrimination purely bilateral bargains become available to all participants, even those with little effective capacity to negotiate. Furthermore, the commitment to nondiscrimination puts the retaliatory power of the strong behind the complaints of the weak. Nondiscrimination, in other words, creates a collective security system out of what would otherwise depend on the relative power of individual states. It disciplines mercantilism.

It is impossible to avoid admiration for those who have thus created a liberal trading system out of mercantilism twice in the past two centuries. But the success resulted from a Faustian bargain. Particularly in the postwar world, liberalization was achieved at the price of constantly reemphasizing an erroneous, essentially preeconomic view of international trade.

One obvious problem is that retaliation is an unreliable means of discipline. Its use cannot be predicted. But the problem with mercantilism is deeper than that. It is psychologically inconsistent with nondiscrimination. Why, countries ask, should they retaliate over discriminatory policies not aimed at their own exports? Are they not, indeed, likely to benefit from such policies? Why should the benefits of nondiscriminatory access be afforded to countries that do not play the liberal game? One now thinks of Japan and the newly industrializing countries in this capacity, but historically the United States created still greater problems. Indeed, one can argue that both the breakdown of the nineteenth century treaty system and the failure to recreate it in the interwar period were largely the result of the largely unilateral protectionism of the United States, its refusal to reciprocate.[11] Again, why should there be liberalization in favor of countries that provide only negligible markets? Also, why retaliate against protection of insignificant markets? It is not difficult to see that mercantilism is unlikely to prove consistent with a commitment to nondiscriminatory and generally liberal policies in a world of many countries with divergent characteristics, and, in fact, it has not.

The system then also relies on some vestigial sense of the benefits of unilateral liberalism, on the fading memory of disasters of half a century ago, and on the consciousness of a once hegemonic power of the consequences of its defection. These are weak foundations, indeed. The system is built on sand.

10. See *International Trade 1983–84* (Geneva: GATT Secretariat, 1984).
11. On this see Tumlir, *Protectionism,* chap. 2.

The Trading System Today

After substantial initial successes in the first twenty years or so after World War II, the trading system has been cumulating difficulties. Many of those difficulties relate to the ease with which political problems have been resolved by discriminatory arrangements that are also very attractive to the producer interests involved. With the growth of discrimination—one estimate from the GATT secretariat is that discriminatory export restraint arrangements covered 12 percent of world nonfuel trade in the mid-1980s—protection can no longer be stabilized.[12] What is agreed in multilateral trade negotiations is, accordingly, of declining relevance.

Another, not at all unrelated, problem is that of contingent or administered protection.[13] It is the problem of securing the desired stability in trade policy. In order to reach agreement on a GATT, it was necessary to permit action to increase protection or violate other norms. There were clauses permitting protection for balance of payments reasons (articles 12 and 18), infant industry protection (article 18), emergency safeguard protection (article 19), quantitative restrictions against imports of agricultural products (article 11), protection against dumped or subsidized goods (article 6), discrimination against particular contracting parties (article 35), and finally discrimination in the case of customs unions and free trade areas (article 24).

The various loopholes and escape clauses, and corresponding domestic laws, have operated in the context of a general unwillingness to adjust to changes of foreign origin and are associated with a rejection of comparative advantage in favor of the mercantilist framework of GATT. To take one somewhat paradoxical example, the American countervail against the adjustment-resisting subsidies of others has itself protectionist force, especially as cases can be resolved via export restraints.[14]

12. See Michel Kostecki, "Grey Area Trade Policy" (Geneva: GATT Secretariat, February 1986), p. 6.

13. These terms have gained wide currency. See, for example, Rodney de C. Grey, "A Note on U.S. Trade Practices," in William R. Cline, ed., *Trade Policies in the 1980s* (Washington, D.C.: Institute for International Economics, 1983), pp. 243–58. See also J. Michael Finger, H. Keith Hall, and Douglas R. Nelson, "The Political Economy of Administered Protection," *American Economic Review*, vol. 72 (June 1982), pp. 452–66.

14. That the countervailing duty and antidumping provisions of American trade law

In short, within a generally mercantilist, import-resisting framework undisciplined by strict adherence to the principle of nondiscrimination, it has proved difficult to stabilize protection. In this fundamental respect it is now increasingly appropriate to refer to an international trading nonsystem, a patchwork of ad hoc arrangements.

Free Trade Agreement between the United States and Canada

The proposal for a free trade agreement between Canada and the United States can be seen in large measure as a reaction to the decay of the international trading system as a whole. For the countries concerned, bilateralism is apparently an alternative to reliance on a flawed multilateralism.

Canada's economic relations with the United States have long been fraught with difficulty, as Canada oscillates between economic nationalism and the notion of closer economic relations with the United States.[15] Whenever one of the two countries has looked toward more liberal bilateral trade, the other has rejected it. In 1866 the United States withdrew from the Reciprocity Treaty. Partly in reaction to American protection, the Canadians then moved in 1874 toward MacDonald's protectionist national policy. In 1896 the Americans turned down Canadian proposals for reciprocity. After 1911, however, it was a Canadian election that ended hopes of substantial bilateral liberalization. In 1947 the Canadian prime minister refused to continue with bilateral negotiations, and Canada instead put its trust in multilateral arrangements, namely, GATT. In the 1980s Canada and the United States are again interested in a bilateral arrangement.

For much of her history Canada has been interested in the idea of preferential trade, alternating between the United States and the British Empire as the appropriate partner. In retrospect, the period ushered in with GATT was exceptional. Canada liberalized substantially within the GATT framework on a multilateral basis and also enjoyed substantial

are protectionist in effect is an important finding of Finger, Hall, and Nelson, "Political Economy of Administered Protection."

15. On the history of Canadian trade policy, see John Whalley with Colleen Hamilton and Roderick Hill, *Canadian Trade Policies and the World Economy* (University of Toronto Press, 1985), table 1-10.

benefit from this process. What is clear now, however, is that many of Canada's most astute observers no longer see the GATT framework as a viable bulwark against protectionist pressures in the world, especially when about three-quarters of Canada's trade is with the United States alone and some of the most visible protectionist pressures are emerging in that country.

The nature of the choice has been put particularly clearly by Richard Lipsey and Murray Smith:

> Some will be willing to rely solely on the multilateral approach. . . . We worry, however, that the gains will be too little and too late. The next round of GATT negotiations will probably take place in the late 1980s and, if the Tokyo Round is any indication, several years may pass before any resulting trade liberalization actually occurs. In any case, the negotiations will probably take place in the present protectionist atmosphere and, thus, the trade-liberalizing results may be disappointingly small. . . . So it seems to us to be unnecessarily risky to rely solely on the next round of GATT negotiations for the trade liberalization that we feel is urgently needed. . . . Furthermore, as was illustrated by the example of the Tokyo Round of procurement negotia-tions, the GATT may not be the best vehicle for achieving trade liberalization with our most important trading partner: the United States.[16]

The authors conclude their analysis by arguing that the best approach for Canada is to push "multilateral liberalization for all it is worth, but also [push] now for a major bilateral trade-liberalizing agreement with the United States."[17]

From Canada's point of view, an important concern appears to be with the predictability of market access to the United States. As another distinguished Canadian international economist, R. J. Wonnacott, has put the point: "Until fairly recently, the major question has been: what would be the net benefits to Canada of moving from our present position to a freer trading arrangement with the United States? However, another question is now also being asked: what would be the further benefits to Canada of being able to secure our *present* access to the US market? In other words, our *present* level of exports to the United States is threatened by a build-up of protectionist pressures in the United States."[18]

16. Richard G. Lipsey and Murray G. Smith, *Taking the Initiative: Canada's Trade Options in a Turbulent World* (Toronto: C. D. Howe Institute, 1985), pp. 70–71. See also Lipsey, "Will There Be a Canadian-American Free Trade Association?" *World Economy*, vol. 9 (September 1986), pp. 217–38.

17. Lipsey and Smith, *Taking the Initiative*, p. 71.

18. R. J. Wonnacott, "Canada/United States Free Trade: Problems and Opportu-

Normal trading rules, it is suggested, no longer provide the stability Canada needs, given her extraordinary dependence on the American market. This failure, in turn, reflects protectionist pressures in the United States, which show themselves in increasingly frequent complaints about unfair trade and growing use of the "less than fair value" provisions of American trade law. In fact, the way the contingent protection system is being used reminds the observer increasingly of the old notion of the "scientific tariff," the tariff that will offset comparative cost disadvantages. If this analysis is correct, then the direction in which American trade policy is going merely reveals the extent to which the basic logic of trade has never been accepted.

From the point of view of the United States, security of market access per se is less of a concern. The current talk about bilateral and multilateral approaches, of which the proposed free trade area with Canada is merely a salient example, largely reflects a profound frustration with the whole multilateral machinery of the GATT system and growing skepticism about the unconditional most-favored-nation (MFN) principle. What appears to be happening is that the United States is moving—in an inchoate and ill-thought-out manner—to a new trade policy that combines a measure of a conditional MFN principle with a large degree of trade policy autonomy, its traditional combination of the nineteenth century. This movement is partly evidence, it must be admitted, of an attempt to preserve a degree of liberalism in actual trade policy.

The reasons for this drift in American trade policy appear to be two: the failure to obtain satisfactory agreement to further global liberalization within the GATT framework, revealed most painfully at the GATT ministerial meeting of November 1982, and the growing feeling that the whole trading system in which the United States has embedded itself is unfair, that the United States is being "taken for a ride" by protectionists and interventionists elsewhere. Whatever the reasons, such a move would amount to a clear rejection of the seventy years of history during which the United States painfully learned and then successfully played its role of global leader; this period's main landmarks were the acceptance of the unconditional MFN principle in 1922, the abandonment of congressional control over an autonomous tariff in 1934, and the agreement on GATT in 1947.[19]

---

nities," Special Research Report, Series on Canadian Trade at a Crossroads (Ontario: Ontario Economic Council, 1985).

19. See Tumlir, *Protectionism*, pp. 22–25.

There can be no question, it appears, that the proposed free trade agreement is in accordance with GATT article 24 and is not in violation of international trade law. In this respect the proposal is quite unlike the majority of such agreements of the past quarter century or so, especially those among developing countries and between the European Community and certain groups of developing countries. The questions that must be raised refer to the spirit, not the letter, of the agreement.

Again, it is impossible not to sympathize with Canada. Canada has to adapt to the world in which it finds itself. The chances must be high that such an agreement with the United States will be immensely beneficial to Canada as the economy is forced to increase its efficiency and especially if secure access to the American market is indeed achieved.

The difficult questions are inevitably those facing the United States. In what sort of world does it want to find itself? Does it wish to have a separate trade policy for every trading partner with the bitterness inevitably caused by constantly changing positions in an unstable hierarchy of privilege? Is it conceivable that any sort of stability in global trade policy can be secured if the United States does get involved in an increasingly complex network of preferential trading arrangements, both interlocking with and rivaling those of the European Community? Would one not expect Japan to follow the example of the two great economic powers, especially when so much discrimination is already directed against her? Would the world not then start to look progressively like that of the 1930s with "co-prosperity spheres" and trading blocs in ceaseless conflict?

There are cases when the spirit rather than the letter of the law is what matters. That letter—article 24—was itself a defeat for liberal principles. If the United States goes much further with the sorts of policies toward which it now appears to be leaning, the multilateral trading system is unlikely to survive, let alone prosper.

Free Trade Agreement and a New GATT Round

Rather than just leave things as they are, it is worth asking whether such an agreement between the United States and Canada could be the start of something better, of a reaffirmation of global order.[20] Since a

20. Many of the ideas in this section come from Martin Wolf, "Fiddling While the GATT Burns," *World Economy*, vol. 9 (March 1986), pp. 1–18.

new GATT round has just begun, consideration of this idea would also appear to be timely. Indeed, this idea appears in some of the literature on the proposed free trade agreement. Harold Koh refers to the idea as a "shot in the arm that would both complement and invigorate the new MTN round." The question is, then, how to make such an agreement a shot in the arm rather than one in the heart.

The norms of GATT are moribund and the forces that have made them so are deep-seated. The proposed free trade agreement reveals this. Yet that proposal, along with all the other things that are happening in trade policy, suggests that the trading system is heading for ever greater difficulty. Furthermore, the long agenda of separate problems to be addressed in the new round is more a symptom of the state of the system than a diagnosis of the illness, let alone a cure.

These considerations lead to the idea of a negotiation with the restoration of a generally applicable system of norms, rules, and procedures as a major element. The balance of my discussion considers two broad strategies: tighter international discipline and disciplined unilateralism.

Tighter International Discipline

The strong interest in free trade areas suggests an important truth about mercantilist trade policy. The goal of reciprocity is most easily achieved, and that achievement is most acceptable politically, when the partners simply abolish their barriers to trade with one another altogether. This would be the trade policy equivalent of the "zero option," a clear commitment to complete multilateral disarmament.

It follows that the most radical and exciting of all possible ways of building on the proposed free trade agreement between the United States and Canada would be to return to the old idea of a North Atlantic free trade area.[21] For such an agreement to strengthen the system as a whole, however, rather than further fragment it, there would have to be willingness to accept any country, developing or developed, that offers free trade to the other members.

21. On the idea of a free trade treaty among developed countries, along with rules of competition on nontariff interventions in the market, see Hugh Corbet and Harry G. Johnson, "Optional Negotiating Techniques on Industrial Tariffs," in Frank McFadzean and others, eds., *Towards an Open World Economy* (London: Macmillan for the Trade Policy Research Centre, 1972).

In effect, the proposal would amount to creating a new GATT under article 24, which would obviously imply a conditional MFN principle, but it would be an outward-looking, encompassing conditionality, just as was the case for GATT itself. GATT offered unconditional MFN treatment only to contracting parties, and one of its main problems, politically speaking, has been the arrival of an ever-growing number of free riders (contracting parties that are apparently not bound by any contract), one of the main sources of current American frustration. Accordingly, the proposed free trade area compact might be described as GATT as it should have been, a politically effective balance between nondiscrimination and penalties for free riding.

While a proposal of great charm and simplicity, it is probably unrealistic, not least because a free trade agreement that could not possibly exclude Japan would be difficult to sell to the publics of the other developed countries. A somewhat less ambitious plan to deal with the system as a whole is "GATT plus," a term that appears in a little-known report of the Atlantic Council of the United States.[22] The report elaborates a specific proposal for a comprehensive and tighter agreement than that embodied in GATT itself.

It is the basic approach, rather than the precise details of that proposal, that is the issue here. The guiding ideas are, first, that no country will agree either to a significantly greater degree of discipline in any area painful to itself or to a significant liberalization of its own barriers to trade unless other countries accept corresponding increases in discipline, not only in that area but also in others of particular importance to the first country. At the same time, it must be rendered impossible for a country to substitute another barrier to trade for one that has been ruled out within a specific code. For both these reasons, codes that tighten GATT discipline must be negotiated and adhered to as a package, as was the case for GATT itself. Second, countries will not continue to permit those who do not abide by any of the disciplines to have a voice in the administration of the rules. Third, the obligations accepted must be seen as of equal weight both ex ante and ex post. Finally, the agreement must be open, that is, one that any country willing to abide by the relevant disciplines can join. Perhaps the idea of GATT plus could be described as embodying the discipline of a free trade agreement without free trade itself.

Such a tightening of GATT disciplines in one coherent package would

22. See *GATT Plus: a Proposal for Trade Reform* (Washington, D.C.: Atlantic Council of the United States, 1975).

raise formidable difficulties in two different respects. The first would relate to the coverage of such an agreement and the second would relate to whether the benefits of such an agreement would be limited to the signatories.

Broadly speaking, the aim would be to create a transparent, liberal, and stable trade regime based on market-conforming instruments of policy. In order to achieve this, the package of agreements would have to cover safeguard protection, subsidies and countervailing duties, dumping and antidumping measures, protection for balance-of-payments reasons, public procurement, infant-industry protection, other nontariff measures, dispute-settlement procedures, and administration of the agreement. It would be highly desirable if there were also agreement on agriculture, trade in services, protection of intellectual property rights, and investment, including rights of establishment and national treatment. Furthermore, plans for the liberalization of barriers to trade would also have to be included.

The assumptions underlying this approach are both that a piecemeal reform of GATT is unlikely to go very far and that no reform is possible if all members of GATT are to be involved. In this way, the free-rider problem would be reduced, but whether it would be eliminated depends above all on whether conditional or unconditional MFN treatment would be afforded. In practice, it would probably be impossible to reach such a tighter agreement without conditional MFN treatment, again open to any that are prepared to live by the rules, as has already happened with a number of the codes agreed during the Tokyo round.[23]

In favor of conditionality are the following considerations:

1. GATT itself is a conditional MFN agreement in the sense that only contracting parties are entitled to the benefits of article 1 (requiring nondiscrimination). Generally, the benefits, especially of tariff reductions, are accorded to nonmembers, but this is a favor rather than a right.

2. The conditional element in GATT was based on the assumption that all members would undertake substantially equivalent obligations and so be entitled to equal treatment according to mercantilist logic. In practice, however, obligations are by no means universally accepted, thereby violating the implicit bargain.

3. Accordingly, conditional MFN obligations would do no more than

23. On the idea of developing a series of codes on the basis of conditional MFN treatment, see Gary C. Hufbauer and Jeffrey J. Schott, *Trading for Growth: The Next Round of Trade Negotiations*, Policy Analyses in International Economics no. 11 (Washington, D.C.: Institute for International Economics, 1985).

reestablish GATT as it should be. It would not rule out the extension of the relevant treatment, but it would be as a matter of favor rather than of right.

4. Furthermore, without conditional MFN treatment there would be no incentive for nonsignatories to adopt the package of new and tighter obligations, and the free-rider problem would merely be reinstated.

If it were decided on balance that the right approach is to try to improve trade policies through tighter international agreements, then a conditional MFN approach would appear to be politically inevitable. It seems increasingly unlikely that countries would accept tighter obligations without trying to curb free riding.

Disciplined Unilateralism

One element of any improvements in the international trading system would have to be better domestic laws and procedures for considering pleas for protection. The purpose of such changes would be twofold: to make the process of granting protection more transparent and to introduce some economic rationality into discussions of protection. Furthermore, insistence on more transparent forms of protection such as tariffs, auctioned quotas, or subsidies would have to be an element of any proposal for tighter international discipline (presuming that complete free trade were not achieved). By making the economic costs of protection more visible, the process of public education would be improved and, it may even be hoped, the mercantilist fallacy that underlies so much trade policy would wither away.

Two ways of achieving the goal of improved domestic discussion have been proposed.[24] One would be essentially legal, namely a nondiscrimination treaty. The point of a nondiscrimination treaty is that it would make illegal various kinds of covert administrative measures of protection such as voluntary export restraints. Furthermore, under a plausible interpretation of the concept of nondiscrimination, the only quantitative restrictions that would be permissible would be auctioned quotas. Thus the possibility of public and legislative oversight of protection would be greatly increased.

The second method would focus on the economic content of proce-

24. On greater unilateralism in trade policy, see J. M. Finger, "Incorporating the Gains from Trade into Policy," *The World Economy*, vol. 5 (December 1982), pp. 367–77. On the case for a nondiscrimination treaty, see Tumlir, *Protectionism*, pp. 62–64.

dures for granting protection. All requests for protection need to be publicly evaluated and the economic costs and benefits assessed. Estimates of the costs of such measures as voluntary restraints on exports of motor vehicles from Japan to the United States have influenced the debate on protection. The second approach would therefore involve a technocratic rather than a legal approach to improving the domestic context for trade policy formation.

It may be argued that the most important reform would be to make the domestic costs and benefits much more obvious and correspondingly give domestic political forces more room for maneuver. After all, protection is not mainly about international relations. It is primarily about the internal distribution of income, a truth that the present framework of trade policy obscures. The answer then might be to allow bound tariffs to rise, sometimes referred to as "retariffication," and to concentrate on reaching international agreement less on the level of protection than on its form and on the procedures for changing it. The eventual result might be to create a clearer domestic understanding of the implications of decisions on trade policy.

Need for Fundamental Reevaluation

While Canada and the United States are discussing their free trade area, the governments of the world appear to have arrived at the beginning of another major adventure in multilateral commercial diplomacy. There is a long list of unfinished and new business, but that list is in large measure indicative of cracks in the foundations of the system itself. Put most simply, the generally mercantilist attitudes that underlie, and are reinforced by, GATT make it increasingly difficult to sustain equal treatment of all GATT members when their policies or trade behavior diverge radically. Differences in resource endowment, in government involvement in economies, and in the acceptance of international obligations on trade policy all affect the willingness of trading partners to afford liberal and equal treatment. The result has been a strong impulse toward discrimination that is sometimes tacit and sometimes overt. Yet, with discrimination now well established, stabilization of the conditions of trade is virtually impossible.

If the new GATT round is to create a durable framework of liberal and stable policies in as wide an area as possible, these basic flaws have to be addressed. Two approaches have been considered above, which may be summarized as follows: either use mercantilism more fully or try at last to transcend it.

In practical terms, the new GATT round will have to start with an appreciation of the problem as a whole and not just with a long list of particular demands. Bargaining over specific issues may make sense within a sturdy system but does not when the system itself is flawed. A logical first step, therefore, might be a comprehensive review of the working of the GATT system as a whole.

Challenge to North America

It is to this wider view that the two parties to the present agreement need to be called. A quotation from Lord Robbins indicates the danger of "exclusive preserves" in economic life in general and the implications of the collapse of the United Kingdom into an illiberal and discriminatory trade policy in the 1930s in particular.

> The administration of the free trade empire is not one of those episodes of history of which Englishmen need be ashamed. . . . But with the passing of free trade . . . all this has changed. We have joined with the protectionist parts of the Empire to exclude the products of the foreigner. . . . In this we are no worse than the other Protectionist Powers. It is not to be believed that if the Empire as a whole were handed over to Germany or Japan it would be administered on free trade lines; it is indeed the victory in Great Britain of the retrograde German ideology of exploitation and power which has been responsible for the ruin of the splendid principles of internationalism and freedom.

Lord Robbins also remarked:

> It is not the possible self-sufficiency of the area [of the United States] as a whole, but the absence of self-sufficiency on the part of the constituent states, which is the advantage of the Union. It follows, too, that any gain in productive efficiency which is secured by the abolition of "internal" obstacles is a gain that has its cost if it is secured only by the erection of obstacles around the area.[25]

As the experience of the European Community has shown, regional liberalization can all too easily become not a step toward wider liberalization, but an obstacle to it.

More specifically, there is a challenge to the United States. The

25. Robbins, *Economic Planning and International Order*, pp. 121, 127.

tragedy of the interwar years, it may be recalled, was largely the result of the congruence of the growing inability and unwillingness of the United Kingdom and the continued unwillingness of the United States to pursue policies compatible with international economic order. During this interregnum all the evils of unbridled nationalism, of mercantilism without any notion of disarmament, reigned supreme.

What is worrying about the present juncture, including the proposal of a U.S.-Canadian free trade agreement, is that the United States appears—understandably, but tragically—to be forgetting what it then learned and to be turning back toward the discriminatory and protectionist policies of its past. It is catching the disease from which the main European powers have failed to free themselves ever since the end of World War I. If so, the world is moving not so much into a new interregnum as into a vacuum of responsibility. To discover ways of combating this danger is the challenge to North American policymakers, especially those of the United States. Only thus can they make the simultaneous discussion of a free trade area in North America and a GATT round not the end of something, however flawed, that worked, but the beginning of something that works still better. Furthermore, what is needed for that is not so much the standard European perspective of the title of these remarks, but an explicit rejection of the defensive mercantilism that all too often underlies it.

HAROLD HONGJU KOH

A Legal Perspective

ON St. Patrick's Day 1985, Prime Minister Brian Mulroney and President Ronald Reagan met in Quebec. Their "Shamrock summit" culminated in a joint declaration agreeing "to give the highest priority to finding mutually-acceptable means to reduce and eliminate existing barriers to trade in order to secure and facilitate trade and investment flows." One year later, in March 1986, the two leaders met again in Washington, D.C., and confirmed their intention to begin bilateral free trade negotiations without preconditions.

The inauguration of these bilateral talks, however, proved to be anything but smooth. After last-minute maneuverings, the twenty-member Senate Finance Committee split evenly on April 23, 1986, on a motion to disapprove the agreement. This legislative deadlock permitted formal negotiations to begin in Ottawa on May 21, 1986, but side disputes over matters including softwood lumber, red cedar shingles and shakes, and American corn have continued to cloud the talks.

Other contributors to this volume offer econometric models designed to forecast the likely economic consequences of a U.S.-Canadian free trade agreement. I attempt here to offer a legal "model" with analogous predictive capacity about future legal developments surrounding such a free trade agreement. My central premise is that the FTA negotiations will occur within and among three discrete legal "markets" governed respectively by U.S. law, Canadian law, and international law, as reflected in the General Agreement on Tariffs and Trade (GATT). By systematically examining each market and exploring their interrelation-

An expanded and modified version of this paper, with full supporting legal citation, appears in *Yale Journal of International Law*, vol. 12 (Spring 1987).

ships, I seek to predict how legal, as opposed to economic, considerations
will influence and channel the course of the negotiations.

The U.S. Legal "Market"

To predict how the FTA negotiations will unfold, one must first
recognize that they arrive at a historical moment of nearly unprecedented
congressional control over U.S. trade policymaking. As I have elaborated elsewhere, this state of affairs did not always exist; rather, it has
evolved after a struggle between the president and Congress for dominion
over international trade matters that has spanned much of this century.[1]
In large measure, this struggle has resulted from an unresolved ambiguity
in U.S. constitutional law regarding the precise division of labor among
the branches of government in international trade matters.

Despite the textual paucity of his foreign affairs powers, enumerated
in article II of the Constitution, the president has historically asserted
dominance over foreign affairs generally and international trade in
particular. In so doing, the president has often claimed an unenumerated
constitutional authority to conduct foreign affairs, usually citing famous
Supreme Court dicta proclaiming him to be the "sole organ of the nation
in its external relations."[2] In response, Congress has traditionally
asserted that the president's authority to regulate trade derives entirely
from statutes passed pursuant to its own foreign affairs powers. These
powers, enumerated in article I of the Constitution, include explicit
authority to "regulate Commerce with foreign Nations" and to "lay and
collect Taxes, Duties, Imposts and Excises." This constitutional tension
has manifested itself in five identifiable regimes of congressional-
executive relations in the trade field, each associated with a particular
trade statute or set of statutes. As these five regimes have succeeded
one another, the pendulum of trade policymaker power has swung first
from Congress to the president, and gradually back to Congress again.

1. This discussion derives largely from a more detailed historical analysis in Harold
Hongju Koh, "Congressional Controls on Presidential Trade Policymaking after *I.N.S.
v. Chadha*," *New York University Journal of International Law and Politics*, vol. 18
(Summer 1986), pp. 1192–1205.
    2. Cited in *U.S.* v. *Curtiss-Wright Export Corp.*, 299 U.S. 304, 319 (1936).

The First Two Regimes: From Congressional to Presidential Management

During the first ill-fated regime, initiated by the now infamous Smoot-Hawley Tariff Act of 1930, Congress attempted to manage trade itself, with disastrous consequences. By setting the highest tariff levels in U.S. history, Congress triggered a series of foreign retaliatory measures that fueled the worldwide depression. This debacle left a lingering public impression that congressional trade management is synonymous with protectionism and destructive of foreign trade.

In response to the Smoot-Hawley fiasco, Congress passed the Reciprocal Trade Agreements Act of 1934, which for the first time delegated to the president broad advance authority to negotiate and conclude reciprocal tariff-cutting executive agreements with foreign nations. The act authorized the president not only to bind the United States under international law, but also to implement the new duties as domestic law by proclamation, thereby eliminating the need for further congressional reference or subsequent approving legislation. As a constitutional matter, trade agreements that were negotiated and concluded during this regime were not "treaties" made by the president with the advice and consent of the Senate in the strict sense referred to by article II of the Constitution. Rather, they were "congressional-executive agreements" negotiated by the president pursuant to prior specific congressional authorization or approval.

During this second regime, which ushered in twenty-eight years of presidentially managed trade, Congress retained only a minimal check on presidential initiative via "sunset" provisions that terminated the president's negotiating authority after brief periods. This political compromise proved both domestically stable and internationally successful in promoting U.S. adherence to evolving norms and structures of international trade law. Under the 1934 act's broad advance delegation, the president concluded thirty-two bilateral agreements between 1935 and 1945 and accepted GATT, thereby consummating the United States' postwar entry into multilateral trade management.[3] Meanwhile, the need for frequent congressional renewal of the president's negotiating authority enhanced Congress's ability to review and monitor executive

3. See John H. Jackson, Jean-Victor Louis, and Mitsuo Matsushita, eds., *Implementing the Tokyo Round: National Constitutions and International Economic Rules* (University of Michigan Press, 1984), p. 141.

trade actions. As the price for renewed negotiating authority, successive Congresses extracted a variety of concessions from the president, including the now defunct peril-point reporting requirement, the first legislated version of the escape clause, and the first legislative veto found in the trade laws.

The Kennedy Round Regime

The Trade Expansion Act of 1962 triggered a third regime of international trade policymaking, which expired in 1967 along with the Kennedy round multilateral trade negotiations. President John F. Kennedy's call for greater negotiating authority to deal with the emerging European Economic Community provided the main political impetus for the act's passage. Yet during this era, congressional-executive legal disputes centered around the precise form and timing of legislative approval necessary to effect the U.S. entry into international trade agreements. While conceding that the president needed broad advance negotiating authority to conduct the upcoming multilateral trade talks, Congress feared that a runaway president might unilaterally negotiate reductions in nontariff as well as tariff barriers. Because the authority to grant nontariff concessions appeared to fall outside its constitutionally enumerated powers to "lay and collect . . . Duties," Congress was concerned that the president might grant such concessions by invoking his inherent constitutional authority to accept executive agreements. Congress therefore sought to shorten the president's leash by authorizing him to negotiate multilateral trade agreements, but requiring him to bring them back for subsequent congressional approval. Admittedly, several of the Trade Expansion Act's provisions expanded the president's negotiating discretion; others, however, reflected Congress's growing distrust of the president, by denying him discretion to grant most-favored-nation status to communist countries and creating the Office of the Special Trade Representative as a new—and presumably more independent—agency to represent the United States at the upcoming multilateral trade talks.

The congressional-executive battle over the U.S.-Canadian Automotive Products Agreement of 1965 (auto pact), a sectoral free trade accord negotiated during this period, typified the legal tensions of the Kennedy round era. This bilateral pact eliminated most transborder tariffs on motor vehicles traded between the countries, as well as parts and accessories intended for use as original equipment in such vehicles.[4] Yet rather than treating the pact as a treaty or congressional-executive agreement previously authorized by existing legislation—options that would have required prior consultations with Congress—the Johnson administration chose to negotiate the pact without congressional involvement, presenting it for legislative approval two months after the deal had been struck.[5] This fait accompli not only triggered congressional protest, but also inspired Congress to pass implementing legislation—the Automotive Products Trade Act of 1965—that strictly conditioned the president's future ability to enter such bilateral accords.[6]

During the Kennedy round itself, these executive-legislative tensions escalated. Over congressional objection, the executive branch agreed to a comprehensive antidumping code, invoking the president's implied authority to accept executive agreements without congressional approval. Partly in response, Congress refused to endorse another nontariff concession that the executive had also negotiated without prior congressional approval. In exchange for certain European and Japanese concessions, U.S. negotiators had agreed to eliminate the so-called American Sales Price method of customs valuation, which based tariff rates not on import prices, but on higher domestic wholesale prices. When the Senate learned of the proposed repeal, it adopted a concurrent resolution urging the president to instruct U.S. negotiators to bargain only on provisions upon which Congress had specifically authorized negotiations in the Trade Expansion Act of 1962. Subsequently, Congress refused to implement the agreement domestically, and when the European parties to the agreement could wait no longer, the agreement lapsed.[7] Not

4. Materials relating to the negotiation and conclusion of the auto pact are reproduced in Abram Chayes, Thomas Ehrlich, and Andreas F. Lowenfeld, *International Legal Process* (Little, Brown, 1968), vol. 2, pp. 307–83.

5. Treating the pact as a treaty would have required the president to secure the approval of the Senate Foreign Relations Committee and two-thirds of the Senate. Because the auto pact eliminated all duties on covered auto parts, the president could not claim to have negotiated it under authority previously granted him by the Trade Expansion Act of 1962, which authorized him only to enter international agreements that reduced tariffs by no more than 50 percent. Treating the pact as a congressional-executive agreement, however, would have obliged the executive branch to gain the approval of the House as well as the Senate and to consult during negotiations with the House Ways and Means and Senate Finance committees.

6. The act required prior consultation with Congress, specified subsequent reporting requirements, and subjected the president's future negotiating authority to a legislative veto.

7. See John H. Jackson and William J. Davey, *Legal Problems of International*

surprisingly, the incident marred the president's negotiating credibility with U.S. allies. Moreover, for the next eight years no further grants of negotiating authority were forthcoming from Congress.

The Tokyo Round Regime

By the early 1970s, congressional-executive clashes over international trade had grown increasingly commonplace. A Congress bloodied by these clashes enacted the Trade Act of 1974, which simultaneously authorized U.S. participation in the Tokyo round of multilateral trade negotiations while imposing further constraints on the president's discretion to conduct foreign trade policy.

This fourth statutory regime rigorously tightened congressional controls on executive discretion. Congress manifested its pervasive post-Watergate, post-Vietnam distrust of unchecked executive discretion in foreign affairs by combining in the 1974 act several tools first applied in earlier regimes. It sought to limit presidential discretion by specifying negotiating objectives and by subjecting the president's negotiating authority to a sunset provision. It also required the president to engage in extensive prior consultations with an elaborate structure of congressional and private-sector advisory committees. Congress also imposed upon the president a wide range of formal certification and subsequent reporting requirements, such as the famous Jackson-Vanik amendment, which required the president to certify a country's compliance with freedom-of-emigration requirements as a condition of granting it various trade benefits. In addition, Congress wreathed the 1974 trade act with six legislative vetoes, a device that during the post-Vietnam era had become the statutory tool of choice for enhancing congressional control over foreign affairs.[8] Finally, Congress enhanced indirect third-party leverage on executive action through the "judicialization" of existing trade remedies. This category of U.S. statutory law included the modified

---

Economic Relations: Cases, Materials and Text on the National and International Regulation of Transnational Economic Relations, 2d ed. (West, 1986), p. 385.

8. A legislative veto is a simple resolution (approved by a majority of the House or Senate) or a concurrent resolution (approved by majority votes in both houses) that purports to alter or override completed executive action. The Constitution (article I, sec. 7) requires that all legislation be approved by a majority of both houses and then presented to the president for his signature or veto. Thus both forms of legislative veto are actions that are legislative in effect, but do not satisfy this constitutional definition of legislation.

escape clause, antidumping and antisubsidy provisions, customs fraud penalties, and remedies against patent and trademark infringement and unfair practices.[9] In providing these remedies, Congress chose to police executive discretion in the trade area by empowering private individuals to initiate proceedings directly against foreign industries by private complaint. Executive branch action on those private complaints was then required within strict statutory time limits and subjected to extensive judicial oversight.

Against these strict controls on executive discretion, the 1974 act balanced a competing objective: to bolster the executive branch's international negotiating credibility, which had been weakened in the aftermath of the Kennedy round. The act delegated to the president broad advance authority to negotiate agreements reducing nontariff barriers. At the same time, however, Congress limited that authority by creating an innovative legislative mechanism, commonly called the "fast-track" procedure. Under this procedure, House and Senate rules were modified to guarantee an up or down vote, without amendments, on negotiated trade agreements and implementing legislation within sixty legislative days after their introduction.[10] In exchange, the president was obliged to notify the House Ways and Means Committee and the Senate Finance Committee at least ninety days before entering any such agreement and to satisfy numerous reporting and consultation requirements.

The legislative treatment of the Tokyo round results showed that the fast-track procedure could accommodate executive and legislative interests, as well as promote the rapid conclusion of multilateral trade

9. Current "judicial" import relief provisions of this type are catalogued in Michael Sandler, "Primer on United States Trade Remedies," *International Lawyer*, vol. 19 (Summer 1985), pp. 761–91. Also see John H. Jackson, "Perspectives on the Jurisprudence of International Trade: Costs and Benefits of Legal Procedures in the United States," *Michigan Law Review*, vol. 82 (April–May 1984), pp. 1570–87; and Peter D. Ehrenhaft, "The 'Judicialization' of Trade Law," *Notre Dame Lawyer*, vol. 56 (April 1981), pp. 595–613.

10. Sec. 151 of the 1974 act, which created the fast track, modified existing House and Senate rules in three important respects. First, it prevented a negotiated nontariff barrier agreement and its implementing legislation from being bottled up in committee by specifying that such a package would be automatically discharged from committee consideration after forty-five legislative days, regardless of whether the committees had taken action upon it. Second, it provided that a bill or resolution approving an agreement would be placed on the calendar for a final vote on the floor of each house without possibility of amendment. Finally, it limited debate on the floor of each house to twenty hours and required that the package be voted on within fifteen legislative days.

accords. The entire U.S. legislative process for approving the nine multilateral agreements negotiated during that round consumed only thirty-four legislative days from presidential notification to final bicameral approval.

Overlooked during this period, however, was the fact that the fast-track procedure functionally resembled the legislative veto, inasmuch as it authorized either house to prevent a fully negotiated trade agreement from being implemented simply by voting down the agreement or its implementing legislation. As would become more apparent during the next trade regime, the fast-track device constituted yet another executive discretion-controlling device of the 1974 act, even as it facilitated the process of international trade negotiation.

As the Tokyo round closed, Congress enacted the Trade Agreements Act of 1979, which strengthened four of the discretion-controlling devices of the 1974 act. First, the 1979 act specified negotiating objectives in even greater detail than did the 1974 act. Second, Congress failed to renew the president's tariff-cutting authority after 1982, creating the anomalous situation that after that date the president would have statutory authority for the next five years to negotiate with respect to nontariff, but not tariff, barriers. Third, the 1979 act stiffened consultation requirements by preserving the committee advisory structure established in the 1974 act and broadening its mandate. Finally, Congress greatly accelerated the trend toward judicialization of trade remedies, and enhanced third-party leverage over the trade process, by adding numerous provisions to the antidumping and countervailing duty laws and upgrading the Customs Court into the Court of International Trade in 1980. Thus the fourth regime of trade management ended with Congress tightening its grip still further over the U.S. trade policymaking process.

The Post-Chadha Regime

In 1983, as the statutory authority provided in the 1979 act was expiring, two events set the stage for the current U.S.-Canadian FTA discussions. First, the Supreme Court declared the legislative veto unconstitutional in *Immigration and Naturalization Service* v. *Chadha.*[11] The *Chadha* decision invalidated the one-house legislative veto provision

11. 462 U.S. 919 (1983).

of the Immigration and Nationality Act, ruling that such a veto violated the constitutional prescription for legislative action contained in article I, section 7 of the Constitution, namely, passage by a majority of both houses and presentment to the president. The broad reasoning of this decision had sweeping implications for hundreds of statutes and invalidated legislative veto provisions in the Trade Act of 1974 and four other major trade laws. Second, at the same time as a post-*Chadha* legislative overhaul of the trade laws was taking place, the United States and Israel were announcing their intent to conclude a comprehensive bilateral free trade agreement. These events contributed to the enactment of the Trade and Tariff Act of 1984, which ushered in the fifth, current regime of U.S. trade policymaking.

The Trade and Tariff Act of 1984 both repaired unconstitutional legislative veto provisions and prospectively authorized the president to negotiate a comprehensive FTA with Israel. The most significant feature of the 1984 act, however, was its modification of the fast-track procedure in order to anticipate and authorize future bilateral free trade negotiations with nations *other* than Israel. Congress was particularly concerned that nations to whom the United States had promised most-favored-nation treatment in reciprocal trade agreements or bilateral treaties might demand the same trade concessions being extended to Israel.[12] Congress drafted the modification with Canada particularly in mind, well aware of Canada's recent free trade overtures to the United States. Indeed, the 1979 Trade Agreements Act had included a provision directing the president to "study the desirability of a trade agreement" in North America. The Office of the U.S. Trade Representative had completed that study in 1981 and had concluded that a U.S.-Canadian FTA would be premature.[13] Two years later, however, the Trudeau government had proposed a sectoral free trade arrangement. Accordingly, in drafting the 1984 act the Senate had originally included Canada along with Israel for special consideration, but the two houses ultimately deleted that special treatment after several U.S.-Canadian trade disputes dampened the enthusiasm of key congressmen.[14]

12. See Alexander H. Platt, "Free Trade with Israel: A Legislative History," in Andrew J. Samet and Moishe Goldberg, eds., *The United States-Israel Free Trade Agreement* (International Law Institute, forthcoming).

13. See *North American Trade Agreements, a Study Mandated in Section 1104 of the Trade Agreements Act of 1979* (Government Printing Office, 1981).

14. See Joseph H. Price, "The Trade and Tariff Act of 1984: An Analytical

As modified, the fast-track procedure required the president, when negotiating a bilateral FTA with a country other than Israel, to notify and consult with the House Ways and Means and Senate Finance committees for a period of sixty legislative days *before* giving the statutorily required ninety-day notice of his intent to sign an agreement; if he failed to do so, the agreement would not receive fast-track consideration. This seemingly modest revision has constituted the most restrictive congressional control upon executive negotiating authority yet devised. On its face, the modified fast-track procedure has significantly enhanced both the influence of Congress as a whole, and that of the House Ways and Means and Senate Finance committees in particular, by offering them not one, but three, bites at any given international trade agreement. First, the sixty-day prenotice consultation period secures the involvement of the two key committees months before negotiations begin and allows them to extract concessions from the president as a condition of letting negotiations proceed. Second, the administration's awareness that any negotiated agreement must return to these same committees for subsequent approval has promoted continuing consultation as the agreement evolves. Third, either house has retained the option to vote down a fully negotiated agreement even after it has been discharged from committee. Significantly, nothing in the language of the 1984 act requires the president to engage in the sixty-day committee consultation period *before* negotiations begin. In theory, he could discharge his statutory duty to consult 150 legislative days before the day an agreement was to be signed, or just as several years of negotiations were coming to a close. However, the Reagan administration has chosen to construe the provision cautiously, notifying the committees of its intent to negotiate a U.S.-Canadian FTA sixty legislative days before the date it intended to begin formal negotiations.

Coupled with numerous other discretion-controlling devices dotting the 1984 act, the modified fast-track procedure has made the current U.S. trade policymaking regime the most congressionally dominated trade regime since Smoot-Hawley.[15] Consequently, the legislative veto's

---

Overview," *International Lawyer*, vol. 19 (Winter 1985), pp. 321–42; and Gary Clyde Hufbauer and Andrew J. Samet, "United States Response to Canadian Initiatives for Sectoral Trade Liberalization: 1983-84," in Denis Stairs and Gilbert R. Winham, *The Politics of Canada's Economic Relationship with the United States* (University of Toronto Press, 1985).

15. This conclusion is further developed in Koh, "Congressional Controls on Presidential Trade Policymaking."

demise has not, as some observers had predicted, diminished Congress's influence over trade policymaking. Inasmuch as the legislative veto represented only one of a broad array of congressional oversight devices in the international trade field, by replacing it with devices such as the modified fast-track procedure, Congress has seized more, rather than less, effective control over trade policy.

Recent Illustrations of the New Congressional Influence

Three events have already dashed the Reagan administration's hopes of steering a U.S.-Canadian free trade agreement cleanly through Congress: the effort by members of the Senate Finance Committee to disapprove the Canadian FTA negotiations and two bilateral skirmishes over Canadian softwood lumber and cedar shingles and shakes. Each dispute graphically illustrates how extensively the various congressional restrictions described thus far have narrowed presidential discretion to conduct the FTA negotiations.

The FTA's brush with extinction came shortly before the sixty-day prenegotiation consultation period specified in the 1984 act was scheduled to expire. Until this point, preliminary negotiations had proceeded uneventfully. Under the 1984 act's modified fast-track procedure, four steps must occur before formal negotiations may begin: (1) the other country—in this case, Canada—must request negotiations; (2) the president must give sixty legislative days' notice of the impending negotiations to the Senate Finance and House Ways and Means committees; (3) the president must consult with those committees during the sixty-day period; and (4) either committee may disapprove of the negotiation of such agreement before the consultation period closes. The first three steps occurred without incident. On September 26, 1985, Prime Minister Mulroney requested formal negotiations. On December 10, 1985, President Reagan notified both committees of his intent to enter bilateral free trade talks with Canada, and both committees proceeded to solicit public comments on the proposed negotiations.

To the surprise of both the U.S. and Canadian negotiators, however, in April 1986 a majority of the twenty-member Senate Finance Committee threatened to disapprove the FTA negotiations and urged the president to withdraw his request for negotiations. After intensive presidential lobbying and a last-minute switch by Senator Spark M. Matsunaga, Democrat of Hawaii, the committee divided evenly on the motion to disapprove, thus permitting formal FTA negotiations to begin as of May 21, 1986.

The incident reveals how seriously the U.S. and Canadian negotiators had underestimated the Finance Committee's extraordinary power under the modified fast-track procedure. In this case, for example, the vote of one more senator on the Finance Committee would have effectively doomed the FTA talks, even though those talks enjoyed general congressional support and had encountered no opposition before the House Ways and Means Committee. As the incident made clear, the modified procedure empowers an ad hoc coalition of key committee members to signal general discontent over trade matters to the president by jeopardizing even a proposed agreement that enjoys general congressional support. Although some of the objecting senators were concerned about Canadian trade issues, the majority claimed no animosity toward Canada, but rather voted for disapproval in order to signal the administration that they desired a greater voice in overall trade policymaking.

Perhaps more significant, fallout from the incident continued, months after formal FTA talks began. Although insiders dispute exactly what concessions were made in exchange for key Senate votes to avert committee disapproval, President Reagan publicly promised committee members that they would be deeply involved in the upcoming talks. In addition, timber-state senators on the Senate Finance Committee reportedly extracted a presidential promise to take some action against Canadian lumber products in exchange for their vote against disapproval of the FTA.

Only two days before formal FTA talks began, the U.S. softwood lumber industry filed a countervailing duty petition alleging that Canada's administrative pricing system for collecting stumpage fees constituted a subsidy that should be subject to a 27 percent U.S. countervailing duty. That petition not only triggered a formal Canadian protest before GATT, but also led to a preliminary determination by the International Trade Commission (ITC) that the Canadian practice had threatened or caused material injury to the U.S. lumber industry. Under the rigid statutory deadlines for countervailing duty actions, the action would have triggered imposition of duties on Canadian lumber imports in early 1987, but for a last-minute pact signed between the two governments at the end of 1986. In that settlement, Canada narrowly forestalled U.S. imposition of countervailing duties by agreeing to impose a controversial 15 percent surtax on Canadian softwood exports to the United States.

A third issue, involving cedar shingles and shakes, also grew out of private U.S. parties' petition for another legal remedy provided by the 1974 trade act. In late 1985, Western U.S. red cedar shakes and shingles producers filed an action against Canadian imports under the so-called escape clause. Under this clause, the ITC may recommend that the president proclaim import relief for a domestic producer who can demonstrate that foreign products are "being imported into the United States in such increased quantities as to be a substantial cause of serious injury" to U.S. industry. In February 1986 the ITC determined that Canadian imports of cedar shingles and shakes were a "substantial cause of serious injury" to the U.S. industry and recommended relief in the form of a higher tariff.

Shortly before the statutory deadline for presidential action, and just one day after formal FTA talks began, President Reagan announced that he would raise tariffs on Canadian shingles and shakes ranging up to 35 percent. That action, taken without prior consultation with the Mulroney government, set off a storm of Canadian protest and provoked the retaliatory imposition of Canadian duties on a range of U.S. goods. While the Reagan administration made concerted efforts to salve Canadian sensibilities, the shingles and shakes case measurably worsened trade relations already strained by the Finance Committee and softwood lumber incidents.

Viewed in isolation, none of these three skirmishes seems significant enough to undermine the FTA negotiations. Taken together, however, they demonstrate that, under the current U.S. trade policymaking regime, Congress must be treated virtually as a coequal player with the president. The near-miss before the Senate Finance Committee reveals the costs of underestimating Congress's direct influence over the negotiating process, while the softwood lumber and cedar shingles controversies illustrate the extent to which Congress now indirectly influences that process by empowering private domestic parties to exert pressure upon the executive branch to force action against foreign governments. The lumber and shingles incidents further demonstrate not only how statutory deadlines imposed by Congress have limited the president's flexibility in dealing with particular trade disputes, but also that the president cannot pursue comprehensive FTA talks without considering and appeasing the interests of even relatively insignificant domestic industries.[16]

16. The effect of statutory deadlines was illustrated by the awkward timing of the president's announcement of the shingles and shakes tariffs, only forty-eight hours

The Course Ahead

This historical record teaches that one must identify the key institutional players in the United States, as well as the legal constraints to which they are subject, in order to predict what political and economic compromises will be struck as FTA talks progress. Domestic industries will be able to influence the substance of the U.S. bargaining position, as well as the tone of the talks—both directly, by pursuing existing statutory trade remedies, and indirectly, through their congressional representatives. Moreover, presidential promises made to avert Senate Finance Committee disapproval of the FTA negotiations significantly limit the trade concessions the administration will be able to offer to Canada. Thus, while the U.S. executive branch publicly favors a comprehensive free trade approach, rather than a sectoral one, these countervailing pressures within the U.S. market will almost certainly operate to contract the FTA's substantive scope. One would expect U.S. interests generally to prevail in bargaining over particular concessions, because of the simple political reality that the key Canadian decisionmakers desire an FTA more than their U.S. counterparts. While concluding an FTA stands at the very top of the Mulroney government's national priorities, the FTA has received only sporadic presidential attention in the United States and has encountered both public indifference and a Congress hostile to trade liberalization.

From the Israeli FTA experience, it seems clear that Congress would willingly approve an FTA of fairly limited scope, which would reduce both tariff and nontariff barriers across the board, establish rules of origin, and set forth mutual understandings regarding trade in services, foreign investment restrictions, licensing of intellectual property rights, and dispute settlement mechanisms. The FTA might also address the question of whether local "buy-national" laws should be excluded from any government procurement accord and whether tariff reductions

---

before the statutory deadline for escape clause action and just hours after the first round of formal FTA talks had concluded. By shrewdly utilizing these statutory remedies, particular industries have exerted an influence on intergovernmental negotiations that is grossly out of proportion to their relative importance. The U.S. cedar shingles and shakes industry, for example, currently employs only about 1,650 people, and U.S. imports of Canadian shingles and shakes comprise less than one-seventh of 1 percent of the total volume of U.S.-Canadian trade. See "Chop, Chop," *The Economist*, June 7, 1986, p. 83; and "Canada's Quick Retaliation for Shingles Tariff Prompts Some on the Hill to Rethink Protectionism," *Wall Street Journal*, June 19, 1986, p. 64.

should be phased in at the same pace in both countries. It is noteworthy, however, that although the Israeli FTA received overwhelming congressional support in 1984, Israel was unable to secure an exemption for its exports from U.S. antidumping and countervailing actions. This experience, underscored by recent cedar shingles and softwood lumber episodes, strongly suggests that Congress would refuse to approve any Canadian effort to modify the availability of countervailing duty and antidumping actions to combat Canadian trade practices that U.S. industries deem unfair.

As for legal form, the final negotiated pact will be brought back to Congress for expedited subsequent approval in the form of a congressional-executive agreement, rather than as a treaty to be submitted to the Senate for advice and consent. As in the case of both the Israeli FTA and the 1965 auto pact, the parties would agree to abstain from putting the agreement into force until after the respective legislatures had enacted the agreement into domestic law. Accompanied by draft legislation (likely resembling that which implemented the U.S.-Israel FTA), the agreement would be submitted to the Senate Finance and House Ways and Means committees, then to both houses for approval by a majority vote. Should Congress and the president differ at this point over the wisdom of the particular trade package proposed, the critical question would become whether this package would be entitled to expedited approval under the fast-track procedure.

If, after negotiations, either committee or either house were to pass a resolution that rejected fast-track approval for the free trade package or that imposed particular requirements upon the package as a precondition for fast-track treatment, the president would still retain three options. First, he could resubmit the agreement and implementing legislation for congressional approval under normal unexpedited congressional procedures. In this case, the package would become vulnerable to post-negotiation amendment, could be bottled up in committee, or could be halted by filibuster on the floor. Given the importance of the FTA, however, the possibility would remain that Congress might choose to approve it—as it did the auto pact—even after its derailment from the fast track. Second, the president could resubmit the package, but request that it be given ad hoc fast-track consideration, notwithstanding the prior committee or house disapproval. Third, he could accept the FTA on behalf of the United States on his own constitutional authority, as occurred during the Kennedy round with the antidumping code. Such an action, while legally possible, would be politically risky and could trigger a constitutional confrontation between Congress and the president. Whether such a dispute could be resolved politically would largely depend on the prevailing level of congressional distrust for the president in the realm of foreign affairs.

In light of recent experience demonstrating Congress's clout under the current trade policymaking regime, however, U.S. negotiators would be wise to avoid such a constitutional showdown by keeping Congress fully apprised of and involved in the negotiations as they progress. In so doing, the FTA negotiators could use procedures employed during the Tokyo round as a model for executive-congressional cooperation. During those negotiations, members and staff of the House Ways and Means and Senate Finance committees directly discussed trade issues with foreign officials in Geneva. The committees and the Office of the U.S. Trade Representative even entered a formal memorandum of understanding whereby the USTR agreed to supply the two committees with classified cables relating to the negotiations. Full-time committee staffers monitored the negotiations and were sometimes even present during negotiating sessions.[17] The extent of congressional input into the negotiation of the Tokyo round codes surely speeded their passage through Congress. Similar ongoing consultations between Congress and the executive—the two key players in the U.S. market—would therefore appear to be prerequisite to the U.S.-Canadian FTA's enjoyment of a similar fate.

The Canadian Legal "Market"

A similar institutional analysis aids understanding of the Canadian legal market. Like the United States, Canada is a federal nation with a national executive and legislature and subnational provincial governments. Canadian domestic law differs from that in the United States, however, in two crucial respects. First, Canadian treaty law has no

17. See Robert C. Cassidy, Jr., "Negotiating about Negotiations: The Geneva Multilateral Trade Talks," in Thomas M. Franck, ed., *The Tethered Presidency: A Study of New Congressional Restraints on Presidential Power and Their Effect on America's Ability to Conduct an Effective Foreign Policy* (New York University Press, 1981), pp. 264, 273; and Jackson, Louis, and Matsushita, *Implementing the Tokyo Round*, p. 153.

requirement that the Parliament approve either the signing or the ratification of an international agreement. Canada's law of international agreements finds its root not in domestic constitutional law, but in unwritten custom, which recognizes the Canadian executive's sole prerogative to enter solemn treaties with other nations.[18] Second, although under Canadian law the federal government as a whole has full power to bind Canada to the FTA internationally, there is no supremacy clause analogous to article VI, section 2, of the U.S. Constitution to bind the provinces to abide by such an agreement.[19] From these two distinctions, one may conclude that the domestic institution with which the Canadian executive must most carefully reckon will not be the federal legislature, as in the United States, but rather the provinces.

Constraints on Parliamentary Action

Given that treaty making in Canada lies within the executive's sole prerogative, the Canadian government theoretically retains the option of not submitting a negotiated FTA to Parliament at all. However, the Canadian government has traditionally obtained parliamentary approval of important treaties during the interval between signing and ratification by laying the treaty before Parliament and either moving a resolution of approval (to be adopted by a majority in each house) or asking Parliament to enact by statute any treaty provisions that are to have municipal effect. Alternatively, the Canadian government might choose to implement the treaty immediately by an order-in-council (the equivalent of a presidential executive order in the United States) while seeking legislative approval some months later, a course it pursued in the case of the 1965 U.S.-Canadian auto pact. In that case, the Pearson government claimed that the auto pact was not a treaty, but merely an agreement between the administrations of two countries. The governor general put it into effect immediately, under his preexisting powers to remit duties under existing customs and tariff legislation. The government did not introduce a motion calling for parliamentary approval of the agreement until nearly one and one-half years after the agreement was entered and never admitted any legal obligation to obtain such approval. In the end,

18. See Chayes, Ehrlich, and Lowenfeld, *International Legal Process*, p. 338.
19. See Allan E. Gotlieb, *Canadian Treaty-Making* (Butterworth's, 1968), pp. 28–29; and Peter W. Hogg, *Constitutional Law of Canada*, 2d ed. (Carswell, 1985), pp. 254–56.

however, both houses approved the pact, in much the same way as Congress did in the United States.

While legally permissible, a decision by the Mulroney government similarly to delay legislative consideration of the FTA would seem politically impractical, given the enormous nationwide impact and high public profile such an agreement would carry. One measure of how much parliamentary criticism such an action might arouse was the hostility triggered by the Pearson government's actions regarding the auto pact, which was an accord of far less national significance. Pragmatic and symbolic concerns, rather than strictly legal ones, would therefore likely determine what legal form the agreement would take. The government's perception of the FTA's importance might lead it to insist that the pact be concluded with all the solemnities of a treaty, a proposal that would have to be reconciled with the intention of the U.S. government to accede to the same pact as an executive agreement.

Regardless of how the Canadian government chooses to characterize the FTA, the next question would be whether the cabinet could implement the agreement domestically in the face of parliamentary refusal to approve it. Numerous influential national interest groups have opposed the FTA, which has spurred growing parliamentary opposition. Given that a failure to obtain parliamentary approval of the FTA would amount to a failure on a confidence motion of the highest national importance, implementation without its approval would seem legally possible but politically untenable. So long as the tradition of parliamentary discipline remains stronger in Canada than the tradition of party loyalty to the U.S. president, however, the Canadian majority party seems virtually certain to secure parliamentary approval for a fully negotiated FTA.

The possibility does remain, however, that even if private Canadian interests cannot affect negotiations indirectly through their parliamentary representatives, they will still be able to exert influence on the negotiations directly by invoking Canadian analogs to U.S. import remedies. In November 1986, for example, a complaint filed by the Ontario Corn Producers' Association triggered Revenue Canada's preliminary determination that U.S. corn exports are subsidized. Based on that determination, Revenue Canada imposed a 67 percent tariff against U.S. grain corn, the first countervailing duty ever imposed by Canada and the first ever imposed on the United States by any trading partner. Should such private suits proliferate in Canada, private Canadian industries could begin to exert pressure on the executive analogous to that currently being exerted on the U.S. executive by private U.S. industry under congressional sanction.

The Power of the Provinces

The structure of the Canadian legal market strongly suggests that the most thorny challenge to the FTA's approval will come not from Parliament or private industry, but from the provinces. The two largest provinces, Ontario and Quebec, have already expressed doubts about the wisdom of concluding a comprehensive FTA with the United States. Moreover, the provinces have historically exploited Canada's lack of a supremacy clause to create problems during several past treaty-making debates.[20] Once again, this problem has legal roots. It arises principally because Canadian constitutional law does not recognize a concluded international agreement as part of national municipal law; for that reason, a fully negotiated FTA would not be self-executing. Under the famous *Labour Conventions* doctrine, international agreements may not be enforced as domestic law in Canada unless specifically implemented by the particular legislature vested by the Constitution Act with jurisdiction over the agreement's subject matter.[21] The federal government would presumably argue that all of the domestic changes required to implement the FTA fall within its exclusive power over the regulation of trade and commerce under section 91(2) of the Constitution Act, and thus are susceptible to domestic implementation through federal statute alone. In response, the provinces would likely assert that some changes would fall within their exclusive jurisdiction to make laws in relation to property and civil rights in the province under section 92(13) of the act; thus, they would argue, the administration and Parliament lack the power to implement the FTA domestically unless each affected province also enacts concurrent implementing legislation. The province of Ontario has claimed, for example, that the FTA cannot be implemented without changing a number of local laws that fall within its exclusive provincial jurisdiction.

If concurrent provincial implementing legislation were legally unnecessary, the federal government could simply negotiate the FTA by itself.

---

20. See Ivan Bernier, *International Legal Aspects of Federalism* (Archon Books, 1973), pp. 152–60.

21. See *Attorney General of Canada* v. *Attorney General of Ontario*, A.C. 325 (1937) (the *Labour Conventions* case).

If the FTA could not be domestically implemented without concurrent provincial legislation, however, then the provinces could secure a de facto veto over the FTA simply by withholding the necessary legislation. The provinces will probably argue that their veto gives them a right not merely to be consulted, but also to protect their interests directly by participating in the negotiations.

Under prevailing practice, the federal government could forestall direct provincial participation in negotiations by asking the provincial governments informally by letter whether they would be willing to take the action necessary to implement the FTA within their jurisdiction. If, for some reason, the federal government could not secure advance provincial approval, it could theoretically ratify the agreement with a reservation declaring that the federal government did not thereby bind itself to carry out obligations that lie within exclusive provincial competence; alternatively, Canada might seek to add a "federal-state" clause to the FTA itself, under which the federal government would undertake to perform only those obligations that lie within its exclusive competence while agreeing to recommend that the provinces implement the FTA by local legislation. Either option, however, would probably deny the FTA much of its attractiveness to the United States and thus would probably be deemed unacceptable.

Additional opportunities for provincial veto would arise if, as some provincial officials are urging, the FTA were deemed sufficiently important to be adopted via constitutional amendment. Under the Constitution Act of 1982, such amendments may be made only by Parliament and at least seven of the ten provinces having 50 percent of the country's population. Even if the provinces were able to force application of constitutional amendment procedures to the FTA, however, the dissent of at least four provinces would be required to veto its adoption.

In short, Canada's ability to negotiate the FTA will hinge crucially on the federal government's ability to secure some advance assurances from the provinces that they will abide by the results of the FTA negotiations. The federal government will most likely seek to win such assurances by negotiating a federal-provincial agreement whereby the provinces would commit themselves to implement a negotiated FTA as provincial law. To be effective, however, such an agreement would have to address the controversial question of whether the provinces may reject those portions of the FTA that fall within their exclusive jurisdiction and erect independent barriers to U.S. imports. For example, some

Ontario officials have apparently discussed the possibility of the Ontario Securities and Exchange Commission excluding U.S. financial institutions from their province even after the FTA were signed. Although the United States might seek to include in the FTA a provision precluding the provinces from enacting such laws or authorizing the United States to retaliate directly against noncomplying provinces, the Canadian federal government could not enforce such a treaty provision against the provinces by legislation. The more likely consequence of a Canadian failure to secure a binding provincial-federal agreement would be to dampen, if not kill, the ardor of both the U.S. executive branch and Congress for the agreement itself. Indeed, the chief U.S. negotiator, Peter O. Murphy, has declared his belief that the FTA will not receive congressional approval without assurances from the Canadian government that all portions of the agreement relating to provincial jurisdiction will be implemented.

The International Law "Market"

The international issues surrounding a U.S.-Canadian FTA should closely resemble those surrounding the 1985 U.S.-Israeli FTA and the 1965 U.S.-Canadian auto pact, particularly if, as seems likely, the U.S. negotiators insist on modeling the new pact on these earlier ones. Both pacts raised two GATT-related questions that now seem likely to recur: whether the bilateral agreement comports with the substantive and procedural requirements of GATT's article 24, and, if not, whether the two nations must obtain a waiver from that article's provisions.

Article 1, section 1, of GATT embodies the most-favored-nation principle: each contracting party's cardinal commitment to accord "any advantage, favour, privilege or immunity granted by any contracting party to any product originating in or destined for any other country immediately and unconditionally to the like product originating in or destined for the territories of all other contracting parties." Even the first GATT drafts, however, carved out an exception to this rule for free trade areas, an exemption which, ironically enough, was drafted at least partially in anticipation of a U.S.-Canadian free trade accord.[22]

22. See Hufbauer and Samet, "United States Responses to Canadian Initiatives for Sectoral Trade Liberalization," p. 181.

That exception, now embodied in article 24, exempts from the MFN requirement customs unions, free trade areas, and "interim agreements" leading to the formation of either of the other two arrangements. These arrangements must meet three basic criteria: first, that duties and other restrictive regulations are eliminated on "substantially all the trade between the constituent territories"; second, that duties and regulations retained in the constituent territories are no "higher or more restrictive than the corresponding duties and other regulations of commerce" previously in effect; and third, that the FTA is implemented "within a reasonable length of time." In addition to these three substantive criteria, there are also two procedural requirements. Other contracting parties must be notified of the intent to negotiate an FTA, and after an agreement has been negotiated, it has to be submitted to a GATT working party for study and evaluation. Most commentators agree that the U.S.-Israeli agreement satisfied each of the three substantive criteria, while the Canadian auto pact, which was limited only to the automotive sector, unambiguously violated the first substantive criterion and satisfied only the second of the two procedural requirements.[23]

A comprehensive U.S.-Canadian FTA would probably pass muster under article 24's three substantive criteria, particularly if it were modeled on the U.S.-Israeli FTA. Satisfaction of the first criterion would depend upon both the percentage of trade freed (the quantitative dimension) and the extent to which the FTA would effect an overall liberalization of trade between the two parties (the qualitative dimension). Although no clear definition of either requirement has emerged from GATT's jurisprudence, both requirements would probably be evaluated in light of the breadth of the sectoral exclusions condoned by the agreement and the character of the tariff and nontariff reductions undertaken within it. Numbers alone suggest that if the agreement provided for the phased elimination of both tariff and nontariff trade barriers on 80 percent or more of the trade between the two countries,

23. See "The U.S.-Israel Free Trade Area: Is It GATT Legal?" *George Washington University Journal of International Law and Economics*, vol. 19, no. 1 (1985), pp. 199–228; "International Trade—Agreement for the Establishment of a Free Trade Area between the Government of the United States of America and the Government of Israel," *Harvard International Law Journal*, vol. 27 (Winter 1986), pp. 289–94; and "Recent United States Trade Arrangements: Implications for the Most-Favored-Nation Principle and United States Trade Policy," *Law and Policy in International Business*, vol. 17, no. 1 (1985), pp. 209–36. Also see Kenneth W. Dam, *The GATT: Law and International Economic Organization* (University of Chicago Press, 1970), p. 48.

GATT would probably not condemn it. By way of comparison, the European Free Trade Association, which covers 90 percent of all trade in industrial goods among the constituent territories, won GATT approval in 1960, while other FTAs covering between 50 and 77 percent have won toleration, although not unanimous endorsement, from GATT. Moreover, the two parties would probably satisfy the qualitative dimension of the first criterion by making few exclusions and expressly incorporating GATT principles and trade-liberalizing nontariff accords into the overall agreement. A prudent model for the negotiators would again be the U.S.-Israeli FTA, which expressly operates within a GATT framework and directly incorporates GATT principles into the text of the bilateral accord.

The second substantive requirement, that the pact not be designed to raise any additional barriers to trade, would also seem easily satisfied. Safeguard provisions modeled on those found in the Israeli pact would not qualify as raising additional barriers to trade. Nor would the third requirement, that the FTA be phased in within a "reasonable period of time," pose a serious obstacle. Although GATT does not define "reasonable," and working parties have developed no consistent definition of it, phase-in periods ranging from ten to twenty-two years have historically been sustained. The U.S.-Israeli FTA, for example, phases out all duties on both industrial and agricultural products in four stages over a ten-year period. Even if the U.S.-Canadian proposal were to fall short of article 24's FTA criteria during its phase-in period, it would almost surely qualify as an "interim agreement" toward the formation of an FTA under that article. Because such interim agreements comply prima facie with GATT, the burden would rest on other GATT members to object to it. As a political matter, most of the potential objectors would be impeded from doing so by their own regional arrangements or past public remarks.

Even if the FTA should prove inconsistent with any of these article 24 prerequisites, it seems unlikely that GATT would actually disapprove it, if only because article 24 has historically been so laxly enforced. The contracting parties have traditionally taken an extremely liberal attitude toward literal compliance with the article's terms, focusing instead on whether the challenged agreement promotes trade liberalization in some general sense. As of 1974, thirty-four regional arrangements had been presented to GATT, apart from those specifically exempted upon its drafting, and the contracting parties had condemned none of them. As a consequence, some commentators have argued that GATT has wholly failed to discharge its responsibility to regulate the formation of FTAs.[24]

Even in the unlikely event that a working party should find the FTA inconsistent with GATT, the two countries could still pursue the option of applying for a waiver from GATT's provisions. Such waivers have been liberally granted, particularly when the parties seeking the waiver assert that the FTA will not divert trade from third countries. Of the thirty-four regional arrangements presented to GATT before 1974, eleven, including the U.S.-Canadian auto pact, were granted waivers. Once again, the auto pact precedent illustrates the liberality of the waiver procedure. After various auto-exporting GATT members had protested that pact, the United States appeared before a working party to request a waiver of its MFN obligations, claiming that the auto pact violated the letter, but not the spirit, of GATT because it diverted no trade away from any third countries. Although some working party members expressed concerns about preferential treatment, the contracting parties unanimously granted the auto pact a waiver, conditioned on U.S. willingness to consult with any requesting party that alleged that the agreement had diverted imports away from that country.

In sum, one may expect GATT to play some role in the formation of a U.S.-Canadian FTA. So long as the two countries make a good-faith effort to satisfy article 24, however, it appears most unlikely that GATT will stand in the way of the FTA's implementation.

Toward a General Equilibrium Analysis of the FTA

The preceding "partial equilibrium" analysis of each of the U.S., Canadian, and international law "markets" reveals how one may use legal analysis to predict the likely course of the proposed FTA. By systematically studying historical precedents that have transpired within these markets (for example, the U.S.-Israeli FTA and the U.S.-Canadian auto pact), identifying the institutions within each market that are legally entitled to participate in the making of the FTA, and examining the legal constraints that affect those institutions and structure their relationships,

24. See *Executive Branch GATT Studies*, Committee Print, Senate Committee on Finance, 93 Cong. 2 sess. (Government Printing Office, 1974); and Kenneth W. Dam, "Regional Economic Arrangements and the GATT: The Legacy of a Misconception," *University of Chicago Law Review*, vol. 30 (Summer 1963), pp. 615–65.

one may predict with unusual precision what compromises will be struck within each market with respect to particular legal questions.

What the above analysis excludes, however, is the simple fact that these three legal markets are inextricably interdependent. Negotiating decisions made by the key institutional decisionmakers to satisfy legal constraints imposed by any one of those markets will inevitably cause ripple effects in the other two, which will in turn affect the original market. Thus an understanding of the FTA is further enhanced by subjecting these three markets to a legal "general equilibrium analysis." Such an analysis would not view each market in isolation, but would trace the ripple effects of a compromise struck in one market through each of the other two markets and back to the first. By so doing one may derive general equilibrium solutions, that is, overall policy compromises that are most likely to satisfy the interests of all concerned institutional players and the legal constraints fixed by all three legal markets.

Space does not permit a full-fledged version of this analysis here. Nevertheless, two questions crucial to the future of the FTA illustrate how such an analysis might operate: how long negotiations will probably last, and how to reconcile such a bilateral accord with the goals of the upcoming GATT round of multilateral trade negotiations.

Length of Negotiations

In determining a likely termination date for negotiations, a general equilibrium analysis would ask what date would best satisfy the interests of the key institutional players in all three legal markets. At the same time that the United States and Canada have been pursuing their bilateral FTA talks, the two nations have also been pressing for the new round of multilateral trade negotiations (the "Uruguay round"), which began in September 1986. Assuming that the two countries' executive branches would prefer to present a united front on matters of mutual interest at the Uruguay round, it would make sense to conclude their bilateral talks sometime before the MTN negotiations hit full stride in mid-1988.

On the Canadian side, Prime Minister Mulroney and his party are required to call national elections before February 1989; thus the Canadian executive branch and parliamentary majority have a strong political incentive to forge a federal-provincial agreement and conclude bilateral talks well before that date.

From the U.S. perspective, President Reagan has nearly as great a political incentive to conclude negotiations before he leaves office in January 1989 and preferably before his successor is elected during the previous November. Working backward from the statutory notification period required by the modified fast-track procedure, the U.S. executive branch would therefore wish to conclude negotiations at least by the middle of 1988. The president's desire to keep a protectionist Democratic Congress at bay, however, would probably advance that date into 1987. If negotiations were to extend into the fall of 1988, for example, protectionist pressures engendered by the November elections might influence Congress's reaction to them. More important, were negotiations not completed before January 1988, the president's statutory authority to negotiate nontariff barriers under the 1979 Trade Agreements Act would expire, requiring him to seek new negotiating authority from Congress in order for talks to continue. Current signs are that Congress would grant the president such new authority subject only to even more restrictive conditions than those placed on him by current law. To avoid these congressional pressures, the president therefore has a powerful motivation to complete the talks before 1987 ends.

Thus the timetable that would represent a general equilibrium solution, accommodating the interests of all key players in all three markets, would bring negotiations to a close in the early autumn of 1987. Such a schedule would permit the agreement to be legislatively approved and domestically implemented in both countries sometime in 1988.

Compatibility with the New GATT Round

Another question a general equilibrium analysis can address is how to reconcile a comprehensive bilateral FTA between the world's two largest trading partners with a process of multilateral trade liberalization exemplified by the Uruguay round. Although the United States and Canada have pushed for that round to extend GATT coverage to areas such as services, the so-called Gang of Ten developing nations has just as vigorously opposed GATT's extension into those areas on the ground that the industrialized countries should eliminate their own market barriers to developing country exports before extending GATT's reach.

One can envision the U.S.-Canadian FTA playing three different but interrelated roles in these GATT talks: first, as a bludgeon to bring the developing countries to the GATT bargaining table and to keep them there; second, as a fallback liberalization measure for the United States and Canada if the Uruguay round should fail; and third, as a shot in the arm that would both complement and invigorate the new round. Key U.S. officials have virtually conceded that the threat of a Canadian FTA has already been used in the first way, that is, to get GATT members, particularly the developing nations, to agree to the Uruguay round. Were this its only purpose, however, the FTA would already have played its role and would lack continuing significance.

But the fact that the two nations continue to pursue the FTA suggests that the bilateral talks must serve a broader purpose. As Canada and the United States now recognize, the extended preliminary sparring over the scope of the Uruguay round discussions portends a significant likelihood of multilateral deadlock during that round. A U.S.-Canadian FTA can therefore provide a fallback form of trade liberalization for both countries in case the new round should prove unproductive. Through the FTA, the two countries may secure broadened access to each other's markets long before any market-opening effects from the multilateral talks could be realized.

Both of these explanations, which focus primarily on the GATT market, cast light on the FTA's relationship with the Uruguay round. What neither fully accounts for, however, is the interaction between the internal dynamics of the U.S. legal market and its Canadian and GATT counterparts. Since World War II, U.S. trade policy has been characterized by two overriding legal commitments: a substantive commitment to trade liberalization, whereby the United States has espoused a legal obligation to offer trade concessions to foreign countries on a non-discriminatory basis, and a procedural commitment to multilateralism as the appropriate framework within which the negotiation and resolution of trade disputes should take place. Both commitments, I would argue, are embodied in the continuing U.S. adherence to GATT.

The president has historically exhibited a greater commitment than has Congress both to trade liberalization as a substantive norm of international conduct and to multilateralism as a procedural norm. Much of U.S. willingness to resolve trade matters within the framework of GATT, therefore, can be attributed to historical presidential domination of international trade policymaking. Under the current U.S. regime, however, Congress has seized an increasingly active role in trade policymaking, spurred by an unprecedented trade deficit and protectionist pressures from powerful domestic interest groups. The Uruguay round thus arrives at a time of intense congressional questioning not only of the substantive goal of trade liberalization, but also of the appropriateness of GATT as the best procedural forum within which to conduct international trade discussions.

I would argue that this evolution of the U.S. domestic legal structure for international trade management from a presidentially managed regime into a regime of shared congressional-executive control has effected a profound change in the type of international trade structures that the United States is now willing to enter. As I have argued elsewhere, the United States' procedural flight from multilateralism in trade matters has not been an isolated phenomenon, but rather is symptomatic of a pervasive loss of faith at all levels of the U.S. government in multilateralism as the principal procedural mechanism for international conciliation and dispute resolution.[25] In some areas, such as international trade, the Reagan administration has acquiesced in a congressionally led flight from multilateralism. In other cases, such as the United States' recent withdrawal from the World Court's compulsory jurisdiction, the executive branch has led the flight and Congress has acquiesced in it. As the balance of power between the Congress and the president for the management of international trade has begun to shift in Congress's favor, Congress's biases toward protectionism and against GATT have weakened both the United States' substantive commitment to free trade and its procedural commitment to multilateral decisionmaking. Congressional agitation has not only placed intense pressure upon the Reagan administration's rhetorical commitment to free trade as the substantive core of U.S. trade policy, but has also spurred an extraordinary array of unilateral, bilateral, and plurilateral presidential trade initiatives.

In addition to the tariff imposed on Canadian shingles and shakes, recent unilateral U.S. actions have included punitive trade sanctions against South Africa, Libya, Nicaragua, and Japan; a spate of "self-initiated" presidential trade investigations under section 301 of the Trade Act of 1974; narrowing of duty-free preferences to certain developing and communist nations; self-initiated investigations of Japanese computer components and Taiwanese export performance requirements in the automotive sector; and a national security action on behalf of domestic machine tool builders against Taiwan, West Germany, Japan, and Switzerland. In addition to the Canadian softwood lumber accord and the U.S.-Israeli FTA, recent U.S. bilateral and plurilateral efforts

25. Koh, "Congressional Controls on Presidential Trade Policymaking."

have included voluntary restraint pacts on automobiles, steel, and semiconductors; the so-called Caribbean Basin Initiative; bilateral textile quota agreements with Hong Kong, Taiwan, and South Korea; free trade feelers toward the Association of South East Asian Nations and Egypt; market-oriented sector-specific trade liberalization talks with Japan; the Treasury Department's 1985 intervention with other developed nations to bring down the value of the dollar; and the ongoing Bilateral Investment Treaty program with ten developing countries.

Each of these actions, I would argue, may be viewed as a reactive or preemptive presidential strike designed to head off even more drastic or protectionist congressional action. Taken together, these actions represent a self-conscious presidential effort to preserve some of the United States' substantive commitment to trade liberalization, by softening its procedural commitment to pursue that liberalization in multilateral forums. As the Office of the U.S. Trade Representative has expressly acknowledged:

> Bilateral trading relationships are of growing importance to the United States. While our government remains strongly inclined to pursue a broad multilateral trading system based on the GATT, . . . a growing body of opinion in this country holds that we should not place exclusive reliance on GATT negotiations involving all trading countries, but rather should pursue negotiations among what we call "like-minded" countries to achieve higher levels of trading discipline than are possible if more countries are involved.[26]

Turning to the Canadian market, it becomes clear that the Reagan administration's new procedural approach fits neatly with the Mulroney government's own goals for the MTN round. A comprehensive FTA serves not only the Mulroney government's intrinsic interest in securing Canadian access to U.S. markets, but also its instrumental interest in using the FTA as a forum for forging bilateral compromises on matters of intense mutual concern, which the two nations may then present to GATT as a united front. To the extent that the new round will focus principally on establishing clearer multilateral rules of trade conduct, rather than on actual liberalization of market access, the bilateral FTA will almost certainly provide Canada with a better forum for meaningful reductions of tariff and nontariff barriers than will the Uruguay round.

Turning finally to the international market, it could be argued that a bilateral FTA between the United States and Canada violates the spirit,

---

26. Office of the U.S. Trade Representative, *1983 Annual Report of the President of the United States on the Trade Agreements Program* (USTR, 1984), p. 67.

if not the letter, of an international process ostensibly committed to multilateral trade management through GATT. This need not be the case, I would argue, if one views the FTA as merely one manifestation of an emerging, more complex international economic order that de facto, if not de jure, currently dominates international trade management. That order incorporates not only GATT norms and procedures, but also unilateral actions, bilateral trade accords, and multilateral trade coalitions that coexist with and complement the GATT framework. While an accord like the FTA may potentially detract from the Uruguay round, it may also invigorate and spur the sagging multilateral trade process by providing an opportunity for two sophisticated, economically developed neighbors and political allies to reaffirm, in a bilateral setting, their shared trade values regarding services, investment, intellectual property, agricultural trade, and dispute-resolution regimes.

Although the congruence of the two nations' interests in some of these areas has yet to be tested—particularly in the areas of investment and intellectual property—the basic compatibility of the two nations' trading philosophies makes the FTA a good test of whether the upcoming trade round has any hope of success. As one U.S. official recently observed, "These negotiations also will say a lot about international trade relations in the years to come. If the U.S. and Canada can't work out their differences, there's not much hope for the next GATT round."[27]

Successful U.S.-Canadian accords in these areas, concluded under the umbrella of the FTA, could provide momentum for a more global grappling with those issues during the Uruguay round. By adding to the body of state practice regarding highly controversial trade issues, the legal terms outlined in the U.S.-Canadian FTA could contribute to the development of an international legal consensus regarding these issues and instruct other GATT parties on how to develop substantive rules to deal with them. By serving as an experimental laboratory for addressing numerous substantive legal issues that will likely arise during the Uruguay round, the FTA can demonstrate to the world at large that, notwithstanding the decline of multilateralism as the exclusive procedural forum for rule change, the substantive norm of trade liberalization remains alive and well.

27. Statement of Deputy Assistant USTR William Merkin, reported in "Prospects of U.S.-Canada Free Trade Talks Assessed at Conferences in Ottawa, New York," *International Trade Reporter*, vol. 3 (May 14, 1986), pp. 665, 667.

Comments by Michael M. Hart

Harold Koh's paper is organized around three themes—U.S. law, Canadian law, and international law—and he examines each in the light of their historical development. I would like to focus on certain aspects of two of these three themes: the U.S. trade policymaking system and the nature of GATT obligations. In light of these two factors, I propose to review Canadian interests in the area of contingency protection.[28]

U.S. Trade Policymaking

U.S. interests and objectives in a bilateral trade agreement with Canada are neither simple to determine nor readily analyzed. The U.S. political decisionmaking process virtually guarantees imprecision and frequent changes in direction. Koh demonstrates that this has been the case for most of the twentieth century. In Canada, while there are many actors and various levels of influence, in the final analysis federal policy emerges from one source: the cabinet. Canadian interests and the pursuit of these interests are, therefore, clearer and more easily discerned. A role for the provinces in the trade policymaking process is relatively new, and the details of provincial involvement remain to be determined. In the United States, federal policy emerges from a highly brokered political market involving the administration, Congress, the courts, and various special interest groups. Even within the administration, there are shifting alliances and conflicting priorities. Successful policymaking, therefore, requires coalitions, many of which are temporary and forged out of what appear to be unrelated interests.

Second, the role of and attitudes toward trade policy differ in the two

---

28. I do not propose to comment on Koh's characterization of Canadian law, where he admits he is on weak ground and which is not essential to the case he makes. Suffice it to say that in Canada, a government with a majority in the House of Commons has the political, legal, and constitutional capacity to negotiate an international agreement and to implement the results of that agreement in federal law as regards areas of federal jurisdiction. The tensions and difficulties a U.S. administration faces in negotiating an international trade agreement are not present in Canada. Nevertheless, the increasing interest of the provinces in international trade matters and the increasing reach of international trade negotiations into areas of provincial jurisdiction (or, conversely, the decrease in the instruments of trade and industrial policy solely within the purview of the federal government) have underlined the need for the two levels of government to work together.

countries. In Canada, trade policy is at or near the top of the political agenda. It is a central element of economic policymaking, and even foreign policy may be deployed to achieve trade objectives. In the United States, from the administration's point of view, trade policy is of a second order of priority. It can be used, for example, as a tool to be deployed in the achievement of broad strategic foreign policy objectives. Traditionally, the administration has been largely oriented toward a "free trade" ideology. It prefers to use negotiations to pursue broad and long-term U.S. interests. Its trade policy tends to focus on reducing barriers to trade and on increasing opportunities for U.S. exporters, and thus it is generally outward looking. International negotiation and the management of trade relations are the central elements in trade policymaking. While aware of current problems, administrations tend to look more to future opportunities for U.S. business.

Within Congress, however, trade policy is viewed as an important ingredient in domestic economic policymaking and in meeting the needs of individual interest groups. Congress tends to be oriented toward a "fair-trade" ideology. Its trade policy focuses on the U.S. market and tends to be inward looking. It is more easily alarmed by merchandise trade deficits. Members of Congress tend to be preoccupied with current problems, rather than any long-term plans to increase U.S. trade performance, and they tend to respond to local and regional interests. Legislation is the central element of trade policymaking. While not at the top of the agenda, trade policy occupies a more important place in Congress than it is accorded by the administration. Koh's paper clearly shows the historical cleavage between the administration's approach to trade policy and that of the Congress. This cleavage was also demonstrated in the easy passage of a blatantly protectionist trade bill by the House of Representatives in May 1986.

Under the U.S. Constitution, Congress is responsible for the making of trade policy, but in practice the administration is responsible for its execution: modern trade negotiations require that the executive branch be able to conduct negotiations for the United States. This division of responsibility must further be qualified, as Koh notes, by the president's foreign policy and treaty-making authority. Both the president and Congress guard their authority with care. The potential for conflict between the two branches, therefore, was built into the Constitution, will remain a feature of U.S. trade policymaking, and will continue to frustrate U.S. trading partners. Most, however, have learned to work (if not enthusiastically) with this unique American feature and view it as a price to pay for negotiating with the United States.

In order to mitigate this problem, the administration and Congress jointly developed the special provisions known as the fast-track procedure. From the administration's point of view, they were adopted in order to facilitate negotiations and avoid the risk of a bilateral agreement being compromised by the normal congressional procedure of amending any legislation by responding to a variety of special interests. But from a congressional point of view, they safeguard its constitutional authority.

The Senate Finance Committee's consideration in April 1986 of the administration's request for fast-track authority to enter into bilateral negotiations with Canada demonstrated the extraordinary tension that has developed between the administration and Congress on the objectives and conduct of U.S. trade policy. Koh's paper shows that these tensions are not new, are deep-seated, and derive from the constitutional allocation of powers. A number of more immediate factors, however, were also at play:

—*Dissatisfaction with U.S. trade policy.* U.S. legislators were profoundly unhappy with the administration's seeming reluctance to tackle the trade deficit by, for example, taking a tough stance against perceived violators of U.S. economic interests.

—*Dissatisfaction with administration tax and economic policy.* Neither house was happy with the strength of the administration's commitment to the market, its reluctance to tackle the deficit through reduced defense spending and an increase in taxes, and its initial refusal to use monetary policy to reduce the U.S. trade deficit.

—*Tension between committee members.* Senate committees consist of strong-minded individuals, each of whom has his own agenda.

—*Party politics leading to the 1986 congressional election.* The nine Democrats on the committee saw the Republicans as vulnerable on the trade issue and were keen to use this issue for electoral gains in November.

—*Special interests.* More than half the senators on the Finance Committee represent regions that are vulnerable to protectionist concerns with Canadian exports or policies that directly engage U.S. interests. During the course of the hearings, however, it became clear that these concerns are more likely to be met in the course of a trade negotiation than on their own merits. Originally considered a liability, the hearings demonstrated that special interests can, in fact, be an asset, even where the motive is protectionist.

Like the House Ways and Means Committee, the Senate Finance Committee was not scheduled to hold hearings. The decision to hold hearings, however, opened an opportunity for various senators to use the hearings to further their own agenda. The fact that their collective agenda amounted to a majority of committee members being prepared to deny the administration fast-track authority (but not to deny negotiations) came as a surprise. Ironically, some senators who had publicly spoken against the negotiations proved in the end to be strong supporters. All twenty senators took a keen interest and were present for the discussions. In the final analysis Congress granted the administration its negotiating authority.

In addition to the decision not to disapprove, these committee hearings had other positive dimensions, including:

—*Clearer commitment from the administration.* The president expended considerable political capital to gain a favorable decision. The administration demonstrated that it was prepared to become more fully engaged, not only at the political level, but throughout the various agencies. The administration also made a clear commitment to work with the congressional committees and to take their oversight responsibilities seriously.

—*Stronger and more positive interest by the U.S. business community.* The possibility of rejection by the Senate awakened a largely apathetic business lobby to the point where even those with a previously negative interest expressed support for negotiations.

—*Strong editorial support.* The *Wall Street Journal, New York Times, Washington Post, Washington Times, Detroit News, Detroit Free Press, Long Island Newsday,* and the *Los Angeles Times* all characterized the Senate Finance Committee as parochial, protectionist, and working against U.S. interests. No major newspaper expressed doubts about the negotiations.

For good or ill, Canadians gained a better and more realistic appreciation of the tension between the administration and Congress and the workings of Capitol Hill. In order to conclude the negotiations successfully, Canada will have to ensure that sufficient attention is paid to this dimension in order to head off any potential problems in the ongoing and concluding phases of the negotiations. Canada will be negotiating with a more politically constrained administration, which will see a need to demonstrate that it is capable of tough negotiations and of meeting the concerns of Congress and U.S. business interests.

GATT and Bilateral Trade Negotiations

Although it is technically correct, Koh's presentation of the GATT dimension of the bilateral negotiations, however, is not as perceptive as his carefully argued discussion of U.S. policymaking. He does not fully appreciate the dynamic nature of GATT and its rather unique character as a multilateral contract administered by its participants. GATT provides a forum and a framework of rules for almost continuous negotiations aimed at reducing barriers to trade. Such negotiations are based on the principle of a multilateral balance of benefits and can include bilateral negotiations.

The existing GATT arrangements also constitute a binding international agreement between the United States and Canada covering their trade in goods—and this agreement conveys rights and imposes obligations upon both countries. As noted, the GATT rules specifically provide that participants can negotiate bilaterally to reduce barriers between them. GATT provides that they can enter into a free trade area or customs union, as long as certain requirements are met. Previous free trade area negotiations, however, do not provide much guidance for Canadian-U.S. negotiations because they have not dealt comprehensively with such difficult areas as services, subsidy practices, government procurement, contingency protection, intellectual property, and investment. These issues dominate the late twentieth century trade policy agenda and may well figure prominently in the negotiations.

GATT article 24 is a derogation from the most-favored-nation (MFN) obligations in article 1. It was originally conceived as part of the compromise required to deal with the U.S. desire to dismantle imperial preferences. The United States was prepared to see new preferences established, but only within the tight confines of a customs union. The addition to article 24 of the concept of a free trade area widened the scope for exceptions to the MFN principle.

A free trade area in effect denies MFN treatment to the nonpartners and establishes new preferences that are available only to the partners in the free trade area agreement. It requires that "duties and other restrictive regulations of commerce . . . are eliminated on substantially all the trade between the constituent territories."

Free Trade Areas and Contingency Protection

GATT negotiations originally concentrated on tariff issues: the binding against increase of the tariffs of industrialized countries and the reduction of high tariffs. By the time of the Kennedy and Tokyo rounds, in addition to continuing the process of cutting and even eliminating tariffs, industrialized countries began a process of harmonizing tariff schedules and remaining rates. With adoption of the harmonized system by all major trading countries by the end of this decade, the end of the next round should result in tariff schedules and rates in the industrialized countries that are more uniform.

Starting with the Kennedy round and continuing during the Tokyo round, the major traders also began systematically to attack nontariff barriers. The aim was not their elimination, but the introduction of greater discipline and transparency. Among the nontariff issues addressed in the resulting codes were countervailing and antidumping duties and subsidy practices. The codes recognized the increasing importance of these and related issues (safeguards).

Most of the industrialized countries now have highly sophisticated, multilaterally sanctioned, and basically discriminatory commercial policy instruments available to deal with politically intolerable imports. These have been characterized by Rodney Grey as the instruments of contingency protection, that is, protection extended when certain factors are present such as injury, dumping, and subsidization. Even where multilateral sanctions remain lacking (for example, when voluntary export restraints are invoked), there is increasing multilateral tolerance. These instruments are much more effective in dealing with politically intolerable imports than tariffs are.

Thus, while the result of seven rounds of GATT negotiations has clearly been a reduction in tariff barriers, GATT members have not dealt as successfully with liberalizing nontariff trade barriers to economically and politically sensitive imports, but in effect have sanctioned the exchange of one instrument of protection for another, albeit now more highly disciplined and regulated. A significant dimension is the change from reliance on a nondiscriminatory instrument to the use of discriminatory instruments. Rodney Grey has argued that contingency protection requires an army of technicians and a learned trade bar to operate successfully. If true, this means that it is a weapon that can be used successfully by only a few countries and thus again is admirably suited to discriminatory application. The United States has taken the lead in adopting this system. The European Community has opted for an administrative system similar in intent but potentially even more discriminatory in its effect. Canada has by now copied much of the U.S. system.[29]

Article 24 requires neither that the instruments of contingency protection be eliminated nor that they be retained in a free trade area or a customs union. For the record, all customs unions have eliminated or highly disciplined the use of the instruments of contingency protection between the parties, while free trade areas have provided for the continued application of these measures.

As a practical matter, a customs union or a common market presumes a high degree of integration, that is, a willingness to tolerate a high degree of policy harmonization and the development of common administrative procedures and institutions. Such policy harmonization facilitates the elimination of the instruments of contingency protection and other nontariff barriers to trade. Nevertheless, a free trade agreement should also result in commerce between the two or more participating countries being conducted on the same basis as commerce within each country. In effect, there should be no impediments to the movement of each other's goods either at the border or once in the domestic market.

Contingency Protection between Canada and the United States

Between Canada and the United States, measures of contingency protection, both actual and threatened, are now among the most important barriers to trade. The system is easily accessible to private parties and the threat of its use has become a significant barrier against Canadian export penetration of the U.S. market. The U.S. penchant for litigation, the ease with which U.S. competitors may initiate multiple actions, the relatively low standards that need to be met to initiate an investigation or for penalties to be imposed, and the high costs involved in contesting an investigation make this a powerful weapon for harassment. Canadian

---

29. The fact that Canada has copied much of the U.S. system, however, should not be mistaken for symmetry in effect. The Canadian system has little effect on U.S. economic interests, while the U.S. system affects Canada on an almost daily basis.

exporters are increasingly engaged in preventing the imposition of a special duty or quota of one kind or other. The uncertainty thus generated acts as a significant disincentive to Canadian exporters, as well as to Canadian and third-country investors wishing to serve the U.S. market from Canada.

The controversy over Canadian softwood lumber exports, as recounted by Koh, presents an apposite illustration of the use of U.S. trade legislation as a harassing tactic. An integral part of the Canadian government's decision to pursue bilateral negotiations with the United States, therefore, is predicated on a desire to provide relief to Canadian exporters from the uncertainties created by the U.S. contingency protection system. Without this certainty, the type of dynamic investment required to take advantage of the other provisions of the agreement will not take place. It is key to providing the stable access that is vital to future growth and investment. It is also a one-sided issue. Canadian nontariff barriers do not pose a similar threat to U.S. growth and investment. U.S. producers already enjoy the benefits of a large continental market. It is difficult for them to appreciate the importance of this issue to their Canadian counterparts. Failure to grasp the importance of this issue, however, could well doom the negotiations.

Prominent in the bilateral negotiations, this issue is also of concern to other U.S. trading partners. They also worry about the direction being taken in U.S. trade policy. The widely shared belief in the United States that the country is being victimized by its major trading partners and constrained by multilateral trade obligations that favor foreign competitors has led to strong pressures to further strengthen and extend trade remedy legislation, both in terms of providing relief from imports and increasing opportunities for U.S. exporters. Given the relatively low level of the U.S. tariff, the relatively higher value of the U.S. dollar, and the enormous U.S. trade deficit, the instruments of contingency protection are perceived as the only means available to redress the imbalance through attacking "unfair" imports and reducing the U.S. merchandise trade deficit.

The Subsidy Dimension

Fairness is an increasingly central preoccupation of U.S. legislators— "fairness" being a code word for doing things the American way. This is not an atypical perspective for a major power. The best example of this mindset is afforded by the deep and abiding concern about foreign subsidies. There is no question that increasing government assistance to industry in one form or another is a matter of international concern. GATT from the outset has been hostile to subsidies. It proscribed export subsidies for industrial products and provided remedies against other forms of subsidization. Article 6 permits aggrieved countries to levy compensatory tariffs (countervailing duties) to offset harmful foreign subsidies, provided that the imports benefiting from the subsidy cause material injury to the domestic industry. Article 16 entails a measure of self-restraint on the use of subsidies, and article 23 permits unspecified countermeasures when actions nullify or impair the benefits that a government can rightly expect from GATT.

Subsidies have an effect similar to tariffs. They distort prices and profits and thus provide some producers with an ability to compete internationally that is not commensurate with their efficiency or productivity. Tariffs distort trade by increasing prices and thus decreasing consumption, while subsidies distort trade either by increasing exports or displacing imports. Nevertheless, GATT article 16's prohibition of export subsidies does not extend to similar restrictions on domestic subsidies. Indeed, the GATT subsidies code recognizes the legitimacy of domestic subsidies for socioeconomic development, while also recognizing the right to impose countervailing duties to offset injurious domestic subsidies.

Subsidies, however, were not a major problem in international trade (with the possible exception of agriculture) until the 1960s. A variety of factors since then have increased not only the absolute level of subsidization, but also the perception of subsidies as a trade-distorting practice. Industrialized countries sought to improve their relative positions by offering various forms of incentives to attract multinational investment, especially in the knowledge-intensive industries. Less developed countries sought to industrialize through subsidization. Industrialized governments countered by subsidizing modernization and rationalization. All governments sought to increase employment by keeping uncompetitive industries alive through a combination of restrictive border measures and financial assistance.

The United States took the lead in attacking the problem of subsidization, partly through more aggressive use of the countervailing duty statute and partially through international negotiations. The U.S. position is understandable. OECD statistics suggest that the United States has the lowest level of subsidization among industrialized countries. This is partly a result of definition and partly a result of the different kinds of programs used in the United States to help domestic industry. The central element in U.S. industrial strategy is defense spending. The United States uses the defense and related budgets (for example, NASA) to maintain U.S. leadership in industrial research and development and to provide strategic industries with a securely funded base. In addition, through the tax system and such programs as Buy America, the United States provides other advantages to domestic industry.

The problem is that the trade-distorting effect of subsidies is often perceived to be directly related to a country's export performance. In a small country such as Canada, which exports a narrow range of products representing a large proportion of total production, almost any domestic subsidy is likely to have a direct impact on exports. In calculating its export effect, the margin is likely to be significant. For a large industrial economy such as the United States, subsidies are distributed over a much wider range of sectors, industries, and regions. Exports represent a relatively small proportion of total production. The average margin on exported products, therefore, is likely to be minuscule. It is not an accident that the first Canadian countervail case involving the United States is in the agricultural sector, where the level of subsidization is high and the range of affected products is narrow. However, subsidization in the large economy is also trade distorting. The distortion in the small economy is likely to be in its export effect. The distortion in the large economy is likely to be in its import displacement effect or in its ability to stimulate product innovation and variety. It is not neutral or benign.

The strong antisubsidy sentiment in the United States and the objection of U.S. business to foreign subsidies should not be mistaken for a willingness by the United States to give up its own subsidies. Congress and the states continue to add to and increase funding for a large variety of aids to industry, many of which may not be perceived as subsidies but whose effect is very similar to the subsidies Americans complain about in other countries.

Assistance programs and subsidies abound in the United States, especially in the areas of agriculture, energy, transportation, and defense. As in other countries, the federal government argues it is merely honoring its constitutional duty to promote industry and commerce and, in the case of defense-related industry, national security. In 1984 a special study by the Congressional Budget Office estimated that federal aid and subsidies to business would exceed $130 billion. Defense spending on goods and services amounted to another $140 billion, while housing and medical subsidies covered a further $110 billion.[30]

Not all of the programs and policies identified as subsidies by the CBO should be considered subsidies as these are understood in the context of the countervailing duty statute or GATT obligations. What is interesting, however, is that even discounting the broad swath cut by the CBO analysis, the degree of subsidization practiced in the United States is at a level that Americans believe is practiced only by other governments. U.S. negotiating objectives in the area of contingency protection, which often revolve around concepts such as fairness, would be significantly improved if U.S. negotiators and legislators had a clearer and more realistic appreciation of the similarity between their country's domestic practices and those complained of in foreign countries. The issue is not whether one country's practices are legitimate and another's are not; the issue is creating barrier-free trade.

Conclusions

Canada and the United States share many objectives in the bilateral trade negotiations, as they do in the multilateral GATT negotiations. Both have long been committed to a gradual process of negotiating meaningful reductions in barriers to trade. For the bilateral negotiations, President Reagan and Prime Minister Mulroney have jointly declared that their aim is to achieve the broadest possible package of mutually beneficial reductions in barriers to trade in order to foster a more open and more certain trade and investment climate. An important test of this determination will be whether the two leaders can develop a mutually agreeable approach to the issue of contingency protection, especially in the light of the historically different perspectives to trade policy taken by the Congress and the administration and the different methods by which both countries pursue their economic development objectives.

For Canada, given developments over the past decade in the application of U.S. trade remedy law, this issue assumed central importance in the debate leading up to the government's decision to pursue bilateral

30. Congressional Budget Office, *Federal Support of U.S. Business* (Washington, D.C.: CBO, 1984).

negotiations. For the United States, in light of the traditional tension between the administration and Congress in the making of trade policy, the issue also looms as central. Unfortunately, for Canada, the aim will be to supplant the U.S. system with a distinct regime insofar as Canadian exports are concerned. For Congress, preoccupied by concerns with fairness, the issue is to increase the automaticity and reach of the system. The administration will need all of its ingenuity and imagination to satisfy both parties. Failure to meet this challenge, however, may well doom the success of the bilateral negotiations, which in turn would cast doubt on U.S. credibility in the multilateral negotiations.

Given Koh's perceptive description and analysis of the tension between the administration and Congress, policymakers in Canada would do well to pay heed to this built-in problem in the U.S. system throughout the negotiations and especially in the ratification and implementation stage should negotiations conclude.

MARGARET BIGGS

An International Perspective

THE IMPLICATIONS of Canadian-U.S. bilateral trade negotiations for third countries and for the international trading system are not being given the attention and analysis they deserve. A major reason, in Canada at least, is the understandable preoccupation with assessing the domestic benefits and costs of a bilateral trade deal and with assuring our American counterparts of our unity and resolve. A further reason is the highly complex and speculative nature of these implications. Even when analytic tools are available—customs union theory, for example—the required analysis is complex and little has been attempted. The international political reactions and reverberations are even more difficult to model and are inevitably the subject of opinion more than fact. Finally, some policymakers and analysts may not consider the international implications of a Canadian-U.S. trade pact to be of much concern, either because they do not attach any political or economic importance to them or because they assume that they are likely to be largely positive.

This paper outlines some of the possible international consequences, positive and negative, of a Canadian-U.S. trade agreement. It does not even begin to satisfy the need for more in-depth analysis of the possible international ramifications of such an agreement. I do hope that it demonstrates that the international implications of a bilateral free trade agreement (FTA) are likely to be of considerable, possibly critical, consequence.

Any analysis of the proposed FTA's international ramifications de-

The author would like to thank Janette Mark for her research assistance and John Curtis, Gerald Helleiner, David Richardson, and Frank Stone for their comments and criticism.

pends upon a reading of a number of key factors: the underlying motivations behind negotiating an FTA and the objectives of the bilateral trade partners; the nature and provisions of the bilateral agreement, particularly its "extendability" to other countries; the health and stability of the global trading and financial systems and the relationship between negotiations on the bilateral and multilateral levels; the trade policy posture likely to be taken by Canada and by the United States vis-à-vis third countries; possible parallel initiatives designed to minimize any economic distortions and political fallout; and other countries' reactions to a Canadian-U.S. trade initiative.

Motivations and Objectives

A major premise of this paper is that the motivations and objectives driving the pursuit of an FTA in Canada and in the United States will go a long way toward determining its likely global effects; that is, will it be inward or outward looking, and will it promote or undermine international discipline, liberalization, and cooperation? The third-country and global implications of Canadian-U.S. trade negotiations will obviously differ depending upon where the objectives, process, and results fall on the bilateral-multilateral spectrum.

For both Canada and the United States, a full FTA with their largest trading partner would represent a significant departure from their own traditional postwar multilateral approaches.[1] Yet both countries have stated their belief that bilateral negotiations could have a positive impact, as a precursor or spur, on the multilateral front. To what extent, therefore, do bilateral negotiations represent just a change in approach and not in objective? The answer to this question appears to be less straightforward in Canada than the United States. In order to discern

1. Canada and the United States have a long history of joint bilateral trade arrangements, the most important being the 1965 Automotive Products Trade Agreement and the 1941 Defense Production Sharing Agreements. Each country also has a range of supplementary bilateral trade agreements with other trading partners. However, in contemporary commercial policy history neither country has entered into a wide-ranging bilateral free trade arrangement, except for the 1985 U.S.-Israeli free trade area agreement. A U.S.-Canadian free trade agreement would be qualitatively different— there would not be the same kind of foreign policy rationale to it—and it would be quantitatively different—their trading relationship is America's largest and the largest in the world.

Canadian objectives one must glean clues from the thinking behind the Canadian decision to propose bilateral trade negotiations.

The most important rationale motivating Canada's bilateral push is twofold: improved and more secure access to the U.S. market is essential to protect and promote Canada's main economic interests, and multilateral trade negotiations will come "too late" and result in "too little" progress to meet these needs.[2] Care is taken to affirm the importance of the multilateral trading system, and the bilateral decision is usually reached as a "second-best" option after discounting the likelihood of achieving a "first-best" multilateral solution to Canada's market access problems.

However, in the process of rationalizing this historic shift away from Canada's past preference for multilateral and nondiscriminatory trade approaches, those advocating a bilateral route sometimes adopt a rather one-sided assessment of Canada's prospects in bilateral as distinct from multilateral trade negotiations (MTN) and a rather narrow interpretation of what constitutes Canada's international interests. For example, in 1984 and early 1985 when the idea of a bilateral agreement was gaining momentum in Canada, multilateral talks were considered to be some time away, whereas a bilateral agreement was thought to be a much quicker "fix." It is now apparent that the "two tracks" are in train at the same time, with bilateral negotiations no doubt concluding much sooner but probably not as easily as was once assumed.

More important, the preference for bilateral over multilateral negotiations reveals not just a concern for expediency but an assessment that Canada could fare better dealing with the United States directly rather than in the context of wider multinational talks. Considerable weight is attached to those examples from the Tokyo round, where the most-favored-nation (MFN) principle worked against Canada's receiving certain concessions from the United States because the Americans did not want them to be generalized to other trading partners. Little mention is made of the fact, on the other hand, that Canada would not have achieved its key Tokyo round objective of getting the United States to

2. See, for example, Canadian Department of External Affairs, *Canadian Trade Negotiations: Introduction, Selected Documents, Further Reading* (Ottawa, 1985); *Report of the Royal Commission on the Economic Union and Development Prospects for Canada*, vol. 1 (Ottawa: Minister of Supply and Services Canada, 1985); and Richard G. Lipsey and Murray G. Smith, *Taking the Initiative: Canada's Trade Options in a Turbulent World* (Toronto: C. D. Howe Institute, 1985).

accept the injury test in countervail cases if it were not for European influence and leverage.

Further, the discounting of talks under the General Agreement on Tariffs and Trade (GATT) often goes beyond just warning of the dangers of putting all the Canadian eggs in the multilateral basket and results in the contention that the multilateral forum is not very relevant to the bilateral Canadian-U.S. relationship. As James Kelleher, the former minister of international trade, stated, "The problem, concerns, and aspirations that we have, quite frankly, are different from and do not coincide with those of the whole trading world." As a result, the need to protect and strengthen the international trading system has increasingly been divorced from the bread-and-butter concerns of Canadian trade policy and its salience effectively downgraded.

This is not to say that multilateral concerns have been discarded. Even the fact that considerable care has been taken by those advocating bilateral negotiations to portray bilateral talks as a complement, not a hindrance, to multilateral negotiations is in itself an indication that a healthy multilateral trading system is considered to be important to Canada. Yet the absence of much substantive analysis examining how and where bilateral negotiations might serve to help (or harm) multilateral discussions and rule making suggests that multilateral ends have not been a major preoccupation or high priority. Indeed, there are indications that some Canadians hope to secure a preferential arrangement with the United States, not so much as a means to an end, but as an end in itself. For example, Canada's former minister of international trade has spoken of "privileged access" analogous to that achieved by the European Common Market.

> I presume it quite possible . . . that we will have better terms of access in certain areas and regarding certain goods . . . than will other countries around the world. But as long as this complies with Article XXIV of the GATT, there is not legal ground for complaint.[3]

In sum, there are a number of reasons to believe that Canada might be satisfied with a bilateral agreement that met its immediate needs on a continental basis; there is an unapologetic and bold preoccupation with gaining access to the large U.S. market and an unduly critical assessment of GATT's relevance and benefit for Canada. Perhaps both of these positions are merely the result of overcorrections for other tendencies—

---

3. Canada, Senate, Standing Committee on National Finance, *Proceedings,* no. 21, 33d Parliament, 1 sess. (October 16, 1985), p. 36.

the preoccupation in the past with reducing dependence on the United States and the unquestioning allegiance of some Canadians to multilateral approaches. However, the lack of a clear and overriding statement by the Canadian government that its principal aim is to open up the process and product of bilateral negotiations wherever and whenever feasible has reinforced the expectation and desire of some Canadians of preferential access in the U.S. market.

The U.S. interest in an FTA with Canada is rooted in some of the same disenchantment with the progress and relevance of GATT. In particular, there is a frustration with the lowest common denominator and free-rider effects of multinational negotiations and MFN requirements. There is also a widespread perception that the United States has done more than its share to buttress the international trading system and defend the principle of nondiscrimination. The result has been a growing acceptance of more aggressive and discriminatory trade policies. The particular disappointment with the 1982 GATT ministerial meeting resulted in the authorization to negotiate bilateral free trade agreements being written into the Trade and Tariff Act of 1984.

There is reason to believe, however, that the United States has not discarded its preference for multilateral solutions and that it favors bilateral negotiations with Canada primarily because of the leverage and possible demonstration effect it can create for multilateral liberalization and rule making. Given that 80 percent of its trade is *not* with Canada, the United States is unlikely, on the one hand, to forgo using access to its market to lever concessions from its other major trading partners, and is certain, on the other, to try to use selective "minilateral" actions to pave the way toward broader plurilateral or multilateral agreements. The latter objective is strongly endorsed by several agencies of the U.S. government, as evidenced by the following statement by the U.S. General Accounting Office:

> Bilateral agreements could undermine the multilateral trade system created by the GATT because of their discriminatory nature. However, such agreements do not inherently violate the MFN principle. . . . If genuine attempts are made to expand the application of bilateral agreements, such agreements could serve as useful tools in bridging the gap between a lack of international consensus in a given area . . . and conclusion of a full-fledged multilateral agreement. . . . Thus, if bilateral agreements are to be negotiated, the challenge . . . is to make every effort to negotiate these in accordance with GATT principles and work to bring these into GATT's multilateral framework and discipline.[4]

4. U.S. General Accounting Office, *Current Issues in U.S. Participation in the*

To conclude, it appears that the United States still has a strong incentive to pursue, as a first order of business, multilateral solutions to govern its diverse trading relations, while using more selective (bilateral) actions on the side to help goad and smooth international agreements along. In this context, a Canadian-U.S. FTA is currently viewed primarily as a strategic tool to achieve wider objectives. However, this position is no longer based so much in principle as in pragmatism. If frustrated multilaterally, the United States is likely to pursue much more discriminatory trade measures, and its objectives in an FTA with Canada would likely be much more narrowly conceived.

Trade Effects

Assuming that Canadian-U.S. negotiations will lead to an elimination of all or most remaining tariff barriers between the two countries, there is the possibility that some diversion of trade from third countries will occur. Even if trade diversion is not important in aggregate terms or in relation to trade creation between the bilateral partners, it still represents an inefficient use of global resources and it may be significant in certain industries and for trade relations with particular third countries. For these reasons, the issue of trade diversion needs to be more adequately investigated.[5]

In Canada, trade diversion will not be large, primarily because a high percentage of Canadian imports (75 percent in the case of manufactures) already originate in the United States. However, there is the potential for diversion in a number of industries for which the U.S. is often not the lowest-cost world producer, where substantial third-country competition exists, and where a relatively high external tariff has been retained despite successive multilateral tariff-cutting rounds. As tables 1, 2, and 3 indicate, these factors are most evident in the more traditional consumer goods industries, such as clothing, footwear, and textiles, where developing-country competition in particular is quite pervasive. The greatest possibility of import substitution is in clothing, where the

---

Multilateral Trading System, report to the Subcommittee on International Economic Policy, Oceans and Environment of the Senate Committee on Foreign Relations (GAO, 1985), pp. 93–94.

5. Work is currently under way through the Department of Finance to refine and extend the analysis undertaken with the general equilibrium model and include trade diversion effects. This work will be completed in the spring of 1987.

United States still produces and exports a large volume of basic apparel at relatively low unit values, much of which increasingly competes head-on with developing-country products.[6] Other possible areas for trade diversion are auto parts, where countries like Mexico and Brazil are becoming new suppliers; household furniture and appliances, where Asian producers are beginning to challenge American competition; and high technology goods, where U.S. imports might displace some Japanese goods.

There is also scope for trade diversion in the U.S. market, although the situations are not totally analogous. Canadian exports to the U.S. market are more complementary to third-country exports than is the case for U.S. exports to Canada. On the other hand, over 80 percent of U.S. imports come from countries other than Canada (see table 2). However, a fairly similar situation exists in the case of traditional consumer goods industries, where low-cost offshore competition is extensive and relatively high tariff barriers still exist.

One major study of the impact of bilateral free trade on Canadian industry indicates that a number of these import-competing industries in Canada will experience significant gains under an FTA, much greater than would occur under multilateral free trade. For example, the Canadian clothing industry's production is estimated to increase by 478 percent, 6 times that estimated for multilateral free trade; textile production is estimated to grow by 239 percent, 1.5 times the multilateral increase; and knitting output is predicted to rise by 107 percent, 14 times greater than the growth under multilateral free trade.[7] Other instances where third countries might experience lower sales to the United States because of diversion by Canadian imports are in the petrochemical industry (Mexico) and specialty steel (Mexico, South Korea, and Brazil).

Should trade diversion occur in these or other areas of the American

6. In a study of sectoral free trade in the textile and clothing industries, the Textile and Clothing Board asserted that there was likely to be little trade diversion because imported products were highly differentiated by country of origin. This may be true in the high end of the market for both industries, but the middle spectrum is increasingly being occupied by developing-country suppliers (due in part to the upgrading effect brought on by quantitative restrictions) that compete with U.S. producers. See Textile and Clothing Board, *Study of the Impact of Potential Free Trade in Textiles and Clothing between Canada and the United States: Final Report* (Ottawa, 1984).

7. Richard Harris, "Summary of a Project on the General Equilibrium Evaluation of Canadian Trade Policy," in John Whalley with Roderick Hill, eds., *Canada-United States Free Trade* (University of Toronto Press in cooperation with the Royal Commission on the Economic Union and Development Prospects for Canada and the Canadian Government Publishing Centre, Supply and Services Canada, 1985), pp. 167, 176.

Table 1. *Canadian Imports, by Areas and Commodity Groups, 1984*
Percent unless otherwise indicated

Commodity group	United States	Japan	EEC	EFTA	Other Western Europe	Industrial countries	Developing countries	Eastern trading area	Total (billions of U.S. dollars)
Total imports	71.47	6.02	8.69	1.53	0.41	88.12	10.30	0.63	73.23
Primary products	55.94	0.61	10.67	1.10	0.83	69.11	26.95	0.68	13.21
Semimanufactures	67.62	5.52	15.91	2.87	1.00	92.93	5.41	3.32	9.05
Manufactures	74.83	7.32	8.21	1.60	0.32	92.29	6.65	0.61	58.61
Special machinery	77.16	4.17	13.58	3.24	0.15	98.46	1.24	0.15	6.48
Office and telecommunications equipment	86.93	5.30	3.03	0.38	…	95.64	4.36	…	5.28
Road motor vehicles	87.86	7.69	2.58	0.55	…	98.68	0.66	0.06	18.21
Other machinery and transport equipment	78.91	6.06	6.74	1.86	0.10	93.56	6.06	0.29	10.25
Household appliances	37.74	36.23	5.66	1.13	0.38	80.76	18.87	…	2.65
Textiles	48.72	5.77	18.59	2.56	1.28	76.28	17.95	5.13	1.56
Clothing	7.69	1.54	10.77	1.54	0.77	22.31	66.15	10.77	1.30
Other consumer goods	57.82	3.65	15.63	2.08	1.04	80.21	10.42	1.56	3.84

Source: GATT, *International Trade 1984/85* (Geneva: GATT, 1985), table A.35.

Table 2. *U.S. Imports, by Areas and Commodity Groups, 1984*
Percent unless otherwise indicated

Commodity group	Canada	Japan	EEC	EFTA	Other Western Europe	Industrial countries	Developing countries	Eastern trading area	Total (billions of U.S. dollars)
Total imports	19.32	17.85	17.72	3.21	1.07	59.16	37.24	1.69	338.19
Primary products	19.28	1.12	12.33	2.45	1.06	36.22	58.55	2.00	106.77
Semimanufactures	23.76	14.79	27.49	5.16	2.15	73.32	20.40	1.89	44.57
Manufactures	18.87	26.17	20.05	3.48	1.08	69.66	27.50	1.56	224.54
Special machinery	15.57	26.80	37.56	7.99	0.60	88.52	10.58	0.48	16.64
Office and telecommunications equipment	7.02	39.53	7.77	1.14	0.06	55.61	44.28	0.04	25.50
Road motor vehicles	40.20	38.50	16.17	2.83	0.15	97.86	1.96	0.13	47.69
Other machinery and transport equipment	18.44	22.50	27.02	3.63	0.67	72.28	26.82	0.50	30.05
Household appliances	2.02	55.58	5.36	2.40	0.25	65.60	34.03	0.32	15.87
Textiles	3.91	15.18	24.51	3.04	2.17	49.02	40.78	9.54	4.61
Clothing	1.10	3.63	7.26	0.62	0.82	13.49	78.43	7.88	14.60
Other consumer goods	8.08	9.92	22.65	3.32	3.16	47.18	47.54	3.08	24.99

Source: GATT, *International Trade 1984/85*, table A.34.

Table 3. *Post-Tokyo Round Tariffs on Industrial Products,*
by Sector[a]
Percent

Sector	Canada	United States	All industrial countries (average)
Textiles	16.7	9.2	8.5
Wearing apparel	24.2	22.7	17.5
Leather products	6.3	4.2	3.0
Footwear	21.9	8.8	12.1
Wood products	3.2	1.7	1.9
Furniture and fixtures	14.3	4.1[b]	7.3
Paper and paper products	6.7	0.2	4.2
Printing and publishing	1.0	0.7	1.5
Chemicals	7.5	2.4	6.7
Rubber products	6.7	2.5	4.1
Nonmetal mineral products	6.4	5.3	4.0
Glass and glass products	7.2	6.2	7.9
Iron and steel	5.4	3.6	4.4
Nonferrous metals	2.0	0.7	1.6
Metal products	8.5	4.8	6.3
Nonelectrical machinery	4.5	3.3	4.7
Electrical machinery	5.8	4.4	7.1
Transportation equipment	1.6	2.5	6.0
Miscellaneous manufactures	5.4	4.2	4.7
All industries	5.2	4.3	5.8

Source: Alan V. Deardorff and Robert M. Stern,"Economic Effects of Complete Elimination of Post-Tokyo Round Tariffs," in William R. Cline, ed., *Trade Policy in the 1980s* (Washington, D.C.: Institute for International Economics, 1983), pp. 674–75.
a. Weighted by own-country imports, excluding petroleum.
b. Estimated from incomplete data.

and Canadian markets, it could be a source of friction with third countries. (For example, a thorn in the side of Canada's trade relations with Western Europe has been the diversion against Canadian goods, newsprint in particular, that occurred when free trade agreements were struck between the European Economic Community [EEC] and European Free Trade Association [EFTA] countries.) In certain cases, the problems of trade diversion created by preferential North American access will compound the economic distortions and political friction of existing discriminatory import barriers. Protection against developing-country suppliers of textiles and clothing under the Multi-Fiber Arrangement is the most significant case in point.

Beyond the short-run changes in trade patterns that might occur with an FTA, there could be longer-run, dynamic effects that would reduce any global efficiency losses. Trade diversion might increase demand in industries that are subject to scale economies, thereby decreasing domestic production costs and any discrepancy between North American and world prices. Furthermore, it is argued in Canada that scale economies, specialization, and other elements of intra-industry restructuring on a North American basis will help to prepare heavily protected Canadian industries to face global competition. As such, an FTA could be viewed as a helpful interim step in preparation for broader liberalization.

Still, there is reason to doubt, on economic or political grounds, that bilateral liberalization in "sensitive industries" such as clothing and textiles will help smooth the way for multilateral liberalization. First, the reduction of bilateral trade barriers, while no doubt leading to an improvement in the competitive cost structure of the Canadian industry, is unlikely to make the Canadian industry capable of matching global competition. If the lack of a large continental market was such a key variable, one could assume that U.S. firms in these same industries would not be in similar need of special import protection against offshore competition. In this instance, therefore, bilateral liberalization has more in common with the status quo than it does with multilateral liberalization; fifteen years of special import protection has already produced a domestic industry that is more or less on a competitive par with other developed countries but has not yet taken on the qualitatively different restructuring task posed by developing-country competition. Preferential access to the U.S. market is likely to lead to expanded capacity and employment, much of which probably could not be sustained in the face of more global competition.

Expanded domestic clothing and textile industries capable of meeting competition from developed, but not developing, countries are likely to be a source of continued, if not heightened, protectionist pressure in the future. Changes are not likely to occur in the political and economic factors responsible for past protectionist policies in trade-impacted industries—the relatively large number of jobs at stake, the disproportionate number of vulnerable workers, and the concentration of production in politically sensitive and economically depressed regions. Higher growth and more up-market opportunities elsewhere in the economy might help to ameliorate protectionist pressures, but the increased number of jobs at risk and the tendency to protect recent investments could just as easily serve to heighten protectionist demands. Even in the short run, there is a very real possibility that trade barriers could be raised against third countries. In many import-competing industries, aggregate import penetration ("cumulative disruption") is monitored carefully and an implicit import ceiling imposed. Increased bilateral import penetration, even if offset by greater export orientation, may have to be rectified by tightening controls on other suppliers. This kind of scenario could easily unfold, for example, in the case of Brazilian and Korean steel exports to the United States or East Asian clothing exports to Canada.

Overall, a Canadian-U.S. FTA could result in significant trade diversion in certain key industries. Other third-country trade effects could be felt should the price of bilateral integration—greater import penetration—be paid by third-country suppliers. In both cases, developing-country suppliers are likely to be most affected. There is also reason to doubt that adjusting to meet North American competition is a valid means to achieve the objective of facing global competition. The global welfare losses stemming from the creation of an FTA can only be remedied if parallel actions are taken concurrently to phase out external trade barriers where significant trade diversion is likely to take place.

Trade Policy Implications

As discussed above, the pursuit of a bilateral free trade agreement is largely explained as a "second-best" option in both Canada and the United States (although there are narrow economic interests in Canada that would prefer to limit liberalization to bilateral trade). Multilateral approaches based on the principle of nondiscriminatory most-favored-nation treatment still offer a number of advantages. Global economic welfare and efficiency are optimized, political friction and tension among countries are reduced, stability and predictability are enhanced, and administrative and legal problems are simplified.

Of course, the MFN principle is not sacrosanct, as evidenced by the widespread use of discriminatory trade barriers and the existence of numerous preferential trading arrangements. And its value as the modus operandi for the international trading system has increasingly been questioned in recent years. This disillusionment with the principle of MFN treatment has been a cyclical theme in commercial policy history, and it has usually centered, as it does now, on the problems of free riding and trade liberalization lethargy that are engendered by an MFN-based system. As a result, the use of conditional MFN principles came into more favor in the 1970s. The adoption of such principles in two of the Tokyo round's codes of conduct on nontariff barriers was designed to put pressure on free riders and to allow countries that wished to move further and faster to do so. The exclusive nature of these codes, while lamentable because it contributed to a further erosion of the MFN principle, did allow for the extension of some multilateral discipline in an all-important area.

A Canadian-U.S. FTA must be viewed, therefore, in the context of a trading system in which some second-best actions are inevitable, but one that still requires an overriding commitment to the objective of multilateral and MFN disciplines if it is to survive. As Camps and Diebold have said:

> [this] emphasis on the needs of the system runs counter to the current mood almost everywhere . . . but the essential public good of a strong, efficient international system which all countries need if they are to prosper can no longer be supplied unless the U.S. and other key countries are prepared to redefine their national interest in terms which give the preservation of that system real weight.[8]

Second-best solutions such as a Canadian-U.S. FTA must therefore be assessed in terms of their impact on broader multilateral cooperation, rule making, and liberalization.

Bilateral Means to Multilateral Ends?

It has frequently been stated that a Canadian-U.S. bilateral FTA need not conflict with or exclude multilateral commitments if it conforms to the requirements of GATT article 24. Moreover, it is often argued that bilateral negotiations could in fact be highly complementary to multilateral negotiations by creating leverage that could be used to bring other trading partners to the negotiating table, by demonstrating the gains to be had from trade liberalization, or by undertaking spadework on problematic issues that could then be brought forward into the multilateral arena.

At the same time, it has been recognized that the ongoing health of a

8. Miriam Camps and William Diebold, Jr., *The New Multilateralism: Can the World Trading System Be Saved?* (New York: Council on Foreign Relations, 1983), p. 70.

multilateral rules-based trading system cannot be taken for granted. In the words of the Macdonald Royal Commission:

> If North American free trade were to jeopardize or undermine the stability of the GATT system, it would be a steep price for Canadians to pay in order to secure improved access to the U.S. market.[9]

These concerns have not been the subject of much discussion. However, it is not self-evident that selective actions, such as a Canadian-U.S. FTA, will serve as a way station to broader international cooperation rather than as a precedent for a further division of the world into trade blocs or a further weakening of GATT. One seasoned trade analyst has said that it requires "a great act of faith" to accept the view that discrimination can be effectively used as a "transitional, tactical step toward the ultimate objective of global freer trade."[10]

The historical record is mixed. On a number of occasions, the creation of regional agreements has resulted in the hastening of multilateral talks as third countries have sought to work down the preferences and discriminatory effects of integration. The need to deal with the creation of the EEC in 1958 caused the United States to push for the Dillon and Kennedy rounds of MTN. The entry of the United Kingdom into the EEC in 1973 is considered to have been a spur that helped to launch the Tokyo round trade talks.

On the other hand, bilateral or regional agreements themselves have rarely proven to be the vanguard for further multilateral liberalization.[11] The EEC has often been more of an obstruction than a catalyst in international trade liberalization efforts. As a customs union that inevitably must deal with the internal concerns of member countries and the management of a common external commercial policy, it is not exactly analogous to a free trade area like that being contemplated between Canada and the United States. Even with FTAs, however, there is the creation of vested interests concerned with the preservation of their preferential margins. For example, countries in EFTA have frequently appeared to be more concerned with protecting their preferences in the

9. *Report of the Royal Commission*, p. 303.
10. Sidney Weintraub, "Selective Trade Liberalization and Restriction," in Ernest H. Preeg, ed., *Hard Bargaining Ahead: U.S. Trade Policy and Developing Countries* (New Brunswick, N.J.: Transaction Books, 1985), p. 176.
11. Hugh Corbet, "Industrial Tariffs and Economic Spheres of Influence," in Hugh Corbet and Robert Jackson, eds., *In Search of a New World Economic Order* (London: Croom Helm, 1974), p. 181.

EEC market than with broader liberalization. Similarly, if a bilateral or regional agreement governs a large segment of a country's trade, there is a natural tendency for a lessened interest in global trade matters.

An obvious danger with any exclusive agreement is that discrimination might beget discrimination, that GATT will be further weakened, that fewer countries will be left outside of trade blocs to help maintain multilateral discipline, and that there will be a movement toward a world governed by regional trading blocs. As Aho and Aronson have recently stated:

> Even GATT-consistent arrangements can be destabilizing without a strong GATT. The net effect of these actions when coupled with developments in other regions is to raise the possibility of creating rigid regional trading blocs. . . . The experience of the 1930s shows that bilateral arrangements cannot provide a stable, consistent and expanding trading system. . . . Thus, with a large number of countries trying to negotiate through bilateral agreements offering mutually incompatible privileges, predictability and stability are destroyed for everyone.[12]

A further problem with using bilateral agreements to pave the way toward a broader multilateral accord is that such agreements are naturally the product of detailed negotiations and carefully crafted compromises among the parties involved. Accommodating other countries after the fact will risk unbalancing the results of the original agreement, and the original signatories will probably determine who can join and on what terms.

As this discussion indicates, bilateral agreements and other selective actions could potentially harm, not help, the chances of achieving wider multilateral objectives. However in a second-best world, there may be no choice other than to strive for selective agreements that can serve as building blocks for wider agreement. To this end, a number of guidelines can be offered for the negotiation and design of bilateral trade agreements and other "minilateral" actions. These agreements should be consistent with GATT; should be undertaken in parallel with efforts to strengthen GATT and to minimize any of the ill effects of discrimination; should defer wherever possible to multilateral negotiations if there is a reasonable prospect of international agreement within a suitable time frame; should be open to other countries wherever possible (conditional MFN treatment would be preferable to a closed agreement); should be nego-

---

12. Michael Aho and Jonathan David Aronson, *Trade Talks: America Better Listen!* (New York: Council on Foreign Relations, 1985), p. 129.

tiated with a view to third-country accession;[13] and should incorporate procedures for third-country grievances, possibly building upon GATT dispute-settlement procedures.

The Case of a Canadian-U.S. Free Trade Agreement

To this general discussion of the complex relationship between bilateral and multilateral means and objectives one must now add specific questions concerning the context, timing, and forms of a Canadian-U.S. free trade agreement. Such an agreement would, by virtue of its size and membership alone, be an unusually significant event on the world scene. The Canadian-U.S. bilateral trade relationship is the largest in the world, and both countries have played distinctive roles in building and sustaining the multilateral trading system.

Added to this is the fact that Canada and the United States are contemplating an FTA at a most critical time in the history of GATT. The GATT-centered trading system is being threatened from many directions, and a new round of multilateral trade negotiations has just begun its job of strengthening and extending GATT disciplines. The multilateral agenda is daunting. It is dominated by problematic and contentious issues; most of the easy work has already been done.

Obviously the new GATT round will need all the help it can get. It will require a kind and a degree of governmental commitment that has not been in evidence in recent years. Could bilateral Canadian-U.S. negotiations help ease the load by siphoning off contentious issues that may not be ready for action at GATT? How might third countries react to the negotiation of a Canadian-U.S. trade agreement? Might its emergence at this time undermine confidence in GATT and sap its momentum?

The most likely areas where Canadian-U.S. negotiations might help GATT deliberations are subsidies and countervail and the new problems of trade in services, intellectual property, and trade-related investment issues. In the case of subsidies, the goal, bilaterally and multilaterally, is to reach agreement on an accepted practice for calculating the value and trade effects of subsidies and then to determine which subsidies can constitute an unfair trade advantage (or, conversely, are acceptable

13. For example, rules of conduct that would be problematic if generalized should not be established. See Camps and Diebold, *The New Multilateralism*, p. 50.

measures). The services area is largely virgin territory, and international knowledge would be advanced by any work Canada and the United States could do to help develop a better understanding of services trade (definitions and statistics) and to begin to elaborate what measures are acceptable in what circumstances. More important, a bilateral initiative in services could serve to defuse the acrimony surrounding the introduction of this issue in GATT. The developing countries may in fact prefer to see the issue separated from multilateral talks in this way, just as they accept the "twin track" approach being used in the GATT negotiations. As such, bilateral arrangements could help to break the multilateral logjam and would no doubt be designed with an eye to open it up for broader agreement.

Third-country reactions to Canadian-U.S. free trade negotiations will largely be concerned with the meaning of this bilateral venture for future U.S. trade policy. There will be a particular concern about whether the United States is backing away from its leadership role in GATT, is seeking to negotiate a wide range of bilateral agreements, and will be moving toward the use of direct, bilateral reciprocity in other areas as well. How effectively the United States uses bilateral negotiations for its strategic purposes—as a carrot and a stick to induce progress at GATT—and how key third countries respond to this prodding will have a significant impact on the evolution of the international trading system into the next century.

However, the significance of Canada's decision to pursue bilateral free trade talks with the United States should not be discounted. Canada is the fourth most important actor around the table at GATT and it carries additional weight by virtue of the fact that it is the United States' largest trading partner. Although Canadians have become increasingly frustrated by their peripheral status in GATT relative to the dominance of the big three (the United States, the EEC, and Japan), Canada does have influence and Canadian negotiators use it with considerable skill. Should Canada enter into an FTA with the United States, its interest and influence in GATT is likely to be reduced; 80 percent of Canadian trade would be largely dealt with elsewhere and Canada would be significantly less influential. There is a further possibility that the United States and Canada might speak with one voice on certain global issues, as Australia and New Zealand and the ASEAN countries often do. Thus there is the danger that Canada's distinctive voice at GATT—one that speaks to the concerns of smaller industrial countries and often plays an important mediating role—will be lost. For many third countries, especially in the developing world, it will be particularly significant that a small, open economy like Canada—which in theory is dependent upon the protection afforded by a strong nondiscriminatory trading system—feels that it is necessary to pursue its interests primarily by way of bilateral arrangements with the United States. Although understood in terms of Canada's unique trading relationship with the United States, such an initiative could be widely interpreted as a vote of nonconfidence in the GATT process.

Third-country reaction to a proposed Canadian-U.S. FTA has so far been muted, presumably because most countries are waiting to see what negotiations produce and because there is little to be gained by raising objections at this point. Certainly the apparent appeasement of Japanese concerns during Prime Minister Nakasone's visit to Ottawa in January 1986 should be viewed in this light. The EEC cannot credibly object in principle to any economic integration moves, having pioneered in this area thirty years ago, and it has been preoccupied in recent years with the integration of its newest members. The ASEAN countries have been among the few that have publicly expressed some concerns. They believe that they have been hurt by free trade agreements in the past, and they have stated a preference for liberalizing trade and fighting protectionism through GATT.[14]

Most countries will be seeking assurances in the months ahead that their bilateral relations with the United States and Canada will not be harmed. They can be expected to scrutinize carefully and critically the outcome of the Canadian-U.S. negotiations. The EEC's reaction will be important, as its policies are one of the intended targets of American and Canadian efforts. It remains to be seen whether the EEC will react in the same fashion as the United States and others have when faced with European tariff preferences, that is, undertaking to work them down through multilateral tariff cutting. The EEC is probably more concerned that a Canadian-U.S. FTA could be followed by similar actions with Pacific countries.

Japan has a general concern about the drift in U.S. trade policy away from the principle of nondiscrimination for the same reason that it has opposed "selectivity" in the case of safeguards; it will be one of the

14. David Stewart-Patterson, "Canada's Trade Focus Worries ASEAN," *Toronto Globe and Mail*, November 4, 1985, p. B13.

main targets if discriminatory actions become the norm internationally. Already Japan has been forced to negotiate a number of multisectoral market access agreements with the United States, which, Japan is quick to point out, were applied on a multilateral basis. Japan would prefer, however, to negotiate major trade agreements under the umbrella of GATT, where it feels there is protection in numbers and it may not come under such close scrutiny.

The developing countries take much the same view as Japan in this regard. In recent years, many of them have come to recognize the importance of GATT's first principle of nondiscrimination and have become some of the staunchest defenders of the "old trading order" (nondiscriminatory safeguard actions). The quality of their participation in GATT talks and their disposition toward the GATT as a forum have greatly improved. Countries such as Singapore, South Korea, Colombia, and Mexico played an active role in preparations for the new MTN, Mexico having just recently decided to join GATT after years of indecision.

Many developing countries are coming to value GATT late in the game, when Canada and the United States are beginning to question its relevance and to hedge their bets. Unfortunately, one of the effects of a Canadian-U.S. free trade agreement might be to strengthen the hand of those in developing countries who favor more self-reliant, inward-looking, South-South trade approaches. The creation of a major new North-North trade agreement may therefore further estrange some developing countries from GATT. And even moderate developing countries may become pessimistic about the likelihood that their concerns will be adequately addressed in GATT and more reticent about assuming greater GATT responsibilities. The discriminatory and diversionary effects of the EEC in previous years damaged the prestige of GATT in the eyes of many developing countries and contributed to their desire for a new economic order and new trade institutions (for example, the United Nations Conference on Trade and Development).

The developing countries are right to assume that they might bear much of the brunt of any trade diversion resulting from a Canadian-U.S. FTA and that progress on issues of interest to them might evaporate if North-North bilateral or plurilateral agreements were to proliferate. The significance of such a trend for the servicing of third world debt and the economic dynamism of developing countries would be dire. Canada and the United States should take the lead by introducing liberalization measures designed to offset any of the ill effects of their bilateral trade agreement for developing countries.

Conclusions

A number of guidelines for maximizing the multilateral benefits (and minimizing the costs) of selective trade actions were given earlier. All of them would appear to be applicable in the case of a Canadian-U.S. free trade agreement. To them must be added special conditions designed to address the problems of managing simultaneous bilateral and multilateral negotiations and of offsetting the economic and political fallout in the developing world of further North-North economic integration. Outlined below is a set of criteria for guiding Canadian-U.S. bilateral free trade negotiations and managing a two-track trade policy to ensure that bilateral negotiations serve to enhance, not undermine, multilateral objectives:

1. Highest priority must be given to strengthening multilateral stability and discipline. Operationally this must mean assigning the MTNs the resources and priority they deserve; it also means deferring to multilateral negotiations wherever there is a reasonable prospect of a suitable international agreement within a feasible time frame. On occasion this may require forgoing a more immediate, narrower agreement.

2. Bilateral negotiations should seek to achieve the most open and liberal agreement possible and should not seek to establish permanent preferences; plurilateral results (conditional MFN) would be preferable to bilateral agreement, and multilateral agreement would be preferable to plurilateral results.

3. As a minimum, a Canadian-U.S. FTA should be consistent with GATT article 24; to do otherwise would be unnecessarily harmful to GATT.

4. Bilateral negotiations should be undertaken with the possibility of third-country accession in mind. Articles of agreement that would be problematic if generalized should be avoided. Undertaking negotiations on an interactive basis with discussions at the MTN or opening the negotiating process to third countries could help produce a more generalizable product.

5. An FTA should incorporate procedures for third-country griev-ances and possibly draw on the good offices of GATT for this purpose.

6. Parallel actions should be taken to reduce the ill effects of economic integration on third countries, particularly developing countries. For example, Canadian and American leadership in bringing international textiles trade under the Multi-Fiber Arrangement back under the regular discipline of GATT could go a long way toward reducing any new economic distortions created by an FTA and offsetting the disillusion-ment that a further North-North agreement would engender.

Comments by J. David Richardson

Margaret Biggs has written a fine paper on the third-party fallout from a Canadian-U.S. free trade agreement. Fallout? Yes, because she doubts there would be any net benefits for outsider countries. That is why she refers to the initiative for a free trade area (FTA) as "discrimination" rather than constrained liberalization, and why she writes "preferential access" rather than simply "access."

I am more agnostic and optimistic than she is. Maybe there will be fallout—but maybe there will be favorable spillover. Maybe the FTA will discriminate against outsiders—but maybe it will prod them to accede to commercial conventions that are in everyone's national interest. Maybe the more promising alternative to an FTA is a new round of multilateral negotiations under GATT—but maybe this alternative will be hopelessly complex and wasteful, ending in chaos.

In brief, Margaret Biggs and I agree on *how* to analyze the third-party consequences of the FTA initiative. We disagree on the weights to assign to each component of the analysis. And we disagree on whether coop-eration or chaos is most likely to emerge in the absence of an FTA initiative.

I learned a great deal from the Biggs paper. I found her prediction of the industry- and exporter-incidence of trade diversion from an FTA to be quite insightful. She also convinced me to be concerned that outsider countries would bear the burden of *new* Canadian-U.S. trade barriers aimed at facilitating adjustment to the bilateral liberalization. She spelled out very sensible guidelines for making a Canadian-U.S. FTA least harmful, including procedures for third-country grievance and acces-sion.

I take issue with a number of points, however. Rather than viewing the FTA as a "significant departure" from "traditional postwar multilateral approaches," I would describe it merely as sensible "deliberalization insurance"—entirely in keeping with Canada's tradition of being exempted from new U.S. border barriers (for example, recent steel arrangements or investment controls in the 1960s). Any country that can take out insurance against the collapse of open trade with the United States should be encouraged to do so, not because of fear, but to avoid folly. Such countries are smart, not sinister.

I grant that the result might be a world of regional trading "blocs" (I would have chosen a less pejorative term). But I wonder if that may at present be a desirable way station on the path to renewed multilateralism. I'm not persuaded, as Biggs is, that such a pattern would create a less stable, less predictable trading environment. On the contrary, each regional trading bloc might be better able to maintain *internal* GATT-type discipline and dispute settlement than GATT itself can at present; this might more than compensate for any reduced discipline *between* blocs. GATT itself began as a regional trading bloc and is still one to this day, albeit a very inclusive one.

I found the view that "the EEC has often been more of an obstruction than a catalyst in international trade liberalization efforts" to be extreme even under the most generous interpretation. I doubt if it can be persuasively defended from any perspective, much less that of Greece, Spain, Portugal, or associated countries.

All of this is secondary to the major premise with which I take issue. Biggs fears that an FTA between Canada and the United States would damage the rest of the world economically. I fear that about as much as earthquake damage to my house in Wisconsin. The reasoning that she uses to nurse her fears is exactly the same as would support the following provocation: the world outside the United States would be economically *better* off if the entire upper Midwest (very similar economically to Canada) seceded from the union and erected its own trade barriers against the remaining (dis)United States and the world. If you believe that, then you'll worry with Biggs about an FTA between Canada and the United States. If not, then you'll wish their negotiators well, as I do, and hope they hew to the guidelines that she wisely prescribes.

Biggs's preference is for continued reliance on the GATT process; she fears that the FTA "initiative could be widely interpreted as a vote of nonconfidence in the GATT process." My reaction is, "Yup—and it should be." The GATT process has already lost its credibility and its effectiveness. It is perhaps time for both Canada and the United States to admit that this particular emperor has no clothes. The reason for stating the truth so cruelly, if it is truth, is to get on with the task of outfitting the emperor properly for the climate he is in today! Margaret Biggs frets about the interpretation third countries will attach to simultaneous bilateral and multilateral negotiations. I do not share her concern. Maybe countries who have undercontributed to the GATT system will become full and responsible partners only if they *do* question the sincerity of Canada and the United States and fear being shut out of expanded markets. Accession mechanisms for an FTA should be encouraged, but I don't agree that it should be "designed to offset any of the ill effects . . . for developing countries." Some of those ill effects may be sticks necessary to induce them to bite the carrot of accession—as an appetizer to the main course, renewed multilateralism.

That is the metaphor I prefer for assessing the current negotiations between Canada and the United States. They are a timely (maybe even crucial) opportunity to write the recipe for future multilateralism. Dishes for the main course should surely include conventions on investment, services, and what the Canadians call contingent protection. Directions for the chefs should involve more than a dash of defining subsidies and creating binational adjudication and dispute settlement. If this all has to simmer a long time, and if other chefs are slow to help out in the kitchen, then for now half a meat loaf is better than none.

Comments by John Whalley

The interaction of a Canadian-U.S. free trade arrangement with the global trading system poses issues that have not received the attention they merit in the current debate on Canadian-U.S. free trade. Margaret Biggs has performed an important service by raising these issues for further discussion.

In essence, her paper makes three points. First, that there are third-country implications through trade diversion effects. Second, that there is an issue of the balance to be struck between a bilateral and multilateral focus in trade policy arrangements from both a Canadian and a U.S. point of view. Third, that a Canadian-U.S. arrangement may have an adverse impact on developing countries.

On the first of Biggs's points, I have relatively little to say. As the paper indicates, the trade diversion effects on Canada from a bilateral arrangement would be relatively small, because over 75 percent of Canadian trade is with the United States. The larger the share of trade with the partner country in a free trade arrangement, the smaller the trade diversion effects tend to be.

The second point, however, goes to the heart of any assessment of whether a Canadian-U.S. free trade arrangement is desirable for either Canada or the United States. Bilateralism versus multilateralism in both Canadian and U.S. trade policies is often portrayed as an either-or choice. It is important to recognize, however, that this is not the case, particularly in Canada. The bilateral focus in Canadian trade policy begins with the U.S.-Canadian bilateral trade agreements of 1935 and 1938, continues through the 1941 Defense Production Sharing Agreement, the 1965 auto pact, and includes a number of other arrangements, the most recent of which is the 1984 Safeguards Notification Agreement. While it has been true that the debate in Canada on trade policy often implicitly assumes that the policy has been one of exclusive multilateralism through GATT, the bilateral component has nonetheless been there. In turn, the multilateral GATT negotiations are, in part, a way of dealing with bilateral issues in a multilateral framework.

What then is driving the current thrust toward a bilateral negotiation outside the multilateral GATT framework? There is no doubt that from both the Canadian and the U.S. side there is an element of frustration with GATT. Previous GATT negotiating rounds, especially the Kennedy and Tokyo rounds, achieved significant trade liberalization, but further active negotiations face varying degrees of difficulties.

The agenda for a future round has now largely emerged, but there are reasons for caution. At the top of the list is agriculture, where the Europeans appear to be relatively intransigent over the Common Agricultural Policy. Next comes services, on which there is great American enthusiasm, but it is not widely shared by other countries. In addition to the complexities of negotiations dealing with areas previously not covered by GATT, the issue of services is more difficult to deal with because it will involve barriers that are poorly documented and difficult to negotiate. On contingent protection, the division between the Europeans and the Americans on selectivity in the application of safeguards is well known.

With concerns over prospects for substantive progress in a further multilateral GATT round, the effects of an enlarged membership in GATT, and a sense that a lowest common denominator comes to dominate multilateral forums, the argument in favor of bilateralism becomes that one can move further and move faster down the bilateral route.

While frustration with GATT may be behind the current bilateral initiative, one also has to ask whether a bilateral negotiation weakens multilateral arrangements, as Biggs suggests. If this is so, the issue becomes what the costs would be to both of the bilateral partners.

From a Canadian point of view, this calculation is complex. Even if a weakened multilateralism were to emerge from an active bilateral negotiation with the Americans, it is not clear that the costs to Canada would outweigh the benefits to Canada.

Furthermore, there is the issue of whether an active bilateral negotiation between Canada and the United States would accelerate or retard multilateral negotiations. One can look at the historical precedent of the Dillon round, which was accelerated by the formation of the EEC, and argue that bilateral and multilateral negotiations are complementary to one another. The argument is that an active bilateral negotiation by one major prospective multilateral participant accelerates multilateral negotiations because of the increased pressure on other multilateral players to come to the negotiating table.

One can also argue that it is the drive for multilateral negotiations on the part of the Americans that gives Canada one of its strongest bilateral negotiating levers. Within the U.S. trade policymaking community, it is widely recognized that the pressure for multilateral negotiations comes from the executive branch and primarily from the Special Trade Representative's Office.

This being the case, the possibility of an active bilateral negotiation becomes important to the United States as a vehicle to force other multilateral partners to the table. This is one reason why the United States would want to have services included in a bilateral negotiation, and in a form that could subsequently be applied multilaterally. Similar arguments would seem to apply to bilateral negotiations covering trade-related investment issues.

Thus, to the extent that issues of multilateral negotiation intermingle with the bilateral negotiations, the calculation from a Canadian point of view goes beyond concerns over a possible weakening of the multilateral system. There are genuine issues as to whether multilateral negotiations can be accelerated through an active bilateral negotiation and whether the prospect of multilateral negotiations strengthens Canada's ability to negotiate bilaterally. One can indeed argue that Canada may exercise more eventual influence over subsequent multilateral negotiations through a prior bilateral negotiation with the United States.

Finally, Biggs raises a series of concerns over the impact of a bilateral negotiation on developing countries. The trade diversion effects involved are likely to be relatively small. Many of the products that the developing countries currently export to both Canada and the United States (such as textiles) have similar quota restrictions from both countries. The trade diversion effects may thus prove even smaller than one might expect on the basis of the bilateral tariff reductions and current trade flows alone.

In terms of wider regional fragmentation, it is important to keep two points in mind. First, the developing countries are a heterogeneous group, and a trade arrangement between Canada and the United States would have different effects on them. It could help the Asian countries by promoting their trade with Japan. It might hurt the African countries because of trade diversion effects against commodities. Effects on the Indian subcontinent and Latin America are less clear.

A second, wider, issue remains the impact of a North American trade arrangement on other regional trade groups. With a strengthened North American trade arrangement and present arrangements in Europe, the pressures on the Japanese to move to similar regional arrangements could become even stronger. This in turn could yield major benefits for some of the developing countries whose access to the Japanese market has not been liberalized as Japan has grown.

DRUSILLA K. BROWN and ROBERT M. STERN

A Modeling Perspective

FROM Canada's perspective, its trade and foreign direct investment relations with the United States are of predominant importance. It seems natural therefore that Canada might seek ways to enhance and make these relations with the United States more secure in the hope of increasing Canadian economic welfare. The United States might similarly stand to benefit from an even closer and special relationship with Canada.

Indeed, there have been several episodes in U.S.-Canadian relations since the 1850s when actions were taken or initiatives proposed to develop special arrangements for bilateral trade. However, due to the exigencies of nation building and the concern for its political sovereignty, Canada's historical choice before World War II was to foster its economic development and industrialization by restrictive trade measures and a variety of domestic interventions. The United States was also preoccupied mainly with its domestic development until World War II. In the postwar period, when the United States assumed leadership in world economic and political affairs, it favored (though not always consistently) a policy of multilateral liberalization of international trade and invest-

The research underlying this paper was made possible in part by financial assistance from the Donner Foundation and the Ford Foundation. We owe a special debt of thanks to Alan V. Deardorff and Filip Abraham, who contributed greatly to the conceptual development of the model used in the paper; to Christopher Jackson, who was largely responsible for the gathering and processing of much of the data; to John Alfaro for assistance with the computer programming; and to Judith Jackson for the organization, typing, and revisions of the paper. Helpful comments on earlier versions of the paper were received from Alan V. Deardorff and members of the Research Seminar in International Economics at the University of Michigan.

155

ment. But as the U.S. leadership role has diminished, its attachment to the principles of multilateralism has weakened. The United States now appears more prone than before to threaten and actually to carry out restrictive actions when it perceives that its economic interests are being damaged by the policies of other nations. Canada may thus find itself vulnerable to such actions both directly and indirectly.

It is against this background that the current initiative for a U.S.-Canadian free trade agreement (FTA) is to be considered. The possible establishment of an FTA raises many questions concerning its scope and how the economic interests of the United States, Canada, and the rest of the world might be affected. As will be noted, several estimates have been made of the potential effects of an FTA, and the general presumption is that Canada could experience an increase in welfare, possibly as much as 10 percent of GNP. The sources of this gain would be greater efficiency in resource use associated with Canadian tariff reductions, improvements in the terms of trade due to U.S. tariff reductions, and especially the realization of scale economies arising from increased domestic competition and improved access to U.S. markets. However, international trade theory holds that it cannot be determined a priori whether a particular preferential arrangement will be beneficial or harmful. For example, preferential tariff reductions introduce new distortions. Further, there is no presumption that freer trade will result in a particular country specializing in decreasing-cost industries. Accordingly, it is not altogether obvious that Canada would benefit from a bilateral liberalization of trade with the United States.

One way to proceed in analyzing the economic effects of an FTA would be to develop an econometric model of the economic structure and linkages of the countries involved and then to use such a model to assess the quantitative effects of preferential changes in commercial policies (tariffs and nontariff barriers). This is unfortunately a rather difficult task since it requires complex estimation procedures to obtain values of the key parameters. An appealing alternative is to construct a theoretical model that is capable of solution and to use assumed values of the parameters for computational purposes. The question then becomes what kind of model to construct. Here the options range from simple partial equilibrium models to highly complex general equilibrium models that reflect the myriad of market interactions within and between countries. We have chosen this latter option and have constructed a computational general equilibrium model of U.S.-Canadian trade and foreign direct investment for the purpose of analyzing the effects of an FTA between the United States and Canada.

Before presenting our model and preliminary results, we discuss four important modeling alternatives for analyzing an FTA and provide a brief review of previous studies of the cost of protection and the effects of trade liberalization for Canada and the United States.

Modeling Alternatives and Review of Previous Studies

The analysis of the effects of a U.S.-Canadian FTA will depend importantly on how a number of particular issues are modeled. These include (1) whether Canada should be treated as a small country that cannot influence world prices for its imports and exports; (2) whether Canada's trade should be characterized in terms of differentiated (non-standardized) products so that it has some control over its export prices and will experience changes in its terms of trade as a result of changes in trade policies at home and abroad; (3) whether Canadian manufacturing firms have unexploited economies of scale; and (4) whether and how foreign direct investment will be affected by tariff reductions.

Modeling Canada as a Price Taker

The traditional view of the economic effects of an FTA is based on a model of three countries producing and trading two goods. It is assumed that both goods can be produced in all countries with constant returns to scale, that goods and factor prices are freely flexible, and that factors are mobile between industries, but not between countries. If one assumes the United States to be a large country and Canada a small, price-taking country, this model strongly suggests that U.S. welfare would decline if it formed an FTA with Canada, while Canada would gain from the arrangement.

The reason for this probable outcome is found in the price-taker assumption for Canada. In this simplified model, Canada, before an FTA, imports exclusively from the United States at the world price. Canadian consumers pay that price plus the Canadian tariff. Canada also exports to the United States at the world price, although U.S. consumers pay the world price plus the U.S. tariff.

After the two countries remove their tariffs against one another, the price of Canadian imports from the United States falls by the amount of the erstwhile Canadian tariff. Imports rise and Canada gains the full benefits of trade creation. Moreover, Canada now exports to the United States at the U.S. domestic price, that is, the world price *plus* the U.S. tariff (which still applies to all imports except those from Canada). Canada thus retains tariff revenue that would otherwise have been collected by the U.S. government. Canadian terms of trade and Canadian welfare are therefore improved.

In contrast, the United States is clearly worse off. Marginal imports from the rest of the world are still subject to the U.S. tariff. At the same time, the United States will have shifted some imports from low-cost rest-of-the-world suppliers to higher-cost Canadian suppliers. This diversion of trade reduces U.S. welfare.

A number of studies have sought to calculate the cost to Canada of its tariff and the benefits that would result from its removal, both unilaterally and bilaterally vis-à-vis the United States.[1] Several treat Canada as a price taker and conclude that it would experience significant gains from trade liberalization. This is not surprising since it follows directly from the way that Canada's price behavior is modeled.

The welfare implications of the traditional model need not hold if rest-of-the-world prices change as a consequence of a U.S.-Canadian FTA. In the normal case, the expectation would be that the trade of both the United States and Canada with the rest of the world would decline after an FTA came into force. Supply on the world market of the goods that the United States exports would fall, thus raising its price. Similarly, U.S. demand for imports from the rest of the world would decline,

---

1. For a summary, see Roderick Hill and John Whalley, "Introduction: Canada-U.S. Free Trade," in John Whalley, ed., *Canada-United States Free Trade* (University of Toronto Press in cooperation with the Royal Commission on the Economic Union and Development Prospects for Canada and the Canadian Government Publishing Centre, Supply and Services Canada, 1985); John H. Young, *Canadian Commercial Policy* (Ottawa: Royal Commission on Canada's Economic Prospects, 1957); Ronald A. Shearer, John H. Young, and Gordon R. Munro, *Trade Liberalization and a Regional Economy: Studies of the Impact of Free Trade on British Columbia* (University of Toronto Press, 1971); William R. Cline, Noboru Kawanabe, T. O. M. Kronsjö, and Thomas Williams, *Trade Negotiations in the Tokyo Round: A Quantitative Assessment* (Brookings, 1978); Roma Dauphin, *The Impact of Free Trade on Canada* (Ottawa: Minister of Supply and Services Canada, 1978); Hugh McA. Pinchin, *The Regional Impact of the Canadian Tariff* (Ottawa: Minister of Supply and Services Canada, 1979); and James R. Williams, *The Canadian-United States Tariff and Canadian Industry: A Multisectoral Analysis* (University of Toronto Press, 1978).

causing a fall in price. On both accounts, U.S. terms of trade would improve at the expense of its trading partners.

Product Differentiation

A substantial body of literature is devoted to the analysis of possible trade patterns for three or more goods in the context of newly adopted preferential tariff arrangements.[2] Many of the results of the traditional model are observed in these models. It continues to be the case that the large country—the United States—is adversely affected if trade is diverted from the small-country partner, Canada. Similarly, Canada will gain if it trades exclusively with the United States.

However, under the assumption that both countries continue to trade in the world market after an FTA or customs union is formed, both may lose. A selective tariff reduction will remove the distortion between domestic goods and imports from the associated trading partner, which is welfare improving. But a new distortion is introduced between imports from the preferred country and those from third countries. In the realm of the second best, removing one distortion while creating another need not improve welfare. Complete tariff removal on one trade partner will give optimal results only if demand for the import from third countries is completely independent of the price of the import from the preferred partner.

These varied approaches to FTA analysis have been implemented empirically using the Armington model, in which imports are disaggregated according to their places of origin.[3] In this model each country exports a differentiated product—that is, products from different sources are not perfect substitutes. Thus both partners continue to trade with the rest of the world after the FTA has been created.

There are two complicating factors that make welfare analysis in the

2. See especially Eitan Berglas, "Preferential Trading Theory: The *n* Commodity Case," *Journal of Political Economy*, vol. 87 (April 1979), pp. 315–31; W. M. Corden, "Customs Union Theory and Nonuniformity of Tariffs," *Journal of International Economics*, vol. 6 (February 1976), pp. 99–106; Richard G. Lipsey, *The Theory of Customs Unions: A General Equilibrium Analysis* (London: Weidenfelt and Nicolson, 1970); J. McMillan and E. McCann, "Welfare Effects in Customs Unions: Some Long Run Features of Dynamic Time Series Models," *Economic Journal*, vol. 91 (September 1981), pp. 697–703; and Raymond Riezman, "A 3x3 Model of Customs Unions," *Journal of International Economics*, vol. 9 (August 1979), pp. 341–54.

3. Paul S. Armington, "A Theory of Demand for Products Distinguished by Place of Production," *IMF Staff Papers*, vol. 16 (March 1969), pp. 159–76.

Armington model more difficult. First, in this model all countries, large and small, can have some control over their export prices by altering tariffs on imports. For example, a tariff reduction on Canadian imports from the United States will displace domestically produced goods in favor of imports. Generally, the price of Canadian-produced goods will fall on the world market, resulting in a deterioration in Canada's terms of trade. Efficiency gains associated with trade creation may be overwhelmed by that deterioration, thus reducing Canadian welfare. On the other hand, a tariff reduction on U.S. imports from Canada will allow Canadian penetration of the U.S. market. The increase in U.S. demand for Canada's exports will raise the price of Canadian-produced goods on the world market, thus improving the terms of trade.

The welfare implications for Canada will thus depend critically on the relative importance of the trade creation and import penetration effects that will be associated with tariff changes in the two countries. The adverse terms-of-trade effects from trade creation will be comparatively large if Canada's tariffs on U.S. exports are larger on average than U.S. tariffs on Canadian exports. Canadian terms of trade are also likely to worsen depending on whether Canadian and U.S. consumers see U.S.- and Canadian-produced goods as similar or quite different. The closer the two goods are in Canadian eyes, the stronger the trade creation effect. On the other hand, if Americans view the two goods as poor substitutes, the penetration effect will be weak. In either case Canada's terms of trade are likely to deteriorate.

Second, in the differentiated-products model, unlike the traditional model, the relative size of the two countries is less important. Consumers in both countries enjoy lower prices on imports from each other after the tariff reductions, whereas in the traditional model U.S. consumers must pay the world price plus the tariff for marginal imports. Thus in the differentiated-products model trade creation emerges in both countries, rather than in Canada alone as in the traditional model.

A number of Canadian studies are based on general equilibrium models that allow for product differentiation and variable terms of trade.[4]

4. Robin Boadway and John Treddenick, "A General Equilibrium Computation of the Effects of the Canadian Tariff Structure," *Canadian Journal of Economics*, vol. 11 (August 1978), pp. 424–46; Richard Harris, "Applied General Equilibrium Analysis of Small Open Economies with Scale Economies and Imperfect Competition," *American Economic Review*, vol. 74 (December 1984), pp. 1016–32; Richard Jones, John Whalley, and Randall Wigle, "Regional Impacts of Tariffs in Canada: Preliminary Results from

When these models specify a unilateral removal of Canadian tariffs on all imports, the results suggest that the benefits of trade creation will be offset by a deterioration in Canada's terms of trade. A move to multilateral free trade, on the other hand, would give Canada significant welfare gains.

Hamilton and Whalley's study examines the welfare and terms-of-trade effect of a U.S.-Canadian FTA, using 1977 tariff and nontariff barrier data. It shows Canada's welfare *increasing* by $1.3 billion and its terms of trade *improving* by 0.7 percent. U.S. welfare increases by $0.6 billion and its terms of trade are unchanged by the bilateral removal of tariffs and nontariff barriers (NTBs). The authors attribute these findings to the fact that Canada is the small partner in the FTA.

In the same study it is observed that differing levels of initial protection will affect gains and losses from an FTA. Thus the United States could expect to be a large gainer from an FTA with highly protected, newly industrializing countries that have significantly higher levels of protection. The model we shall offer has many features in common with that used by Hamilton and Whalley. It finds the United States the gainer and Canada the loser from an FTA. The reason is that Canadian tariffs are higher on average than U.S. tariffs. That is, an FTA leads to a decline in Canadian terms of trade that outweighs the benefits to Canada of trade creation from tariff reductions.

Scale Economies and Imperfect Competition

The outcome of an FTA may be substantially different from the predictions of the small-country and differentiated-products models if scale economies are present. It is commonly suggested that Canada's import restrictions have resulted in suboptimal plant size, short production runs, and excessive product diversity. U.S. import restrictions are believed to reinforce these characteristics of Canadian manufacturing by limiting the access of Canadian firms to the U.S. market. This line of reasoning argues that an FTA would permit Canadian firms to realize economies of scale otherwise not available.

a Small Dimensional Numerical General Equilibrium Model," Working Paper no. 8510 (University of Western Ontario, Centre for the Study of International Economic Relations, 1985); and Bob Hamilton and John Whalley, "Geographically Discriminatory Trade Arrangements," *Review of Economics and Statistics*, vol. 67 (August 1985), pp. 446–55.

Many of the strongest proponents of an FTA between Canada and the United States stress the importance of scale economies as offering additional gains from trade above those normally associated with greater specialization. However, to date it has not been possible to prove in general in the differentiated-products models that a country gains from trade when scale economies are present. That is, nothing precludes the result that trade may lead a country to *reduce* production in industries with scale economies while specializing in industries with constant costs. It is possible that average productivity within a country may actually decline with trade, thus lowering economic welfare.[5]

In this context, two Canadian economists, Richard Harris and David Cox, have constructed a highly innovative empirical model in which firms in many manufacturing industries face declining average cost.[6] Two different pricing strategies are assumed. Under one set of assumptions firms tacitly collude, setting the market price at a "focal" price equal to the world price plus the tariff. Alternatively, it is assumed that there is monopolistic competition, with each firm assuming a constant elasticity of demand and charging the profit-maximizing price. The actual price in the model is a weighted average of the two pricing strategies.

Unilateral and multilateral free trade experiments were conducted with the Harris model for Canada and the rest of the world. The results suggest that the welfare gains for Canada would be positive for both experiments and much larger than those obtained by the kinds of models described above. The gains from multilateral liberalization were as much as 8 to 9 percent of Canada's gross national expenditure.

Tariff reductions improve economic welfare through several channels. Foreign tariff reductions allow Canada greater penetration of foreign markets, which leads to an increase in the scale of production and lower average costs. Home-country tariff reductions increase welfare for two

---

5. Helpman and Krugman show that a sufficient condition for trade to improve welfare is that the cost of producing the autarky bundle using trading equilibrium techniques of production must be smaller than the cost of the autarky bundle using autarky techniques. This condition may fail if specialization occurs in the constant-costs industries, thus raising the average cost in industries with scale economies. Elhanan Helpman and Paul R. Krugman, *Market Structure and Foreign Trade: Increasing Returns, Imperfect Competition and the International Economy* (MIT Press, 1985).

6. Harris, "Applied General Equilibrium Analysis of Small Open Economies"; Richard G. Harris with David Cox, *Trade, Industrial Policy, and Canadian Manufacturing* (Toronto: Ontario Economic Council, 1984); and David Cox and Richard Harris, "Trade Liberalization and Industrial Organization: Some Estimates for Canada," *Journal of Political Economy*, vol. 93 (February 1985), pp. 115–45.

reasons. First, lower tariffs allow consumers the freedom to choose the utility-maximizing combination of imports and the domestic good, the traditional source of the gains from trade. In addition, lower tariffs promote competition domestically through the focal price mechanism, which further increases the scale of production and lowers average costs.

When these channels are considered in more detail, it develops that the implications of a tariff reduction in the model in question depend in part on the hypotheses about pricing strategy. When monopolistic competition is assumed, the effect of a Canadian tariff reduction is to induce consumers to substitute toward imports and away from the domestic good. Domestic output declines in accord with the changed demand conditions. Firms leave the industry until a new equilibrium is reached, with the remaining domestic firms earning zero profits.

On the other hand, a tariff reduction by the partner country will raise demand for Canadian exports. Positive profits will attract new entrants until profits return to zero. The net effect on demand for Canadian-produced goods depends on whether the decline in production for the domestic market is outweighed by increased production for export. Total demand will generally fall if the original Canadian tariffs were high in comparison with tariffs in the partner country.

The effect on the scale of production by each firm depends on the perceived elasticity of demand. If the net effect of the FTA is to boost demand, entry occurs. Since the elasticity of an individual firm's demand curve is positively related to the number of firms in the industry, entry raises the perceived elasticity and lowers the profit-maximizing price. A lower price requires that firms expand the scale of production in order to satisfy the zero-profits condition. If demand falls, though, scale of output falls as well.

In contrast to the monopolistic competition hypothesis, the focal pricing strategy links the domestic price to the tariff. Initially each firm sets its price at the world price plus the tariff. A decline in the domestic tariff reduces the domestic price by the amount of the tariff. Since the domestic and imported goods sell for the same price on the domestic market, there is no substitution from the domestic variety to the import. Imports rise because the fall in the price of the good increases demand for both the import and the domestic good. The firm responds to the lower price by increasing the scale of production.

The tariff cut by the partner country will raise industry and firm demand for Canadian-produced goods, but the focal price will not be affected. Therefore, the scale of production of each firm will not change. The new demand is satisfied by increasing the number of firms in the industry.

In Harris's model, the industries that expand the most under the assumption of focal pricing are in many cases the same industries that expand the least under the monopolistic competition pricing. For example, industries that have high initial tariffs will lower the focal price the most under unilateral free trade. As a result, domestic and foreign demand will increase and the industry will expand. Moreover, the lower price requires that all firms within the industry increase the scale of production in order to reduce profits to zero. In contrast, with monopolistic competition a unilateral tariff reduction shifts demand toward imports, forcing the domestic industry to contract.

The different implications for the two pricing hypotheses for the level of production are apparent when comparing the depth of tariff cut with the change in production across industries in Harris's multilateral free trade experiment. Of the eleven Canadian industries with the greatest tariff protection, five experience the largest percentage increase in production, which is what would be expected from the focal pricing strategy. However, five of the remaining six industries with the highest tariffs are the only imperfectly competitive industries for which output declines, which is consistent with the monopolistic competition pricing strategy.

The relative contribution of these two pricing assumptions to the welfare improvement from an FTA is apparent in sensitivity analysis, which Harris performs. Welfare gains in the multilateral liberalization experiment fall dramatically as the weight attached to the focal price falls. For example, when a small weight of 0.2 is attached to the focal price, welfare gains for Canada would be similar to those obtained with the conventional models. It thus appears that the substantial welfare gains in Harris's model with scale economies are due in large measure to the assumption of focal pricing. That is, under focal pricing, home-country tariff reductions tend to increase the scale of production. The higher these tariffs initially, the greater the scale economies realized with liberalization. In contrast, under monopolistic competition, reduction of the home tariffs leads to lower firm production. The relative heights of home and partner-country tariffs are therefore critical in determining the scale effects of an FTA in the absence of focal pricing.

In view of the importance of the focal pricing strategy for the realization of scale economies in Canada, it is worth considering the effect of a preferential tariff reduction on the focal price. While it is clear that a global tariff reduction will lower the focal price and lead to an increase in the scale of production, it is not clear that a preferential tariff reduction will have the same effect. If Canada continues to import from third-country suppliers after the formation of the FTA, these goods will sell at the world price plus the tariff. The pressure to lower the focal price is then significantly diminished. Accordingly, it is not clear, given the industry structure that characterizes imperfectly competitive markets, that a preferential tariff reduction will make possible the realization of economies of scale.

In another recent study, Randall Wigle analyzed the effects of unilateral, bilateral, and multilateral tariff reductions on Canada's welfare.[7] He used an eight-region and six-commodity model, with scale economies in the nonmechanical and in the machinery- and equipment-manufacturing sectors. The former sector was assumed to be characterized by monopolistic competition and the latter by focal pricing. Wigle's pricing assumptions differ from those of Harris in that focal pricing occurs in only one of the two decreasing-cost industries. Using pre-Tokyo round tariffs, he concluded that a unilateral removal of Canadian tariffs would *reduce* Canadian welfare by (U.S.) $700 million, or 0.3 percent of 1977 GNP. Bilateral tariff removal by Canada and the United States was estimated to *reduce* Canadian welfare by $100 million and *increase* U.S. welfare by $1.2 billion. In the case of the multilateral removal of tariffs and NTBs, Canada's welfare was estimated to *increase* by 2.5 percent of GNP.

Wigle's results suggest the importance of the point that the relative height of home and partner-country tariffs and the assumptions about pricing behavior are critical in analyzing the effects of an FTA. Since Harris did not model the United States explicitly with reference to Canada but rather included the United States as part of the rest of the world, he did not distinguish the differences in tariff rates for the United States and the rest of the world. As columns 1 and 6 of tables 1 and 2 show, actual U.S. bilateral tariff rates with respect to Canada are considerably lower than the comparable bilateral tariff rates with respect

7. Randall Wigle, "Canadian Trade Liberalization: Scale Economies in a Global Context," Working Paper no. 8604C (University of Western Ontario, Centre for the Study of International Economic Relations, 1986).

Table 1. *Average Tariffs, Pre-Tokyo Round, Weighted for Bilateral and Total Trade, by Sector*

	Bilateral trade-weighted								
	U.S. tariffs		Canadian tariffs		Other country tariffs[a]		Total trade-weighted		
Sector	Canada	Other	U.S.	Other	U.S.	Canada	U.S.	Canada	Other
Agriculture	2.4	2.0	2.8	4.6	14.2	4.2	2.2	3.4	10.2
Food	6.9	6.3	6.6	7.0	13.4	8.8	6.3	6.9	15.3
Textiles	12.7	14.3	19.0	18.5	9.3	19.0	14.4	18.9	9.0
Clothing	22.3	26.1	24.7	23.3	17.8	18.9	27.8	25.4	18.1
Leather products	3.5	4.9	5.9	10.2	1.0	2.5	5.6	8.2	3.6
Footwear	9.0	8.9	24.2	24.2	15.5	15.0	8.8	24.5	14.2
Wood products	0.5	7.8	4.6	8.5	1.1	2.2	3.6	5.8	1.9
Furniture and fixtures	9.1	5.9	19.4	18.7	11.2	21.5	8.1	19.4	9.4
Paper products	0.2	2.8	11.9	11.7	4.8	3.0	0.5	11.8	6.2
Printing and publishing	0.6	1.2	5.6	6.2	1.5	1.5	1.1	5.7	2.2
Chemicals	1.0	5.6	7.9	7.8	8.6	7.3	3.8	7.9	9.4
Petroleum products	0.1	0.3	0.7	0.1	0.7	0.2	1.4	0.2	1.6
Rubber products	5.1	2.9	12.9	10.7	6.0	3.6	3.6	12.2	5.2
Nonmetal mineral products	0.7	11.9	7.0	14.0	1.8	0.1	9.1	9.5	4.5
Glass products	9.9	9.9	11.0	12.5	10.6	9.4	10.7	11.3	10.8
Iron and steel	3.6	5.1	6.5	6.9	3.6	5.0	4.7	6.7	5.6
Nonferrous metals	1.0	1.3	3.0	0.7	3.1	0.4	1.2	2.0	2.0
Metal products	6.0	6.8	14.0	13.9	9.2	12.2	7.5	14.1	9.6
Nonelectric machinery	3.7	5.3	6.2	7.1	7.6	9.1	5.0	6.1	7.8
Electric machinery	7.2	6.1	12.8	12.3	10.0	10.4	6.6	12.9	10.0
Transport equipment	0	3.4	0	3.6	7.8	4.8	3.3	2.4	10.6
Miscellaneous manufacturers	1.1	3.2	7.8	8.4	8.2	8.6	7.8	8.8	7.2
Average	1.2	6.0	5.2	9.7	8.6	3.5	4.5	6.4	5.2

Source: Based on data supplied by the Office of the U.S. Trade Representative.
a. Industrialized countries only.

to Canada for "other" countries excluding the United States.[8] The difference between U.S. and "other" tariffs on Canada appears pivotal. When the rest-of-the-world tariffs (and NTBs) are taken into account in Wigle's multilateral experiment, Canada is shown to benefit. In contrast, in his bilateral experiment in which the relatively higher Canadian tariffs vis-à-vis the United States are at issue in the monopolistically competitive industries, the results suggest a net decline in demand for Canadian goods, worsened terms of trade for Canada, and a decline in scale of production in Canadian manufacturing.

8. The category "other" includes the remaining sixteen industrialized countries as well as the sixteen newly industrializing countries. While we have tariff rates for the individual industrialized countries, we do not have comparable information for the newly industrializing countries. The bilateral and total trade-weighted tariff rates in tables 1 and 2 thus refer to the remaining industrialized countries only.

Table 2. *Average Tariffs, Post-Tokyo Round, Weighted for Bilateral Trade, by Sector*

Sector	U.S. tariffs		Canadian tariffs		Other country tariffs[a]	
	Canada	Other	U.S.	Other	U.S.	Canada
Agriculture	1.6	1.8	2.2	1.8	14.1	4.2
Food	3.8	4.8	5.4	6.1	11.4	8.0
Textiles	7.2	9.1	16.9	16.4	7.6	16.1
Clothing	18.4	21.4	23.7	22.1	15.2	15.9
Leather products	2.5	3.8	4.0	8.7	0.6	1.8
Footwear	9.0	8.9	21.5	21.9	15.2	14.1
Wood products	0.2	3.8	2.5	4.9	0.9	1.8
Furniture and fixtures	4.6	2.9	14.3	14.1	8.0	16.0
Paper products	0	1.3	6.6	6.5	3.9	2.6
Printing and publishing	0.3	0.7	1.1	1.0	1.1	1.1
Chemicals	0.6	3.5	7.9	7.0	5.9	5.3
Petroleum products	0	0.1	0.4	0.1	0.7	0.2
Rubber products	3.2	2.0	7.3	6.0	4.5	2.9
Nonmetal mineral products	0.3	7.2	4.4	8.5	1.4	0.1
Glass products	5.7	5.8	6.9	7.9	8.7	7.5
Iron and steel	2.7	3.9	5.1	5.5	3.1	3.9
Nonferrous metals	0.5	0.8	3.3	2.7	2.6	0.4
Metal products	4.0	4.4	8.6	8.9	7.0	10.2
Nonelectric machinery	2.2	3.2	4.6	4.8	5.1	6.6
Electric machinery	4.5	4.1	7.5	7.1	8.1	8.7
Transport equipment	0	2.5	0	2.5	3.4	3.4
Miscellaneous manufacturers	0.9	2.0	5.0	5.3	5.3	5.8
Average	0.7	4.3	3.8	7.4	6.9	3.0

Source: Based on data supplied by the Office of the U.S. Trade Representative.
a. Industrialized countries only.

We conclude that Harris's choice of tariff rates overstates the benefit to Canada from penetrating the U.S. market, although we do not expect that a revision in the tariff rates would materially alter the conclusion that Canada gains from multilateral tariff removal. However, Wigle's model indicates that with minor changes in the pricing assumptions that reduce the importance of focal pricing, the choice of tariff rates can reverse Harris's conclusion about a U.S.-Canadian FTA. Therefore, the presence of unexploited scale economies may not be sufficient to guarantee that Canada gains from an FTA. The relative depth of tariff cut by the two countries, along with market structure and pricing behavior, becomes critical to the outcome.

Tariff Reductions and Foreign Direct Investment

A final issue concerns the effect of tariff reductions on foreign direct investment. A tariff reduction by a small country lowers its domestic price, thus reducing the marginal value product of capital installed in the home country. Foreign direct investment that is sensitive to the rate of return will exit, reducing the capital stock. On the other hand, a reduction in tariffs in the partner country may encourage foreign direct investment.

It can be argued that the loss of capital due to a tariff reduction may actually be desirable from the point of view of the host country.[9] Protection raises the domestic price above the world price, which raises the return to capital in a protected sector above its marginal product, valued at world prices. Thus, in the presence of a tariff, the host country pays imported capital more than the true value of its output, which results in a welfare loss.

The tariff provides protection to all capital whether or not it is owned domestically. Thus tariff removal will reduce the transfer to foreign capital owners and increase home-country welfare. The higher the tariffs before liberalization, the larger the welfare gain. However, in the traditional model of an FTA, this gain accrues only to the small country. For the large country, marginal trade continues to be with the rest of the world. Consequently, the domestic price does not decline and foreign capital continues to be paid in excess of its true marginal value product.

International capital mobility provides a second source of welfare gain for the small country if capital is sector specific. As some models provide, the small country is able to sell its exports to its larger FTA partner at the world price plus the partner's tariff. The increase in the export price will also raise the marginal value product in the small country's export sector, thus attracting foreign capital.

The same results will not follow from models in which countries specialize completely or from those in which products are nationally differentiated, such as the Armington model.[10] In these cases, goods that are produced domestically are not imported. Thus, with national product differentiation, import tariffs do not alter the equality between the price of the domestically produced good on the domestic market and its price on the world market. As a result, imported capital is paid its true marginal value product, even in the presence of a tariff. Moreover, a tariff

9. Richard A. Brecher and Carlos F. Diaz Alejandro, "Tariffs, Foreign Capital and Immiserizing Growth," *Journal of International Economics*, vol. 7 (November 1977), pp. 317–32; and Richard A. Brecher and Ronald Findlay, "Tariffs, Foreign Capital and National Welfare with Sector-Specific Factors," *Journal of International Economics*, vol. 14 (May 1983), pp. 277–88.

10. G. D. A. MacDougall, "The Benefits and Costs of Private Investment from Abroad: A Theoretical Approach," *Economic Record*, vol. 36 (March 1960), pp. 13–35.

reduction does not directly affect the marginal value product of domestically employed capital. A capital inflow will be stimulated only if there is an increase in the price of the home country's output relative to goods produced elsewhere. In other words, foreign direct investment will increase in countries that enjoy an improvement in their terms of trade. Therefore the same conditions that lead to a terms-of-trade improvement will also result in an increase in the capital stock.

The conclusion to be drawn is that in the traditional model the small country is expected to receive all of the benefits from internationally mobile capital. Both the loss of foreign capital in the import-competing sector and the increase in foreign capital in the export sector are welfare improving. In the Armington model, capital flows will reinforce terms-of-trade gains but are not necessarily expected to accrue to the small country.

The Computational Model

We have constructed a four-region computational model for the purpose of analyzing an FTA between the United States and Canada. Canada, the United States, and a group of thirty-two other countries are modeled explicitly, and the rest of world constitutes an abbreviated fourth region.[11] Our sectoral coverage includes twenty-two tradable product categories based on three-digit ISIC industries and seven nontradable categories based on one-digit ISIC industries.[12] (The full list of industries is in table 5.)

Because of space constraints, the equations and a technical description of our model are not included here, but are available from the

11. The thirty-two countries are sixteen industrialized countries: Australia, Austria, Belgium-Luxembourg, Denmark, Federal Republic of Germany, Finland, France, Ireland, Italy, Japan, Netherlands, New Zealand, Norway, Sweden, Switzerland, and the United Kingdom; and sixteen newly industrializing countries: Argentina, Brazil, Chile, Colombia, Greece, Hong Kong, India, Israel, Mexico, Portugal, Singapore, South Korea, Spain, Taiwan, Turkey, and Yugoslavia.

12. Our choice of countries or regions and sectoral disaggregation was patterned on the same lines as the Michigan model of world production and trade. See Alan V. Deardorff and Robert M. Stern, *The Michigan Model of World Production and Trade: Theory and Applications* (MIT Press, 1986); and Drusilla K. Brown, "A Simulation Model of World Production and Trade with Bilateral Trade and Commercial Policies and Applications to the Tokyo Round" (Ph.D. dissertation, University of Michigan, 1984).

authors on request. Some general remarks may thus be helpful in order to bring out some of the essential features of the model. As noted, there are a variety of modeling assumptions and options for analyzing the effects of changes in trade policy. Some of our important assumptions and the key characteristics of our model are as follows.

1. The production functions assume constant returns to scale. We make no allowance for scale economies, as Harris has done in his modeling efforts.

2. Production is a function of capital and labor. Capital is assumed to be industry specific. The wage paid to labor is fixed and macroeconomic policy is assumed to maintain national employment at the base level. These assumptions are designed to focus attention especially on the short-run allocative effects that may occur in response to exogenous changes such as the removal of tariffs. This is in contrast to other models in that both capital and labor are variable and general equilibrium is to be attained.

3. Although capital is industry specific within countries, we assume there will be industry-specific capital flows between countries in response to differences in rates of return. The idea is to capture certain aspects of the direct foreign investment decision. These capital flows are assumed to respond imperfectly, which means that Canada is not being modeled here as a small country facing a given world interest rate.

4. Goods markets are perfectly competitive and prices of tradable goods are determined in world markets that equate supply and demand for each of the twenty-two tradable goods from each of the four geographical areas, yielding eighty-eight individual markets. The prices of nontraded goods are determined domestically to equate demand and supply within each country. Our model thus does not allow for imperfect competition. Firms follow conventional rules of competitive pricing and profit maximization.

5. Imports are disaggregated by place of production. Each tradable good that enters in the utility and production functions is itself an aggregate of imports and the domestically produced good. In turn, the level of imports is an aggregate of goods produced by each of the three foreign suppliers.

6. Exchange rates for all regions except the rest of world fluctuate to maintain the trade balance at the base level. The rest of world pegs its currency to a basket of the other currencies, but also imposes the condition that expenditure on imports not exceed the available foreign exchange earned through exports. This is accomplished with a tariff

equivalent of an import license, which constrains the value of import demand to be equal to the revenue earned through exports.

7. Although the underlying market structure is perfectly competitive, the solution is constrained by the presence of NTBs, which are measured according to the trade coverage of pre-Tokyo round NTBs of all kinds. The NTBs take the form of quotas and are represented by their tariff equivalents.

8. The base year for data on production, employment, trade, and direct foreign investment for the United States, Canada, other countries, and the rest of the world is 1976. Input-output coefficients for the production function were derived from the U.S. input-output table for 1972 and the Canadian table for 1976.

9. Tariff averages for each product category are *bilaterally* trade weighted, thus yielding a separate set of rates for each partner. These are in contrast to tariff averages that are weighted by total country imports from all sources. This distinction is important because the bilateral composition of imports may vary depending upon the country of origin. So far as we can tell, most previous studies have aggregated tariffs weighted by total country imports, a procedure that is inappropriate for obtaining tariff averages that are to be used in analyzing bilateral changes in tariffs. The bilaterally weighted and total-import-weighted nominal tariff rates for the pre-Tokyo round are as shown in table 1 and the bilaterally weighted post-Tokyo round rates are as shown in table 2. It is evident that the bilateral rates are considerably lower on U.S. imports from Canada than the tariffs on total U.S. imports.

10. The tariff rate actually applied to each product category is a weighted average of the nominal tariff and the tariff equivalent of each of the applicable NTBs. The fractions of trade subject to NTBs for each country are presented in table 3. Other parameters include the elasticity of substitution among sources of imports and between imports and the domestic good, the elasticity of substitution between capital and labor, and the supply elasticities.[13]

Results

We have used our model to investigate the effects of an FTA between Canada and the United States. A number of possible arrangements were

13. The interest elasticity of real capital flows was set at 3.0 in our central experiment, following the suggestions of John Mutti and Harry Grubert, "The Taxation of Capital Income in an Open Economy: The Importance of Resident-Nonresident Tax Treatment," *Journal of Public Economics*, vol. 27 (August 1985), pp. 291–309.

Table 3. Parameters of the Model

Sector	Substitution elasticity between imports and domestic goods[a]	Substitution elasticity between capital and labor		Supply elasticity		Nontariff barrier trade coverage[b]					
		U.S.	Canada	U.S.	Canada	U.S. Canada	U.S. Other	Canada U.S.	Canada Other	Other Canada	Other Other
Agriculture	1.1	0.8	0.8	0.5	0.4	0.01	0.01	0	0	0	0.20
Food	1.1	1.7	1.0	5.5	5.6	0.45	0.45	0.16	0.16	0.16	0.18
Textiles	1.1	1.0	0.7	14.0	6.0	0	0.41	0	0	0.17	0.23
Clothing	4.3	1.2	1.4	26.9	13.4	0	0.66	0	0	0.54	0.38
Leather products	1.8	1.2	1.0	24.2	13.3	0	0	0	0	0	0.02
Footwear	2.8	1.4	1.0	20.4	15.2	0	0	0	0	0.41	0.22
Wood products	1.8	0.9	0.8	3.6	6.5	0	0	0	0	0	0
Furniture and fixtures	3.1	1.1	0.9	10.3	7.1	0	0	0	0	0	0
Paper products	1.6	1.6	0.7	10.1	2.9	0	0	0	0	0	0.01
Printing and publishing	3.0	0.8	1.0	6.5	4.4	0.61	0.61	0	0	0	0.02
Chemicals	2.6	1.1	1.4	3.4	5.2	0	0	0	0	0	0.03
Petroleum products	2.4	2.9	2.9	8.9	7.9	0	0	0	0	0.01	0.40
Rubber products	5.7	1.6	4.7	5.5	39.0	0	0	0	0	0	0.02
Nonmetal mineral products	2.8	1.2	1.1	5.2	3.0	0	0	0	0	0	0.07
Glass products	1.6	1.3	1.1	5.3	3.9	0	0	0	0	0	0
Iron and steel	1.4	1.4	0.4	11.6	4.2	0	0.10	0	0	0	0.04
Nonferrous metals	1.4	1.4	0.4	15.6	5.6	0	0	0	0	0	0.09
Metal products	3.7	0.9	0.7	6.2	3.7	0	0	0	0	0	0.02
Nonelectric machinery	1.0	0.7	1.5	4.3	10.9	0	0	0	0	0	0.03
Electric machinery	2.1	0.5	0.5	4.7	2.6	0	0	0	0	0.10	0.06
Transport equipment	3.6	0.3	0.6	2.4	5.8	0	0.20	0	0	0.34	0.05
Miscellaneous manufacturers	2.0	1.3	1.3	2.1	7.3	0	0	0	0	0	0.03
Mining and quarrying	...	1.5	1.5	1.2	0.6	...	...	...	...	...	...
Utilities	...	2.3	2.3	1.7	1.3	...	...	...	...	...	...
Construction	...	1.1	1.1	9.1	3.9	...	...	...	...	...	...
Wholesale trade	...	2.3	2.3	4.5	6.5	...	...	...	...	...	...
Transportation	...	1.5	1.5	3.3	5.7	...	...	...	...	...	...
Financial services	...	1.7	1.7	1.0	1.2	...	...	...	...	...	...
Personal services	...	1.1	1.1	11.7	1.9	...	...	...	...	...	...

a. Elasticity of substitution among imports equal to elasticity of substitution between imports and the domestically produced good.
b. A value of zero indicates no NTBs on the sectoral trade; a value of 1.00 indicates that all of the sectoral trade is subject to NTBs.

considered, with the central case consisting of a bilateral removal of pre-Tokyo round tariffs. Pre-Tokyo round rates were chosen in order to facilitate comparison with other studies. Other experiments included unilateral removal of tariffs by the United States and Canada on bilateral trade, and multilateral tariff liberalization.[14] All experiments were repeated using post-Tokyo round rates. In each case, it was assumed that the liberalization occurred all at once rather than being phased in over a period of years. An overview of the results obtained is presented in table 4.

The results from all the bilateral experiments based on our model indicate a small increase in welfare for the United States but not for Canada. Removal of the comparatively higher level of protection on Canadian industries apparently reduces total demand for Canadian-produced goods. Equilibrium is restored by a fall in the relative price of Canadian goods and a depreciation of the Canadian dollar. In the central case for the removal of pre-Tokyo round tariffs (section A of table 4), Canada's terms of trade deteriorate by 1.2 percent and the Canadian dollar depreciates by 1.2 percent. The loss of purchasing power reduces Canada's welfare by $684.3 million, based on trade in 1976. This reduction in welfare is only 0.35 percent of Canadian GDP in the base year. In contrast, the U.S. terms of trade improve slightly and welfare increases by $654.4 million, or 0.04 percent of U.S. GDP.

As noted in tables 1 and 2, the Tokyo round tariff cuts by Canada substantially reduced the level of protection of most Canadian industries. Thus an FTA with the United States based on post-Tokyo round rates appears less detrimental to Canadian welfare. Nonetheless, the model results (section B) still indicate a small decline in Canadian welfare of $499.3 million.

In order to determine the effects of each country's own tariffs, we conducted a series of experiments for the unilateral removal of tariffs. The results are summarized in sections C–F of table 4. It is evident that Canada benefits by increased access to U.S. markets. Unilateral removal of U.S. tariffs on imports from Canada increases Canadian welfare by $166.5 million and $102.8 million, based respectively on pre- and post-Tokyo round tariff rates. However, since Canadian tariffs are considerably higher than U.S. tariffs, unilateral removal by Canada reduces

14. Since we did not have comprehensive estimates of NTBs for all countries or regions included in the model, we were unable to conduct an experiment involving removal of both tariffs and NTBs.

Table 4. *Results of a U.S.-Canadian Free Trade Area: Changes in Country Imports, Exports, Exchange Rates, Trade Balance, Terms of Trade, and Welfare*
Millions of U.S. dollars unless otherwise indicated

Country	Imports[a]	Exports[a]	Exchange rate[b]	Current account	Terms of trade (percent change)	Welfare
A. *Pre-Tokyo round: bilateral tariffs only*						
United States	1,456.6	1,307.1	−0.0	293.6	0.3	654.4
Other	−100.4	−197.2	0.2	−167.0	−0.0	−19.6
Canada	1,143.2	1,493.9	1.2	−126.1	−1.2	−684.3
B. *Post-Tokyo round: bilateral tariffs only*						
United States	1,017.8	913.3	−0.0	229.3	0.3	479.8
Other	−75.5	−143.7	0.1	−120.7	−0.0	−19.8
Canada	792.3	1,043.1	0.9	−108.2	−0.9	−499.3
C. *Pre-Tokyo round: unilateral tariff removal on Canada*						
United States	226.2	255.2	0.0	−136.6	−0.1	−259.2
Other	2.6	−0.4	−0.1	−8.6	0.0	−12.8
Canada	275.9	243.3	−0.7	145.5	0.5	166.5
D. *Post-Tokyo round: unilateral U.S. tariff removal on Canada*						
United States	137.1	157.0	0.0	−81.3	−0.1	−161.3
Other	1.4	0.5	−0.0	−4.3	0.0	−13.0
Canada	170.5	147.7	−0.4	85.9	0.3	102.8
E. *Pre-Tokyo round: unilateral Canadian tariff removal on U.S.*						
United States	1,230.4	1,051.9	−0.0	430.2	0.5	909.1
Other	−103.0	−196.8	0.3	−158.3	−0.0	10.0
Canada	867.3	1,250.6	1.9	−271.6	−1.7	−851.4
F. *Post-Tokyo round: unilateral Canadian tariff removal on U.S.*						
United States	880.8	756.2	−0.0	310.6	0.3	633.8
Other	−76.8	−144.2	0.2	−116.4	−0.0	0.5
Canada	621.9	895.4	1.3	−194.0	−1.2	−600.8
G. *Pre-Tokyo round: multilateral tariffs only[c]*						
United States	7,346.1	6,961.3	−0.0	162.0	0.4	−140.4
Other	8,953.9	9,867.9	0.0	59.3	−0.4	660.2
Canada	1,827.1	2,336.9	1.9	−221.1	−1.9	−1,092.3
H. *Post-Tokyo round: multilateral tariffs only[c]*						
United States	5,362.4	5,062.9	−0.0	224.8	0.4	−139.1
Other	6,757.7	7,562.0	0.1	−68.0	−0.4	809.0
Canada	1,349.8	1,699.8	1.3	−156.7	−1.3	−775.7

a. Dollar value of change in trade volume.
b. A positive value indicates depreciation of currency.
c. Refers to tariff removal by the United States, Canada, and the other industrialized countries only.

Canadian welfare by $851.4 million and $600.8 million, respectively. On balance, the terms-of-trade losses from Canadian tariff reductions exceed the gains from Canada's increased penetration of the U.S. market.

It is interesting that Canada appears to fare worse under a multilateral tariff removal, and that the United States is also negatively affected. The multilateral removal of pre-Tokyo round tariffs results in a reduction of

Canada's welfare by \$1.1 billion and of U.S. welfare by \$140.4 million. For removal of post-Tokyo round tariffs, the welfare reductions are \$775.7 million for Canada and \$139.1 million for the United States. The major reason for these results is that NTBs in agriculture, especially in the European Community, diminish the effects of tariff liberalization on both Canadian and U.S. exports, whereas Canadian and U.S. imports of manufactures increase substantially. This suggests that it might be in the interest of the United States to pursue bilateral tariff negotiations with Canada if European Community concessions in agricultural products do not appear to be forthcoming.

The sectoral results of the bilateral experiment using post-Tokyo round tariffs are presented in absolute terms in table 5 and percentage changes in tables 6 and 7. The sectoral changes in U.S. employment are all less than 1 percent. In Canada the percentage changes are larger, ranging from a positive 3.89 percent for leather products to a negative 1.58 percent for metal products. For both the United States and Canada there is an evident shift in employment in favor of tradables and against nontradables, which reflects the lower relative prices of tradables after the tariff reductions. While the results suggest that there might be some employment dislocations in particular sectors, especially in Canada, they would be moderated if the FTA were phased in over a period of years rather than all at once, as we have assumed.

Imports and exports for both the United States and Canada show increases in intra-industry trade for most sectors, but not all. For the United States, the exceptions are in agriculture, petroleum products, and transport equipment, and for Canada, footwear, petroleum products, and transport equipment. The percentage output effects in the United States are all less than 1 percent. The output effects for Canada are larger. It is noteworthy that output rises in the United States and falls in Canada in food and related products, textiles, printing and publishing, chemicals, glass products, metal products, electric machinery, and several nontradables. The opposite pattern occurs in wood products, petroleum products, nonferrous metals, transport equipment, and mining and quarrying.

We would expect increases in intra-industry trade, especially in sectors where tariffs are higher than average in both countries. The reduction of these tariffs will lower prices relative to other products and raise demand, thus attracting resources from other industries. It is also possible that capital may be attracted from countries outside the FTA.

Table 5. *Sectoral Effects of U.S.-Canadian Free Trade, Tariffs Only, Post-Tokyo Round*
Millions of U.S. dollars unless otherwise indicated

Sector	United States				Canada			
	Employment (number of workers)	Imports	Exports	Output	Employment (number of workers)	Imports	Exports	Output
Agriculture	−392.1	37.1	−2.1	2.6	2,807.9	13.0	47.2	23.9
Food	−701.0	27.9	25.9	101.7	192.9	17.5	30.8	−42.8
Textiles	3,616.5	7.2	78.4	119.4	−445.7	68.6	5.6	−17.0
Clothing	982.1	15.2	28.5	25.8	878.0	9.1	9.2	13.8
Leather products	130.2	6.9	7.3	3.9	377.5	4.6	9.3	8.7
Footwear	48.1	11.3	5.0	1.9	356.1	−0.2	6.3	8.2
Wood products	−772.0	42.9	16.5	−24.0	1,312.7	17.9	55.3	44.1
Furniture and fixtures	342.8	67.9	52.4	7.9	1,334.5	48.5	67.8	35.0
Paper products	371.6	73.0	63.0	33.3	961.0	66.7	100.4	39.1
Printing and publishing	1,236.6	2.4	39.1	55.9	−893.0	36.2	3.7	−23.5
Chemicals	1,483.2	96.0	186.4	189.4	−729.0	183.1	96.6	−66.4
Petroleum products	−454.9	107.8	−1.4	59.3	497.8	−19.5	90.2	105.2
Rubber products	216.3	120.1	135.9	24.0	726.8	112.1	121.9	32.9
Nonmetal mineral products	317.1	18.1	29.1	19.1	272.4	25.4	30.3	5.6
Glass products	226.6	12.1	19.1	10.8	−13.4	16.8	12.2	−1.4
Iron and steel	406.2	37.7	23.4	29.6	856.3	22.9	31.8	41.3
Nonferrous metals	−439.0	59.1	9.1	−46.3	1,693.4	6.1	95.8	95.9
Metal products	3,536.5	116.4	270.4	164.0	−2,391.7	253.6	112.1	−126.9
Nonelectric machinery	2,498.8	122.9	149.7	123.9	2,730.2	138.3	123.1	97.2
Electric machinery	4,298.9	86.4	206.3	174.1	−907.9	185.0	74.3	−59.4
Transport equipment	−5,369.8	297.4	−160.5	−398.9	6,195.8	−150.6	292.1	541.1
Miscellaneous manufacturers	2,246.0	90.8	125.6	76.9	1,267.5	88.1	78.0	37.1
Mining and quarrying	−742.1	...	...	−29.2	3,182.1	...	...	99.7
Utilities	336.9	...	...	11.8	−538.6	...	...	−17.0
Construction	1,001.7	...	...	76.6	−493.0	...	...	75.6
Wholesale trade	−9,173.8	...	...	139.7	2,239.1	...	...	−138.2
Transportation	720.6	...	...	45.0	−1,435.5	...	...	−51.8
Financial services	−4,896.3	...	...	187.7	381.6	...	...	−151.5
Personal services	−1,075.4	...	...	3.5	−15,936.8	...	...	−356.5

Table 6. *Sectoral Effects on the United States of U.S.-Canadian Free Trade, Tariffs Only, Post-Tokyo Round*
Percent

Sector	Employ-ment	Exports	Imports	Output	Capital	Rental rate	Prices
Agriculture	−0.01	−0.01	0.46	0.00	0.01	−0.02	−0.08
Food	−0.04	0.49	0.50	0.05	0.13	−0.10	−0.08
Textiles	0.31	2.25	0.36	0.27	0.12	0.19	−0.04
Clothing	0.08	5.36	0.44	0.09	0.11	−0.02	−0.05
Leather products	0.14	0.74	0.84	0.13	0.02	0.10	−0.22
Footwear	0.03	8.93	0.61	0.03	0.06	−0.02	−0.13
Wood products	−0.15	0.68	1.91	−0.09	−0.01	−0.16	−0.21
Furniture and fixtures	0.09	20.86	11.90	0.06	−0.01	0.09	−0.24
Paper products	0.06	2.28	2.19	0.06	0.07	−0.01	−0.15
Printing and publishing	0.12	5.34	0.71	0.11	0.09	0.03	−0.04
Chemicals	0.14	1.62	1.83	0.17	0.22	−0.08	−0.09
Petroleum products	−0.26	−0.03	0.30	−0.07	0.08	−0.12	−0.11
Rubber products	0.08	15.10	7.42	0.15	0.26	−0.11	−0.19
Nonmetal mineral products	0.07	3.27	1.68	0.08	0.11	−0.03	−0.07
Glass products	0.13	3.86	3.33	0.13	0.14	−0.01	−0.14
Iron and steel	0.05	1.12	0.80	0.04	−0.01	0.04	−0.07
Nonferrous metals	−0.14	0.51	1.11	−0.11	−0.01	−0.10	−0.22
Metal products	0.23	9.60	5.10	0.22	0.21	0.03	−0.09
Nonelectric machinery	0.11	0.69	1.52	0.11	0.11	−0.00	−0.18
Electrical machinery	0.23	2.51	1.17	0.23	0.21	0.05	−0.11
Transport equipment	−0.30	−0.79	1.84	−0.28	−0.24	−0.17	−0.16
Miscellaneous manufacturers	0.17	1.36	0.79	0.14	0.12	0.05	−0.12
Mining and quarrying	−0.09	. . .	. . .	−0.03	0.00	−0.06	−0.05
Utilities	0.05	. . .	. . .	0.01	0.00	0.02	−0.01
Construction	0.03	. . .	. . .	0.03	0.03	−0.00	−0.05
Wholesale trade	−0.04	. . .	. . .	0.02	0.11	−0.07	−0.04
Transportation	−0.02	. . .	. . .	0.02	0.02	−0.00	−0.02
Financial services	−0.06	. . .	. . .	0.03	0.07	−0.08	−0.06
Personal services	−0.00	. . .	. . .	0.00	0.04	−0.04	−0.02

These factors may account for the cases in which trade and output and employment of both labor and capital increase in both countries. We noted above that the FTA might result in a depreciation of the Canadian dollar. This could stimulate Canadian exports even in sectors where U.S. tariffs are low compared with Canadian tariffs. By the same token, some Canadian sectors may contract, despite the currency depreciation, if Canadian tariffs are much higher than U.S. tariffs, Canada's exports to the United States are fairly small, or U.S. exports to Canada are substantial. It is mainly for the foregoing reasons that particular sectors may move in opposite directions in the two countries with an FTA.

In addition, there are some other sectoral results that reflect certain characteristics of our model. For example, increased production in

Table 7. *Sectoral Effects on Canada of U.S.-Canadian Free Trade, Tariffs Only, Post-Tokyo Round*
Percent

Sector	Employ-ment	Exports	Imports	Output	Capital	Rental rate	Prices
Agriculture	0.50	1.21	0.76	0.11	−0.01	0.64	0.01
Food	0.07	2.85	1.08	−0.19	−0.58	0.65	−0.20
Textiles	−0.41	3.06	5.49	−0.43	−0.49	0.11	−2.31
Clothing	0.75	15.14	1.27	0.50	−0.51	0.89	−0.95
Leather products	3.89	4.14	1.67	3.28	0.35	3.45	−1.93
Footwear	1.77	20.28	−0.07	1.53	0.09	1.63	−0.76
Wood products	1.08	2.62	3.76	0.85	0.13	1.21	−0.47
Furniture and fixtures	2.42	29.99	26.72	2.12	1.02	1.63	−1.51
Paper products	0.66	2.11	12.45	0.39	−0.07	1.05	−1.00
Printing and publishing	−0.87	4.58	7.48	−0.68	−0.20	−0.70	−0.82
Chemicals	−0.77	6.08	8.02	−0.88	−1.03	0.19	−1.60
Petroleum products	2.49	1.68	−0.45	1.52	−0.21	0.94	0.81
Rubber products	2.40	34.80	23.96	1.67	−0.88	0.69	−1.77
Nonmetal mineral products	0.58	3.67	6.46	0.24	−0.24	0.77	−0.75
Glass products	−0.09	13.69	6.97	−0.27	−0.62	0.49	−2.68
Iron and steel	1.17	4.21	3.24	0.91	0.13	2.59	−0.13
Nonferrous metals	3.06	2.15	0.72	2.90	2.37	1.73	−0.51
Metal products	−1.58	17.18	24.47	−1.54	−1.44	−0.20	−1.28
Nonelectric machinery	2.46	4.06	2.18	1.83	0.45	1.31	−2.88
Electrical machinery	−0.66	10.61	8.73	−0.81	−1.01	0.73	−1.95
Transport equipment	3.32	3.53	−1.54	2.88	1.86	2.37	0.51
Miscellaneous manufacturers	1.59	5.20	3.29	1.11	0.03	1.23	−2.24
Mining and quarrying	2.18	...	...	0.56	0.13	1.33	0.57
Utilities	−0.48	...	...	−0.16	−0.00	−0.21	−0.09
Construction	−0.08	...	...	−0.16	−0.30	0.20	−0.35
Wholesale trade	−0.14	...	...	−0.30	−0.61	0.21	−0.03
Transportation	−0.20	...	...	−0.17	−0.10	−0.07	−0.10
Financial services	0.08	...	...	−0.33	−0.54	0.37	0.06
Personal services	−0.49	...	...	−0.31	−0.03	−0.42	−0.19

particular industries will also stimulate the production of intermediate inputs. A case in point is leather products, which shows a 3.28 percent increase in output in Canada despite the low U.S. tariff. Capital is also attracted to this industry in both countries from outside the FTA. The presence of NTBs is also worth noting since the effects of tariff reductions will be moderated in these instances. An example here is the food and related products sector for the United States, where we set the post-Tokyo round NTB coverage at 45 percent. Canadian exports in this sector show an increase of 2.85 percent, but output declines by 0.19 percent. There is a loss of capital that is so substantial that employment rises despite the fall in output.

There are several product categories in which U.S. tariffs are virtually zero, yet Canadian exports still increase. This occurs because the Canadian tariff cut raises demand for U.S.-produced goods, thus raising prices to U.S. consumers. As a result, U.S. consumers substitute into imports, which increases Canadian exports. Examples here include paper products, printing and publishing, chemicals, and nonmetallic mineral products, all bearing U.S. tariffs of less than 1 percent.

Finally, the increase in the relative price of U.S. goods tends to raise the rate of return to capital in the United States, with the result that capital will be attracted from abroad, particularly from Canada. The largest capital outflows for Canada are in metal products and chemicals. On the other hand, expanding export industries in Canada will attract capital. This is most notable for nonferrous metals, transport equipment, and furniture and fixtures. The loss of capital by Canada tends to raise the rental rate (valued in domestic currency) relative to the wage rate. Thus capital owners in Canada would increase their income share as a result of formation of an FTA. The increases in the rental rate are especially substantial in leather products, iron and steel, transport equipment, nonferrous metals, footwear, and furniture and fixtures.

Sensitivity Analysis

It is evident that computational models that incorporate national product differentiation are characterized by strong terms-of-trade changes. Consequently, the specification of the degree of substitutability among products from different sources may be critical in calculating changes in welfare in a model like ours. To investigate this issue, we conducted a sensitivity analysis of our results (not shown). In each case the bilateral pre-Tokyo round tariffs between Canada and the United States were reduced to zero.

Varying the elasticity of substitution among imports from various sources sharply alters the trade, terms of trade, and welfare effects of the bilateral tariff reductions. The greater the degree of substitutability, the larger the welfare gain for the United States and the smaller the welfare loss for Canada. This is not a surprising result. If imports from various sources are close substitutes, the preferential tariff induces substitution out of goods produced by third-country suppliers toward imports from the preferred partner. In comparison, substitution out of the domestically produced good is fairly small. Thus the burden of the preferential tariff falls primarily (but not entirely) on the third-country supplier, rather than on domestic producers. As demand for output from the third country declines, the price of its export falls, improving the terms of trade for Canada and the United States.

The model nonetheless indicates a decline in welfare for Canada, even for very high values of the elasticity of substitution among imports. This is possibly associated with a loss of capital to the United States. However, a second explanation is possible, which is that the welfare-reducing effects of the distortion between the imports from the United States and those from the rest of the world, created by the preferential tariff reductions, are more severe the greater the substitutability between imports from different sources. When imports and the domestically produced good are regarded as close substitutes, the preferential tariff reduces demand for the domestic good to the same degree as imports from third countries. Thus the results of the model with regard to this parameter appear to be fairly stable.

We also tested the sensitivity of the model to changes in the interest elasticity of capital. In the central case, with the elasticity set at 3.0, the relative price of Canadian-produced goods falls, causing a decline in the relative rate of return on capital in Canada. Canada then loses part of its capital stock to the United States. However, Canada suffers a welfare loss that varies little under a range of assumptions about the sensitivity of capital flows to rate-of-return differentials.

Conclusions and Implications for Research and Policy

Our purpose in this paper has been to review the important modeling issues involved in analyzing the economic effects of an FTA between the United States and Canada and to present some computational results of our own. The major modeling issues identified included whether Canada should be treated as a small country, whether its trade should be characterized in terms of differentiated products, whether Canadian manufacturing firms have unexploited economies of scale, and the impact of tariffs on foreign direct investment.

These issues are important because the way they are modeled may lead to different analytical outcomes and interpretations of the economic effects of an FTA. Thus it appears that when Canada is modeled as a small country it would generally benefit from an FTA with the United States. But when this assumption is modified to take into account the realistic possibility of national product differentiation, there is no presumption that Canada would necessarily benefit from an FTA with the United States. The same conclusion may emerge when changes in foreign direct investment are taken into account. Earlier studies suggest that there may be very substantial benefits to Canada from trade liberalization when departures from the assumptions of perfect competition and constant returns to scale permit scale economies and collusive pricing. The difficulty with these studies is that they do not model the bilateral relationship explicitly. However, more recent analysis suggests that scale economies might be realized by Canada under conditions of multilateral trade liberalization, but not necessarily under bilateral liberalization.

Our computational model incorporates a variety of assumptions and economic characteristics, the most important ones being perfect competition and constant returns to scale, fixed money wages, fixed sectoral capital stocks but intrasectoral capital mobility between countries, and national product differentiation and variable terms of trade. The results of our computational analysis of a U.S.-Canadian FTA using both pre- and post-Tokyo round tariffs suggest that the United States would experience a very modest improvement and that Canada would experience a small decline in welfare and the terms of trade. We noted that there would be a shift in output and employment toward tradable sectors and away from nontradables because of the changes in relative prices due to the reductions in tariffs. While the sectoral effects in the United States were fairly small, those in Canada were more substantial in both relative and absolute terms. Still, it does not seem likely that an FTA would be unduly disruptive to Canadian labor markets if the FTA liberalization were phased in over a period of years.

Our computational results were shown to depend importantly on the elasticity of substitution between imports and domestic products and between imports from different national sources. As we increased the elasticity of substitution among imports, U.S. welfare increased but Canada's welfare loss tended to become smaller. When goods from all sources were regarded as closer substitutes, Canada's welfare loss was not altered materially.

With the exception of Wigle's model, most other major studies of a U.S.-Canadian FTA have produced results suggesting that Canada would benefit from such an arrangement. These other studies use somewhat different modeling assumptions than we do, and this may account for the differences in results. Our model is best thought of as relating to the short run, especially because we do not permit the labor market to clear and we assume that capital is immobile domestically between sectors. The model used by Hamilton and Whalley is premised on the idea of nationally differentiated products and variable terms of trade, but it permits all markets for goods and labor and capital to clear. Harris's model incorporates a variety of industrial organization features involving scale economies and imperfect competition, although he too assumes national product differentiation. His results, which indicate substantial benefits from trade liberalization for Canada, depend importantly on the parameter values chosen to represent scale economies and upon the assumption of collusive pricing by Canadian manufacturing firms. However, if the importance of collusive pricing is diminished, the relative height of home and partner-country tariffs becomes critical in analyzing the effects of an FTA. Since Harris does not model the United States explicitly and bases his computational analysis on rest-of-the-world tariff rates that exceed tariff rates with respect to Canada, his results may overstate the benefits to Canada of an FTA with the United States.

Our main purpose in this paper has been to explore modeling issues and provide some computational results of an FTA based on a model that we believe captures important characteristics of the U.S. and Canadian economies. However, there is a need for additional research to clarify the modeling issues we have identified and provide the basis for a more informed judgment about the economic effects of an FTA.[15]

In particular, more attention should be given to measuring and interpreting the size and significance of scale economies, offering alternative assumptions about the pricing behavior of imperfectly competitive firms, and weighing the role of differences in the degree of substitution between imports and domestic goods and among imports from different

15. It would also be interesting to consider the implications for Canada if an FTA were not possible and if Canadian interests were adversely affected in the future by U.S. trade actions. Wonnacott presents some interesting calculations along these lines that are designed to call attention to Canada's vulnerability and to reinforce the benefits Canada might realize if it could obtain guaranteed access to the United States and exemption from U.S. trade actions aimed primarily at third countries. Ronald J. Wonnacott, "On the Employment Effects of Free Trade with the United States," *Canadian Public Policy*, vol. 12 (March 1986), pp. 258–63.

sources. There is also a need for accurate and up-to-date measures of the tariffs and NTBs that affect each country's bilateral and multilateral trade. Other important items on the research agenda include an effort to update the data and to further disaggregate data at the industry and possibly regional or state levels. Finally, to the extent that the FTA will cover trade and investment in services, existing models covering goods might well be adapted to include services.

Comments by Richard Harris

The Brown-Stern paper represents another high-quality modeling of multicountry trade flows, which has distinguished the work coming out of the Michigan model of Bob Stern and Alan Deardorff for a number of years. What makes this paper of particular interest for Canadians is the emphasis on trade among Canada, the United States, and the rest of the world within an explicit multicountry computable general equilibrium framework. This is a very useful paper from the perspective of someone teaching Canadian trade policy, particularly the discussion of customs union theory in the context of the traditional model.

On the subject of trade liberalization there are three basic questions economic analysis has dwelt on, or at least three questions quantitative analysis has claimed to shed light on. The first is the potential real income effects, or efficiency gains and losses, that might come about as a result of tariff and nontariff trade barrier reductions. From a single country's point of view, an important aspect of these gains or losses is the change in terms of trade as a result of the liberalization. Of additional importance are the efficiency gains in production that might come about as a result of the liberalization. The second question concerns gainers and losers from a trade liberalization, both within a country—usually distinguished by industry or region—and between countries. The third question relates to the short-term impact of protection, or trade liberalization, on employment.

Not surprisingly, the time frame of questions one and two is often much longer than that of question three, and the methods of analysis quite different. Models concerned with employment loss have invariably had particular features associated with macroeconomic analysis, such as rigidities in labor markets so that unemployment was built into the equilibrium of the models. Long-term models, however, often assume some form of price flexibility so that full employment is a characteristic both before and after the policy-induced shock of a change in tariff structures. Both types of models have for the most part lacked specific dynamics and have used a comparative static analysis to generate results. With different time frames, however, choice of parameter values should be affected greatly, with elasticities generally being lower the shorter the time frame.

The first two sets of questions have given rise to a variety of models that are loosely termed "neoclassical" in their basic theoretical structure. In reviewing these models as they apply to Canadian trade, Brown and Stern have noted that on average they give rise to very small efficiency gains and in some cases actual losses. I have reviewed these estimates elsewhere and have concluded that even within the theoretical framework used they provide unreasonably small estimates of the welfare gains of trade liberalization.[16] The result is simply because of the way trade is treated in these models. The critical "Armington assumption" implies that each country produces a set of goods that are specific to its own country but are imperfect substitutes with other countries' goods in a similar commodity category. This assumption, together with elasticities used to quantify the substitutability between imports and domestically produced goods, guarantees large terms-of-trade effects and virtually no changes in the pattern of specialization in production across countries in response to trade liberalization. The net effect is that countries with large domestic tariffs are often losers in bilateral and multilateral tariff cutting, and countries with initially low relative protection levels are the winners. This is true in Brown and Stern's results: Canada loses, assuming it has relatively higher tariffs than the United States in the simulated cuts. Another way of stating this result is that under Armington the optimal tariff for each country is extremely high; countries initially closest to their optimal tariff level suffer when tariffs are reduced across all countries. From the world perspective, given the absence of changes in the pattern of specialization and production across countries, tariff cutting buys very little for world efficiency. In table 4 of the Brown-Stern paper, a mutual cut in Canadian-U.S. tariffs from the pre-Tokyo round levels results in an aggregate loss in world welfare. Even so, the numbers are extremely small.

In assessing employment effects of trade liberalization, a number of

16. Harris with Cox, *Trade, Industrial Policy, and Canadian Manufacturing.*

issues come up. The first, and in many respects the most important, is the inability of static models to deal adequately with the dynamics of labor markets. In recent years our understanding of labor markets has improved and taught us that the flows into and out of unemployment are vastly greater and more important than the stock of unemployment at a given moment in time. For example, it is estimated that in the United States as many as one worker out of four changes jobs every year and experiences brief periods of unemployment. This turnover view of the labor market suggests that adjustment due to trade policy changes is likely to be small relative to the quits, layoffs, and hires that accompany normal economic activity and will certainly be small relative to the changes that accompany the business cycle. A pioneering effort to get at this aspect of the labor market was a paper by Baldwin, Mutti, and Richardson.[17] Making some simple assumptions about the average experience of an unemployed worker due to trade displacement, they computed the dynamic adjustment cost to tariff reductions to be a small fraction of the efficiency gains. Some current research I have been undertaking seems to confirm the conclusions of Baldwin, Mutti, and Richardson in a complete dynamic model. The unemployment conse-quences of bilateral trade liberalization between Canada and the United States are extremely small and transitory in nature.

The second aspect of modeling short-term employment effects of trade liberalization has to do with the nature of the wage rigidities and the existence of short-run capacity constraints in export-oriented indus-tries. Brown and Stern adopt the assumption of rigid nominal wages and a neoclassical description of supply. If short-run supply curves are perfectly elastic due to unused capacity, but nominal wages are rigid, then it comes very close to a Keynesian model. In such a model the trade multiplier plays an important role and in the context of bilateral free trade provides an important mechanism for the reduction of aggregate unemployment. A number of models have focused on the implications of rigid real wages. In this case domestic tariff reductions are typically employment creating, even without foreign tariff reductions, because the lower cost of imported goods in a small open economy with a large tradable-goods sector allows producers to reduce nominal producer

17. Robert E. Baldwin, John H. Mutti, and J. David Richardson, "Welfare Effects on the United States of a Significant Multilateral Tariff Reduction," *Journal of International Economics*, vol. 10 (August 1980), pp. 405–23.

wages, which in turn increases the supply of exports and encourages aggregate employment.

The final aspect of modeling short-term employment is the role for investment flows. Brown and Stern adopt an assumption of capital that is sector specific but flows between industries in different countries in response to differential rates of return. I am not sure this is the appropriate assumption in a short-term model. In the longer term one usually adopts the assumption that capital is malleable and can flow between sectors and possibly countries. Certainly for Canada and the United States this seems the only sensible assumption. In a time frame sufficiently short to hold nominal wages fixed, it seems only reasonable to regard capital as sector specific and possibly firm specific, as well as country specific. In modern industrial sectors most plant and equipment constitutes a sunk cost on the part of the firm. Ability to move that capital geographically is extremely limited in the short run. The possibility of changing the use of that capital by transferring its use to another major industry is limited. If capital were treated as sector and country specific in the Brown-Stern model, my guess is that it would change the results marginally in favor of greater gains accruing to Canada. It would be interesting to do this calculation.

The Brown-Stern model fits somewhere in the middle ground between efforts to quantify the long-run effects of trade liberalization and models that focus on the short run. In their model, governments run compensatory fiscal policy to keep aggregate employment constant. At the same time the nominal exchange rate adjusts to keep the trade account in balance. In the real world neither of these things would necessarily occur during a period of tariff reductions, but that is not a complaint against the model. Indeed, no one has devised an acceptable theory of the short-run determination of exchange rates, albeit to say that capital flows are obviously of great importance. While the model has short-run features, notably unemployment, it has not been designed to look at the central short-run questions of job creation or loss and capital flows. How, then, should one interpret the results? I think the best interpretation is that the Brown-Stern model provides a way of quantifying the potential short-term terms-of-trade effects, given offsetting policies designed to preserve neutral aggregate employment consequences of trade liberalization. This is obviously useful, because of the importance of terms-of-trade effects in analyzing the effects of trade liberalization. Beyond that, however, the results must be interpreted with caution, given the strong nature of the qualifying assumptions.

Comments by Peter A. Petri

It is easy to understand why a policymaker might be frustrated by the economic analysis of a free trade area (FTA). Theoretical models are consistent with virtually any welfare result, ranging from losses to one or both partners to worldwide gains. Empirical results also range widely. In the Canadian-U.S. case, some estimates of Canadian gain are negative, others slightly positive, and still others dramatically positive. Differences at the sectoral level are no less significant; the correlation of sectoral results, say, between Brown and Stern and Harris is negligible.

In this difficult context the Brown and Stern paper performs several important functions. It gives an excellent review of the relevant theory, highlighting the conditions under which trade diversion may lead to losses from an FTA. It identifies the main modeling assumptions of several prior empirical studies and explains why the treatment of Canada as a small country biases previous results toward the FTA. Finally, using an interesting new version of the Michigan model, it shows that Canadian gains evaporate if the (small-country) assumption of a bottomless U.S. market is replaced by trade elasticities typical of actual econometric studies. Their findings add an important perspective to the debate and perhaps help to explain some of the motives behind the ongoing negotiations.

The prediction that Canada might suffer under an FTA rides on the fact that Canadian tariffs facing U.S. products are higher than U.S. tariffs facing Canadian products. The joint removal of tariffs—the main policy change considered—would increase the Canadian trade deficit, and, with capital flows constant, would force a depreciation of the Canadian dollar and losses in the terms of trade. Thus Canadian negotiators may well want something more than tariff concessions from the United States, for example, favored treatment under American fair-trade laws. Judging by the interest in the issue, it would be worthwhile to examine some more "balanced" combinations of concessions, notwithstanding the serious empirical difficulties involved.

To facilitate the comparison of Brown and Stern's findings with those of other studies, table 8 summarizes, in the simplest form possible, the three major welfare consequences of an FTA. These "back of the envelope" results are derived from a much-simplified Armington model and are expressed as formulas, so that anyone can recalculate the table. Rough analysis of this kind cannot replace the comprehensive model of

Table 8. *"Back of the Envelope" Estimate of Welfare Effects of a Free Trade Area*

Effect	Formula	Value for Canada (percent of GNP)
Specialization	$1/2 \cdot t_m^2 \cdot e_m \cdot m \cdot (1 - 2d)$	+0.15
Terms of trade	$\dfrac{t_e \cdot e_e \cdot e - t_m \cdot e_m \cdot m \cdot (1-d)}{e_e + e_m - 1}$	−0.47
Productivity	$b \cdot t_m \cdot h$	+3.33

Symbol	Value (percent)	Definition
t_e	3	U.S. tariff on Canadian exports
t_m	10	Canadian tariff on imports
e	20	Canadian exports to U.S. (percent of Canadian GNP)
m	15	Canadian imports from U.S. (percent of Canadian GNP)
e_e	2.5	Price elasticity of Canadian exports
e_m	2.5	Price elasticity of Canadian imports
d	10	Diverted imports as fraction of new imports from U.S. in FTA
h	1	Percent decline in domestic production cost due to 1 percentage point cut in tariffs
b	33	Protected traded-goods output (percent of GNP)

Brown and Stern (indeed, some of the parameter estimates used in the table are based on their modeling results), but it can make the main empirical properties of different models more intuitive.

The specialization effect reflects the welfare effects of changes in international trade patterns. It is positive to the extent that resources flow from inefficient import-substituting to efficient export-producing activities and negative to the extent that trade is shifted from efficient third countries to an inefficient FTA partner. It is calculated as: efficiency gained per dollar of imports created times the change in imports net of trade diversion, less tariffs lost on diverted trade.[18] Specialization effects are the only effects typically present in models based on the small-country assumption.

The terms-of-trade effect reflects changes induced by the FTA in the

18. The efficiency gain from a dollar of imports created is equal to the tariff rate, since this is the difference between the resource cost of import substitutes and that of the exports needed to buy a dollar of imports. The 1/2 enters because tariffs are assumed to be reduced to zero, and therefore resource savings on the average new import equal only 1/2 of the initial tariff.

real exchange rate. A real exchange rate change is required if the initial (*ceteris paribus*) trade balance effect of the FTA (the numerator of the formula) is not zero. The welfare consequences of the exchange rate change can be calculated by dividing the initial trade imbalance by the sum of the country's export and import elasticities, less one. Since this sum is typically greater than one and less than the infinity assumed in the small-country case, the terms-of-trade effect is a fraction of the initial trade imbalance. Brown and Stern measure the effects of specialization plus terms of trade at − 0.38 percent of GNP.

The productivity effects of an FTA reflect improvements in domestic production efficiency not associated with changes in actual exports or imports. In Harris's models, competitive pressure from abroad causes firms to exploit scale economies and reduce production costs. Other mechanisms could also be at work: World Bank studies based on developing countries show that greater openness increases the stock of technical know-how through intensified contact with foreign markets, suppliers, and competitors. The productivity effect can be crudely quantified as the share of the economy exposed to competition (the deprotected traded-goods sector) times the protection removed, times the fraction of the protection removed that translates into actual cost reduction. In the Harris model—the first to estimate specialization, terms of trade, and productivity effects—efficiency gains match tariff reductions on a rather optimistic one-for-one basis in all import-competing industries that survive trade liberalization.

The magnitudes of the three effects are very different. The specialization effect is a fraction of the change in trade induced by the FTA and is typically small for a moderately open, moderately protected economy. Terms-of-trade effects can be much larger, as Whalley and others working with realistic Armington models typically find. This is also Brown and Stern's conclusion in the present case, due to differences in tariff levels between Canada and the United States. Finally, since productivity effects apply to the whole domestic traded-goods sector, they can be far larger than either of the other two effects, which are associated with actual trade.

In this setting, it is clear why Brown and Stern's negative terms-of-trade results dominate "small-country" specialization benefits and, in turn, why their results can be dominated by positive productivity gains. Ultimately, the evaluation of the FTA swings on the productivity issue. Productivity pessimists, in line with Brown and Stern's results, will want to see significant additional concessions from the United States. But I suspect that most Canadians who support the FTA believe that it will help to raise labor productivity to U.S. levels and are less interested in its immediate impact on the trade balance.

Let me turn to three minor technical observations. First, while the bilateral capital flow model incorporated is novel and interesting, it is hard to know what empirical confidence to attach to its results. Is it really likely that capital crosses international boundaries more easily than sectoral boundaries in a given country? Second, capital flows themselves have exchange rate and terms-of-trade effects (only the income on capital flows is modeled). In particular, capital flows into Canada during the early FTA period would tend to offset the trade effects of the FTA and reduce associated terms-of-trade losses. Third, the sensitivity results suggest that Canada's gains remain slightly negative even when the Armington elasticities are sharply increased (that is, when the specification is pushed toward the "small-country" extreme). This contrasts to previous results, and it would be useful to get a better feel for the trade diversion effects that must underlie the results.

Brown and Stern make a valuable contribution to the analysis of the U.S.-Canadian FTA, not least because they focus attention on modeling assumptions. In an ideal world economists would offer decisionmakers "definitive" evaluations of alternative policies. Yet in this and many other policy contexts, the underlying economic structure is still subject to too much debate for consensus simulations. Each modeler's evaluation is thus conditional on assumptions, and the burden of choosing among specifications is shifted to the users of the analysis. In this undesirable state of affairs, it is important to identify results clearly with assumptions, as Brown and Stern do with exemplary care.

DAVID F. BURGESS

A Perspective on Foreign Direct Investment

DESPITE a growing body of evidence that a U.S.-Canadian free trade area (FTA) would bring substantial economic benefits to Canada, there remains lingering doubt about its effects on long-run investment opportunities and the viability of plant location in Canada. The Macdonald Commission report cites the concern about the consequences of an FTA for long-run investment in Canada.[1] Surprisingly little attention has been paid by researchers to this question and to the closely related questions about the effects of an FTA on the location of new plants and the viability of existing plants, on foreign direct investment flows, and on the degree of foreign ownership and control of the Canadian economy. Would an FTA encourage or discourage firms to locate new plants in Canada? Would an FTA cause widespread disinvestment by U.S.-based multinational enterprises currently operating branch plants in Canada behind trade barriers? Would an FTA stimulate or deter Canadian direct investment in the United States? Would an FTA put many Canadian-owned firms at risk of takeover by large U.S.-based multinational enterprises that can offer assured access to the U.S. market as well as superior marketing and distribution expertise?

My aim here is to examine these questions in more detail and in the process to allay some of the doubts and fears that have often been expressed. If an FTA comes about (or perhaps more accurately, if it is

1. *Report of the Royal Commission on the Economic Union and Development Prospects for Canada*, vol. 1 (Ottawa: Minister of Supply and Services Canada, 1985), pp. 331–33.

to bear any chance of coming about) policymakers will need to understand more clearly the linkages between an FTA, long-run investment
opportunities, and international capital flows. Much of the benefit of an
FTA to Canada might well be dissipated by unwise policies introduced
in anticipation of misperceived side effects that it is supposed to cause.

What Would or Should Be Included in a Free Trade Area Agreement?

The effects of an FTA on international capital flows and plant location
obviously depend upon the precise details of any agreement, which have
yet to be worked out. Nonetheless, I shall assume for purposes of this
discussion that under an FTA both countries agree to eliminate over a
designated time period all tariff barriers on goods and services that flow
between them (provided, of course, that the goods and services are
either produced by the partner or have an acceptable level of local value
added), and to limit substantially the use of nontariff barriers. In the
words of Lipsey and Smith, "The object should be to ensure security of
access for substantially all of each country's goods to the other country's
market on the basis of national treatment."[2]

While the concept of a free trade arrangement is relatively easy to
define, it has proven to be much more difficult to translate into specifics,
much less to implement. Beyond the mutual elimination of all tariffs,
import quotas, and export subsidies, there is a growing consensus that a
meaningful free trade agreement must deal constructively with the
following specific issues.

First, government procurement policies that give preferential treatment to domestic suppliers or to firms that satisfy domestic-content
criteria must be severely constrained and a determined effort made to
adhere to the principle of national (that is, nondiscriminatory) treatment
in the awarding of government contracts, both at the federal and at the
state and provincial level. There are constitutional limits on what an
FTA might accomplish in this regard since it would be an agreement
between the national governments of federal states. However, for
starters an FTA might commit the United States to treat firms located in

2. Richard G. Lipsey and Murray G. Smith, *Taking the Initiative: Canada's Trade
Options in a Turbulent World* (Toronto: C. D. Howe Institute, 1985).

any Canadian province as if they were located in a U.S. state and commit Canada to treat firms located in any U.S. state as if they were located in a Canadian province.

Second, the use of contingent-protection devices (countervailing and antidumping duties) must be clarified and limited to instances of unfair competition, so that the machinery tends to promote fair trade rather than inadvertently serving as an obstacle to trade. Specifically, under an FTA countervailing duties could be imposed only if the subsidies provided by one country confer special advantages to specific industries or groups of industries or to plants in particular regions. Thus a subsidy that was generally available to all firms and industries within all regions of one country would not be deemed countervailable by the other country even though in many instances such subsidies can be shown to distort trade.

Third, with regard to the use of safeguards or escape clauses, which under GATT rules justify the imposition of temporary restrictions on imports in the event or threat of serious injury to particular industries, an FTA would exempt each partner country in cases where it is not the principal supplier. It would, of course, be preferable for each country to exempt the other from the use of such injury clauses without qualification, but this may not be an attainable goal. However, the use of trade controls for balance of payments reasons would definitely have to be ruled out since this is fundamentally antithetic to an FTA.[3]

Fourth, apart from the transition phase there would be no permanent production guarantees in the agreement to ensure the long-run viability of any particular industry or sector. Thus the current provisions of the Canada-U.S. auto pact that guarantee minimum levels of production and value added in Canada would be phased out under an FTA. It should be stressed, however, that there would be nothing in an FTA to preclude either country from supporting specific industries or activities (such as those that serve to promote and preserve national culture) through direct

3. This point is important in view of the large merchandise trade balance surpluses that Canada has run vis-à-vis the United States in recent years. There is nothing irrational or undesirable about the bilateral trade balance being in surplus or deficit in any year or for several consecutive years, and there should certainly be no effort made to constrain it under an FTA through exchange rate policy or by other means. The central point is that, given the existence of a well-developed capital market between the two countries, an FTA should be silent about the size of the bilateral trade imbalance in any year or over a number of years. The aim of an FTA should be to enhance trade between the two countries both at any one time and between time periods.

subsidization. What would be ruled out would be direct restrictions on the importation of substitutes for these activities.

Fifth, each country would commit itself to the principle of national treatment of foreign investment by the other country while reserving the right to restrict the influx of new foreign investment into a limited number of particularly sensitive areas (which for Canada might include banking and finance, printing and publishing, or energy). All foreign investment admitted into each country would be treated on the same basis as domestic investment, with no performance requirements imposed on foreign-owned firms that were not also imposed on domestic firms, and with no restrictions on the subsequent sale of foreign-owned assets to either domestic or foreign buyers. Since the United States is strongly interested in liberalizing trade in services, and since free trade in services often entails the right to establish a physical presence in the foreign market, some conflict is inevitable between the U.S. goal and Canada's desire to limit new foreign direct investment in certain sectors. The outcome would likely be a compromise whereby the principle of free access for new foreign direct investment capital was endorsed, subject to a limited and well-defined list of exceptions.

Finally, it is worth noting that under an FTA Canada would not have to harmonize its tax policies with those in the United States, nor abandon its flexible exchange rate system in favor of an exchange rate pegged to the U.S. dollar, nor abolish its unique social support systems, regional development programs, or industrial policy initiatives (provided that they were broadly based).[4] A similar statement applies to the United

4. The pressure for Canada to harmonize its tax policies with those in the United States would be no more severe under an FTA than it is now and would quite likely be less. Under an FTA the pretax earnings of labor would rise substantially in Canada, thereby reducing the after-tax real wage gap. In any event, to the extent that higher tax rates in Canada support a richer package of public services, the measured after-tax real wage gap is a spurious index of the real income differential. Regarding the tax treatment of capital, there is no doubt that the long-run prospects for investment in Canada depend as much on how capital income is taxed as on an FTA. However, it is false to assume that Canada would not want to set its capital income tax rate above that prevailing in the United States for fear of losing worthwhile investment opportunities or that it could not set its tax rate below that in the United States for fear of being accused of unfairly subsidizing its domestic industries. A tax rate below the U.S. rate would be a subsidy generally available to all firms and individuals throughout the economy and thus would not be countervailable. A tax rate above the U.S. rate would tend to discourage capital formation in Canada, but this would not necessarily be in conflict with the national interest. If Canada does indeed have market power in a wide range of export industries, as econometric evidence suggests, then under an FTA Canada would be inclined to use

States. Finally, neither Canada nor the United States need alter in any way their commercial policies toward third countries.

The above outline of what an FTA would include and not include is admittedly contentious. It may well be too optimistic. However, the following basic point seems important enough to be emphasized. Rightly or wrongly, Canadians have grown to expect a more active role by their government than have Americans, and subsidies have become a major instrument of national economic policy. The economic development of Canada has been very much a cooperative arrangement between the private and public sectors. Therefore it seems crucial for Canada to have formalized in any free trade agreement the principle that general-purpose subsidies (such as Canada's unemployment insurance and health care systems and research and development incentives) are not countervailable provided that they are not targeted at specific sectors or regions, but are generally available throughout the economy.

Regional development grants would require further negotiation. A reasonable outcome would be an agreement that Canadian exports of goods and services produced in low-income regions supported by regional development subsidies would not be countervailable unless the subsidy lowers the cost of production below what it would be in a preferred Canadian location, and if so that the countervailing duty would be limited to removing the differential. Canada's natural resource and energy policies might also be a contentious issue on the grounds that quotas on exports of specific natural resource products and "made in Canada" energy prices below the world level could be interpreted as unfair subsidies. Formal acceptance of the principle that Canada has a legitimate right to price its natural resource products in its own economy and to limit their export without the risk of provoking countervailing action would be an important step toward removing some of the uncertainty that currently deters long-run investment in natural resource processing in Canada. However, the United States may be reluctant to endorse such a principle without further concessions since virtually any restriction that Canada imposes on its exports of energy and natural resource products can be interpreted as a subsidy for the exports of particular industries that use those commodities as inputs.[5]

---

too much capital and rely too heavily on the international capital market for its own best interest. Taxing capital income in Canada at a higher rate than in the United States may then be both a feasible and a desirable policy under an FTA.

5. GATT codes do not formally preclude quotas on exports of natural resource

Some Implications of General Equilibrium Analysis

Standard trade theory in the Heckscher-Olin-Samuelson tradition predicts that the elimination of trade barriers between two countries will tend to lower the rate of return to capital and deter investment in one of them (in the absence of complementary changes in tax policy). However, it is now generally recognized that the basic assumptions of this model are seriously out of focus as a guide to understanding the U.S.-Canadian case. The most glaring deficiency is the failure to incorporate economies of scale and imperfectly competitive market structures, which, thanks to the work of several scholars,[6] is now clearly understood to be the salient feature of secondary manufacturing activity in Canada.[7]

A useful review of the effects of trade liberalization on the Canadian economy is Harris and Cox's computational general equilibrium model. These authors focus primarily on the static effects of bilateral and multilateral trade liberalization on Canada's real wage, real GNP, and industrial structure in a world where Canada is depicted as an "almost" small open economy facing given prices for imports and a given rental rate for capital services but having a degree of market power in its export trade. The amounts of domestic capital and labor services supplied to the production process are taken as given and a perfectly elastic supply of foreign savings finances any gap between the economy's capital requirements and its indigenous capital supply. In short-run equilibrium there are industry-specific quasi-rents, which accrue in part to foreigners in proportion to the degree of foreign ownership of each industry. In

---

products or other commodities, yet such restrictions do in fact confer a subsidy upon sectors that use these materials as inputs. While it can be argued that these subsidies are not directed explicitly at exports, in many instances they have their major impact there.

6. See, among others, Harry C. Eastman and Stefan Stykolt, *The Tariff and Competition in Canada* (St. Martin's, 1967); Ronald J. Wonnacott and Gordon P. Wonnacott, *Free Trade between the United States and Canada: The Potential Economic Effects* (Harvard University Press, 1967); and Richard G. Harris with David Cox, *Trade, Industrial Policy, and Canadian Manufacturing* (Toronto: Ontario Economic Council, 1984).

7. Another weakness of the standard theory is its general underappreciation of the role of risk and uncertainty. In an environment where countries have erected trade barriers against each other there will be underinvestment generally because of a presumption that restrictive trade practices are the norm. A commitment to eliminate trade barriers implies a commitment to a more liberalized trading system and a reduced risk of contingency protection measures.

long-run equilibrium these quasi-rents are driven to zero by the entry and exit of firms so that the industry-by-industry detail of foreign ownership and control is irrelevant. Since all firms are identical in any industry, there are no firm-specific intangible assets, which might explain why a U.S.-based multinational enterprise prefers to establish a subsidiary in Canada rather than simply to rent capital services to Canadian entities. In short-run equilibrium each firm exhibits the same degree of foreign ownership and control as any other firm in that industry; in long-run equilibrium the model admits no difference in the degree of foreign ownership and control across industries.

The static implications of multilateral trade liberalization for aggregate investment, international capital flows, and plant location can only be inferred from the results, but they provide an interesting benchmark from which to proceed. Since the amount of capital services supplied locally is taken as given, the impact of trade liberalization on domestic capital requirements and international capital flows can be determined by observing the change in net exports. If it causes a reduction in net exports, the constraint imposed by the balance of payments must have resulted in a reduction in the amount of capital services supplied from abroad, and therefore a reduction in the economy's total capital requirements. Harris and Cox present only results for the percentage changes in net exports of each industry from trade liberalization; net exports decline for nineteen of the twenty-nine industries in their model. Nonetheless, the model predicts that free trade causes an increase in foreign investment flows into Canada and thus an increase in the economy's total capital requirements.[8] In order for this to be the case the ten industries that experience an increase in net exports must be, on average, substantially more capital intensive than the rest of the economy.

Harris and Cox also assume that the elasticity of substitution between capital and labor is unity in all sectors. This means that the capital requirements for producing a unit of value added in each sector increase by the same proportion as the economywide wage rate, ignoring the reduction in fixed costs that follow from having fewer firms in the

8. See Richard G. Harris, "Summary of a Project on the General Equilibrium Evaluation of Canadian Trade Policy," in John Whalley with Roderick Hill, eds., *Canada-United States Free Trade* (University of Toronto Press in cooperation with the Royal Commission on the Economic Union and Development Prospects for Canada and the Canadian Government Publishing Centre, Supply and Services Canada, 1985), p. 164.

imperfectly competitive industries. Since the model predicts that trade liberalization results in a 25 percent increase in the economywide wage rate and value added increases in twenty of the twenty-nine industries in the model (including all of the constant-cost industries), there is a substantial increase in the economy's total capital requirements even though the forced rationalization of the manufacturing sector economizes on the use of capital. Econometric evidence suggests that the elasticity of substitution between capital and labor is substantially less than unity for most sectors, and certainly for Canada's capital-intensive primary industries. This would tend to reduce the positive impact of trade liberalization on Canada's capital requirements. The inclusion of sector-specific factors (such as land) in the primary industries would have a similar effect.

To summarize, the Harris-Cox model predicts that multilateral trade liberalization will result in a substantial increase in the Canadian real wage and real GNP, an increase in the output and value added of most industries (including all industries in the primary and service sectors), an increase in the economy's total capital requirements (despite a reduction in the number of firms or plants operating in Canada's secondary manufacturing sector and the associated decline in fixed costs), and a net increase in foreign investment flows into Canada. Since almost 80 percent of Canada's trade is with the United States, a bilateral free trade arrangement between Canada and the United States alone would have effects on Canada similar to a multilateral agreement, although not quite as large. Thus the Harris-Cox analysis suggests strongly that Canada need not worry about an erosion of its manufacturing base or being transformed into a resource-rich hinterland of the United States under an FTA. Safeguards will not be necessary to prevent the deindustrialization of Canada, because an FTA will encourage labor to shift from the primary sector into the secondary manufacturing sector, rather than the reverse.

While the Harris-Cox results will be reassuring to many, the analysis upon which the results are based is fundamentally static, focusing on the rationalization of existing plants and the attendant real-wage gains, but saying nothing about the long-run prospects for investment and plant location, which is the central concern of this paper. Two other problems with the model need to be mentioned here.

First, the model assumes that the supply of domestically funded capital is independent of trade liberalization. A plausible life cycle theory of savings would predict that if trade liberalization raises the real wage it will also increase the supply of indigenous savings and the quantity of capital services financed at home. If an induced effect on domestic savings were factored into the analysis, the result could easily be that an FTA would result in a net capital outflow from Canada rather than a net capital inflow.

A second weakness of the model is its prediction that even though trade liberalization causes a reduction in the number of firms or plants in the manufacturing sector there will be a greater degree of foreign ownership and control of those firms that manage to survive the rationalization process. This follows not because of any asymmetry in the response of foreign and domestically owned firms to trade liberalization, but because of the assumed infinitely elastic supply of foreign savings coupled with a perfectly inelastic supply of domestic savings. A plausible hypothesis is that Canadian subsidiaries of U.S.-based firms will have an easier time in coping with rationalization because they can tap the finances and marketing and distribution network of the parent corporation to facilitate access into the U.S. market. An alternative view is that the elimination of trade barriers will cause many Canadian subsidiaries to shut down as the parent corporation retreats to serve the Canadian market via exports from fully rationalized plants in the United States. The Harris-Cox model sheds no light on this issue; since all firms in any industry are identical, the model cannot explain the foreign direct investment process and the possibility of differences in the response of foreign and domestically owned firms to trade liberalization.

The third problem with the model stems from its treatment of all tradables produced in Canada as imperfect substitutes for tradables produced elsewhere. Thus the model specification ensures that export markets for Canadian-made goods expand ineluctably under an FTA as the wedge between producer costs and consumer prices disappears. The model recognizes no "niche" at the level of the individual firm that might explain which firms survive the rationalization process, but the viability of every Canadian industry is ensured by the existence of such a niche at the industry level. In reality, the size of the gains accruing to Canada from an FTA are contingent upon entrepreneurial and managerial skill and drive that result in successful penetration of the U.S. market without government support. The more difficult the process of selling abroad, the smaller the net gains will be. If some firms must close under an FTA, it is better for Canadian real incomes that the industrial attrition involve foreign-owned firms, but this detail is assumed away in the Harris-Cox model because it posits identical, representative firms in every industry.

Implications for Capital Flows and Plant Location

I would argue that the dynamic effects of an FTA are likely to be somewhat different from those predicted by static general equilibrium analysis. Since an FTA will raise real wages and real incomes in Canada, it will also stimulate labor supply and employment. Given the relative importance of the services sector as a source of income and employment and the advantages of transacting internationally in services using direct investment, there is a strong presumption that on balance an FTA will increase the incentive for firms to locate new plants in Canada and to expand existing plants. While the long-run impact of an FTA on foreign direct investment flows remains far from clear, it seems unlikely that there will be extreme shifts in either direction. Some U.S.-based companies may close down their Canadian subsidiaries on account of an FTA, but at the same time some Canadian-owned firms will merge or be taken over by U.S. firms as a means of gaining rapid penetration of the U.S. market. Meanwhile, the new competitive environment, together with more assured access to the North American market, should attract new foreign direct investment into Canada both from the United States and from third countries.

The long-run impact of an FTA on Canadian direct investment abroad is also problematic. On the one hand, an FTA should deter much "defensive" investment now taking place because of a growing risk of U.S. protectionism. On the other hand, a larger flow of Canadian exports into the United States under an FTA should stimulate Canadian investment in complementary assembly, marketing, distribution, and service facilities abroad. Finally, because of the strong positive impact of an FTA on real wages and real incomes in Canada, the amount of internally generated savings should increase substantially relative to the economy's capital requirements. Thus Canada's net international indebtedness position should decrease under an FTA.

If two countries agree to eliminate or substantially reduce artificial barriers to trade between them, the result will almost certainly be to enhance productivity and stimulate investment and growth in both countries as resources get shifted into areas of comparative advantage.[9] Moreover, by further clarifying the rules governing trade, and in particular by removing much of the uncertainty about which policy actions taken by one country are countervailable in the other, an FTA will reduce the considerations of political risk that currently permeate the trade relationship and will provide a climate much more conducive to long-run investment decisions based upon economic efficiency. This seems especially true in the U.S.-Canadian case, where each country is the other's major trading partner and a well-developed capital market exists between them. Canada, with the smaller of the two markets, suffers the most from the uncertainties of trade policy and has the most to gain in terms of investment from an FTA. The burden of proof that Canada's long-run investment opportunities would be diminished by an FTA must surely rest with the skeptics.

Unwarranted Fears

Those who remain skeptical about Canada's ability to attract long-run investment under an FTA raise other concerns, four of which I will address and show to be either groundless or exaggerated.

The first question is, what would prevent U.S.-based firms from closing under an FTA? This is perhaps of greatest concern to those who raise the issue of the impact of an FTA on factor flows and plant location. Their questions take the following general form. Why would a U.S. enterprise want to rationalize its plants in Canada if that would mean competing directly with its plants in the United States, which are presumably already fully rationalized in the large U.S. market? Where is the "niche" that gives a Canadian branch plant its unique existence in an unfettered North American market? If this niche has not already been developed or secured by specialization in a limited number of

9. An FTA will be productivity enhancing for Canada because Canadian firms will gain access to inputs at world prices and receive world prices for their outputs. However, it is an empirical question whether this productivity gain will be capital saving or capital using. If there were no unexploited scale economies in Canada and if the supply price of capital were unaffected by an FTA, the productivity gain from a more efficient industrial structure would lead to more capital formation because resources would tend to shift into the more capital-intensive primary sectors. However, if there are unexploited scale economies in the manufacturing sector, the productivity gain from being able to trade at world prices conceivably could mean a decline in capital-output ratios in many manufacturing sectors and thus a reduced demand for capital.

products, won't an FTA put a great deal of pressure on the Canadian government to subsidize branch plants that are willing to specialize? If an FTA might prohibit the use of such subsidies (which would ultimately be in Canada's best interest, since it can not outbid the United States in a subsidy game), won't Canada's fate be sealed with respect to long-run investment? Finally, since many U.S.-based enterprises owe their existence in Canada to the legacy of protectionism beginning with Canada's National Policy of 1879, won't they leave or at least scale down their operations once trade barriers are removed, thereby transforming Canada from a "branch plant" economy to a "warehouse" economy?

This line of questioning sounds convincing enough, but it is seriously deficient. First, it fails to distinguish between a unilateral and a bilateral removal of trade barriers. There seems little doubt that Canada's protective policies have been at least partly responsible for the decision of some foreign firms to locate branch plants in Canada rather than to export into Canada over the barriers. The removal of such barriers should then tip the balance back in favor of exporting into the Canadian market for many firms. However, an FTA involves a *mutual* elimination of trade barriers, in which Canadian-based firms and plants gain unimpeded access into the U.S. market while losing the protective cushion afforded by Canadian trade barriers against U.S. goods. Since there are unexploited economies of scale attributable to longer production runs within the typical plant operating in Canada, this should encourage many firms to rationalize their Canadian operations and to specialize in product lines that have a particularly strong demand in Canada while exporting any surplus to the United States.

Second, while it may well be true that U.S. trade barriers are irrelevant for branch plants whose sole raison d'être has been to serve the protected Canadian market, it does not follow that these firms will leave once trade barriers are removed. Product cycle theory suggests that foreign direct investment is often a phase in the evolution of a product and its market, and that while such investment may be encouraged to happen sooner by trade barriers, it will happen eventually.[10] As Safarian has stressed, trade

10. It should also be stressed that there is growing pressure for multinational enterprises to shift the production of fairly standardized product lines to the newly industrialized countries, which offer significantly lower labor costs. This process is ongoing and inevitable with or without an FTA, and it will become increasingly costly for Canada to circumvent. While the higher real wages that an FTA induces will undoubtedly give further impetus to such a relocation, there is a strong presumption

barriers are only one of many reasons why firms prefer to establish branch plants abroad rather than export.[11] Other reasons include transport costs, relative labor and materials costs (deflated by the exchange rate), local preferences for product design, the extent to which product demand depends upon reputation for servicing, and the extent to which economies of scale have been fully exploited in the home market. Moreover, there are large sunk costs associated with establishing a subsidiary or branch plant abroad, which are a major deterrent to shutting down once trade barriers have been eliminated. Under the current tax system, foreign firms that decide to leave Canada pay a substantial capital levy to exercise this option.[12]

Even if some U.S.-based firms were to decide that the benefits of closing down their operations in Canada outweighed the costs of doing so, the decision would be a profit-maximizing and cost-minimizing response to the new regime. There is a strong presumption that with market prices more closely reflecting marginal social costs and benefits under an FTA, such a decision will also be resource saving and in the general interest of both Canada and the United States. The relative inefficiency of Canadian branch plants would then not be the result of short production runs and a small market so much as the result of relatively high labor and materials costs (deflated by the exchange rate), the lack of regional specificity in product design, the absence of significant transport costs between the two countries, and the existence of unexploited scale economies at plants located in the United States. But there is no evidence that the erosion of tariff barriers between Canada and the United States during the 1970s caused a major exodus of U.S.-based firms from Canada's manufacturing sector.[13] Rationalization of

---

that more appropriate product lines will be established in Canada to replace them—especially if unrestricted access to the North American market can be assured. A decision to shift a product line within a firm should not be confused with a decision to divest. Under an FTA there is a strong presumption that new direct investment will occur in new product lines to replace the exodus from old ones.

11. A. Edward Safarian, "The Relationship between Trade Agreements and International Direct Investment," in David W. Conklin and Thomas J. Courchene, eds., *Canadian Trade at a Crossroads: Options for New International Agreements* (Toronto: Ontario Economic Council, 1985).

12. Lipsey and Smith, *Taking the Initiative*, pp. 119–20; and Donald J. S. Brean, *International Issues in Taxation: The Canadian Perspective* (Toronto: Canadian Tax Foundation, 1984), p. 88.

13. Economic Council of Canada, *The Bottom Line: Technology, Trade, and Income Growth* (Ottawa: Minister of Supply and Services Canada, 1983).

production facilities and specialization in particular product lines appears to have been the preferred response of both Canadian-owned firms and multinational enterprises to the reduction in tariff barriers.[14]

Third, the view that exporting and establishing a branch plant abroad are alternative ways of capturing the return from certain firm-specific intangible assets gives insufficient attention to the fact that direct investment often is in markets producing nonhomogeneous goods, such as sophisticated consumer and producer durables for which local specification and design and a reputation for servicing are important selling points. It also ignores the fact that rather than directly competing with each other for market share, subsidiaries often trade with their own affiliates, buying and selling components at various stages of processing. Under these circumstances trade and foreign direct investment tend to be complements rather than substitutes, and measures that liberalize trade will also tend to encourage investment. It is well-established empirically that most direct investment takes place between countries that trade large amounts with each other rather than between countries that trade very little.

The second question is, instead of providing a healthier climate for new investment in Canada, won't an FTA deprive Canada of much new investment because without trade barriers the Canadian market can be more efficiently served from the United States?

This argument is fundamentally flawed. It fails to recognize what the base case is, it proceeds from the specific to the general, and it ignores the equilibrating role of the exchange rate. Although some U.S.-based firms currently operating in Canada may decide to retreat to serve the Canadian market via exports from the parent firm, this cannot be a widespread phenomenon because of its general equilibrium consequences. A nation must ultimately export in order to pay for its imports. Under an FTA Canada retains its labor force, natural resource base,

14. It is true that after decades of being a net importer of direct investment capital, Canada has experienced a net outflow in the manufacturing sector every year since 1975. See Statistics Canada, *Canada's International Investment Position 1981–84*, vol. 67-202 (May 1986), and table 1. However, this seems to be more a reflection of Canadian-owned firms deciding to establish production facilities abroad than of U.S.-based firms deciding to divest. The net outflow of direct investment seems to have been motivated more by Canada's deteriorating international competitive position and the lack of secure access to the U.S. market than by reductions in official tariff rates. See John R. Baldwin and Paul K. Gorecki, "The Relationship between Trade and Tariff Patterns and the Efficiency of the Canadian Manufacturing Sector in the 1970s: A Summary," in Whalley with Hill, eds., *Canada-United States Free Trade*, pp. 179–92.

public-sector capital, institutional arrangements, exchange rate, tax provisions, and monetary policy. While these basic elements can be combined wisely or foolishly—and how they are combined will be central in determining the climate for investment—there is no realistic sense in which an FTA of itself can damage Canada's long-run investment prospects.

Even if an FTA did nothing but encourage Canadian and foreign-owned firms to shift their production facilities to the United States, the attempt to divest would put severe downward pressure on the exchange rate and the market value of land and other fixed assets located in Canada. The downward revaluation of fixed assets would impose capital losses on existing owners, but it would attract prospective buyers and thus would eventually restore the climate for investment.

A much more likely scenario would be one in which the static and dynamic gains in production efficiency that accompany an FTA would provide an immediate and strong impetus for long-run investment in Canada, not just by Canadians and Americans but also by investors from third countries. Foreign investors could confidently foresee secure access into the U.S. market, secure supplies of energy and other natural resource inputs, and a uniquely Canadian mix of public services. The type of investment that Canada would attract under an FTA would also be more consistent with its human capital and natural resource endowment, its public-sector infrastructure, and its proximity to markets for raw materials and final goods than the investment Canada has heretofore attracted into its highly protected economy using a variety of ad hoc tax concessions and investment incentives.

The ultimate objective of an FTA is to raise the real incomes of Canadians, not to promote investment. Investment is not an end in itself unless there are important external economies associated with it. Until now Canada has been using too much capital per unit of output because of excess product diversity and short production runs in the manufacturing sector. The amount of capital that can be profitably employed ultimately depends upon the supplies of complementary inputs—labor, land, and public-sector infrastructure—as well as how efficiently these inputs are organized. It is not necessarily the case that if an FTA raises real wages and real incomes it must also increase long-run investment opportunities, but there is a strong presumption that this will happen. Even if the rationalization effects of an FTA were relatively small, comparative advantage alone would predict an increase in investment opportunities in Canada because of a shift of indigenous resources from the manufacturing sector (which is relatively labor intensive) to the primary sector (which is relatively capital intensive). What the Harris-Cox model shows is that even if rationalization effects within the manufacturing sector dominate traditional comparative advantage effects, the economy's overall capital requirements will increase. Thus the prospects for long-run investment in Canada under an FTA seem even more certain than the prospects for higher real wages, which depend critically upon the existence of rationalization effects. Of course, the prospects for investment also depend upon the precise details of an FTA—how comprehensive it is in removing trade barriers, how secure it makes access into the U.S. market for Canadian-based firms, and how much it promotes the development of Canada's natural resources and energy for the North American market rather than for only the Canadian market.

A third concern is, if an FTA succeeds in raising real wages in Canada, thereby reducing the wage differential between Canada and the United States, won't this destroy a major advantage of a Canadian plant location over a U.S. location?

According to this view, Canada's ability to attract long-run investment would be seriously eroded by a rise in real wages, certainly by as much as 25 percent, which has been predicted by Harris and Cox. However, this view confuses cause and effect. In a competitive economy the real wage level is a barometer recording the productivity of labor. An increase in wages that stems from a genuine improvement in productivity is fundamentally different from an increase in labor costs that results from inflexible labor market policies or misguided government regulations. In a competitive economy there is no conflict between a high wage level and long-run investment opportunities. To the contrary, a high real wage will further support investment decisions that favor capital-intensive and skill-intensive activities with high value added over traditional activities that ultimately will be viable mainly in the lower-wage newly industrialized countries. The Canadian real wage level and the size of the U.S.-Canadian real-wage differential will be determined simultaneously with the level of investment. Real wages and investment opportunities will be complementary: the higher real wages, the greater the supply of labor and the greater the need for new investment in a whole range of domestic services.

Ultimately, what will attract new investment to Canada will be the skills of its labor force, the flexibility of labor markets, the willingness of labor to accept innovative techniques like profit sharing, the mix of public services available in Canada, and access to secure supplies of crucial energy inputs. These factors, together with a strong signal from governments that they are committed to the pursuit of policies that promote flexibility and adaptation to change and promote the national interest over the special interest, will ultimately determine the future of long-run investment. A comprehensive free trade agreement would go a long way toward providing this signal.

Opponents of an FTA claim that either Canada will suffer a massive exodus of long-term capital or it will be inundated with so much long-term capital that it will cease to exist as a separate sovereign state. The range of opinion about the relationship between an FTA and long-term capital flows is a telling statement of apparent ignorance about the fundamental forces at work.

The fourth and final question is, won't an FTA expose many small Canadian-owned firms to takeovers by large U.S.-based companies that can offer assured access into the U.S. market as well as a marketing and distribution network that would be costly to develop? Won't an FTA also bring renewed pressure to develop Canada's energy and natural resources for an integrated North American market? Won't the combination of both these forces result in large net capital inflows and an even greater degree of foreign ownership and control?

The precise details of an FTA will clearly be important in assessing its overall impact on international capital flows and the level of foreign ownership and control. Thus it makes a big difference whether and to what extent an FTA leads to fewer restrictions on the influx of new foreign direct investment and embodies a more open and "continental-ist" position about the development of Canada's energy and natural resources. I have assumed that under an FTA Canada will retain the right to limit new foreign investment in designated sectors, but that it cannot interfere with transactions of existing foreign-owned assets. This means that there would be nothing in an FTA to prevent existing multinational enterprises from using their retained earnings to buy out small Canadian-owned firms, other than the provisions of Canada's competition policy.

Some have argued that the national treatment provisions of an FTA would undermine, if not destroy, Canada's ability to repatriate certain sectors of its economy. In fact there would be no conflict between an

FTA and the achievement of any desired level of Canadian ownership and control of any sector. If it were deemed desirable to reduce the level of foreign ownership and control of, say, printing and publishing, the government could outbid foreign investors for the assets or subsidize a domestic firm or consortium of domestic firms to make a winning bid.

Several factors suggest that whatever impact an FTA has on foreign investments inflows will be manageable. There will be a phased removal of trade barriers with adequate scope for government support of adjustment costs. All firms or plants will come under severe pressure to rationalize and some will be forced to close, but there seems no reason to believe that the incidence of attrition should be greater for Canadian-owned firms than the Canadian subsidiaries of foreign firms. Rather, the firms that choose not to rationalize—presumably because they perceive little or no benefit from assured access to the U.S. market—will disappear. This suggests that firms or plants whose sine qua non has been the small, protected Canadian market will be at the greatest risk, and small Canadian-owned firms with aggressive managers and an outward-looking vision will survive and thrive.

To be sure, the degree of foreign ownership and control may well increase somewhat in the short run since foreign takeovers of Canadian-owned firms may provide the preferred route to rapid penetration of the U.S. market in certain cases. But because most of the benefit of an FTA will accrue to labor, Canadian savings will be enhanced and thus in the long run the degree of foreign ownership should decline. Whether the level of foreign control increases or falls depends largely upon the attitudes of Canadians toward expected returns versus risks—whether they prefer to accept the risks associated with having a controlling interest or are content with the relative security of minority ownership or the holding of debt instruments. Aggressive Canadian firms would be more inclined to retain a controlling interest in order to maximize returns on their specific intangible assets. In any event, there is no economic justification for opposing an FTA on the grounds that Canadians might prefer debt over equity and might therefore passively supply the funding necessary to enhance foreign interest in the economy.[15]

15. Direct investment flows as recorded in balance of payments statistics generally overstate substantially any net transfer of capital between countries. Close to half of the direct investment inflows from the United States to Canada have been financed by borrowings in Canada and are therefore offset by corresponding portfolio capital outflows.

Table 1. *Canada's International Investment Position, 1978–85*
Billions of Canadian dollars

Item	1978	1979	1980	1981	1982	1983	1984	1985
Assets								
1. Direct investment	16.4	20.0	25.8	32.5	33.9	35.9	41.7	50.4
2. Investment in U.S.	9.0	12.1	16.4	21.8	23.0	25.0	29.6	35.5
3. Total long-term	32.9	39.8	48.5	57.6	63.1	67.0	79.8	n.a.
4. Gross assets	45.9	56.3	67.2	85.0	93.2	100.6	119.9	132.5
Liabilities								
5. Direct investment	48.3	54.3	61.6	66.5	67.2	74.6	81.8	84.0
6. Investment from U.S.	38.3	42.8	48.7	52.3	53.6	57.4	60.2	63.4
7. Total long-term	117.0	130.6	146.4	166.9	184.8	198.1	219.9	n.a.
8. Gross liabilities	133.5	155.7	173.9	218.2	229.3	247.8	272.9	305.6
Net international investment position								
9. Net long-term (row 3 − row 7)	−84.1	−90.8	−97.9	−109.3	−121.7	−131.1	−140.9	n.a.
10. Net international indebtedness (row 4 − row 8)	−87.6	−99.4	−106.7	−133.2	−136.1	−147.2	−153.0	−173.1
11. Statistical discrepancy[a]	16.3	19.0	20.3	29.5	31.3	36.9	43.9	51.0
12. Foreign direct investment inflows	0.1	0.8	0.8	−4.4	−1.4	−0.2	2.2	−2.9
13. Inflows from U.S.	−0.3	−0.4	−0.3	−3.7	−2.0	−0.9	−0.8	−3.1
14. Canadian direct investment outflows	2.3	2.6	3.2	6.9	0.2	2.7	3.8	5.1
15. Outflows to U.S.	1.0	1.2	2.2	3.5	−0.4	2.1	1.9	3.9

Sources: Statistics Canada, *Canada's International Investment Position 1981–84*, vol. 67-202 (May 1986); and Statistics Canada, *Quarterly Estimates of Canada's Balance of International Payments 1982–85*, vol. 67-001 (Third quarter 1986).

n.a. Not available.

a. If the statistical discrepancy is added to row 10, one obtains a measure of Canada's cumulative current account deficit since 1927. Thus at the end of 1985 Canada's cumulative current account deficit amounted to $122.1 billion.

Canada's Changing International Investment Position

Table 1 provides an interesting review of the changes in Canada's international investment position over 1978–85. The data in the table reveal several points that pertain to the issues raised above. First, the proportion of Canadian direct investment abroad that is in the United States has increased from 55 percent to 70 percent over the period (row 2), indicating that the relative importance of the U.S. market to Canadian-owned firms has been growing quite independently of an FTA. Second, the annual rate of growth of Canadian direct investment abroad (measured at book value) has averaged 18 percent over the period (row 1) despite the fact that it grew by only 4 percent and 6 percent in the recessionary years of 1982 and 1983. Part of this spectacular growth undoubtedly is attributable to the desire of Canadian-owned firms to gain secure access to the U.S. market. Third, the proportion of U.S. direct investment in Canada has fallen slightly from 79 percent to 75 percent of the total over the period (row 6). This modest decline is largely explained by the Canadianization of the oil and gas sector that occurred as part of Canada's National Energy Program of 1980. Fourth, the annual rate of growth of foreign direct investment in Canada has averaged only 8.5 percent over the period (row 5); thus the ratio of Canadian direct investment abroad to direct investment by the rest of the world in Canada has grown from 34 percent to 60 percent (rows 1 and 5). Finally, the increase in the book value of foreign direct investment in Canada from the end of 1978 until the end of 1985 was $35.7 billion (row 5), yet the cumulative inflow of foreign direct investment as recorded in Canada's balance of payments accounts was actually − $4.9 billion (row 12). At the same time, the increase in the book value of Canadian direct investment abroad was $34 billion, and the contribution made by foreign direct investment outflows was $24.8 billion, or 73 percent of the total (row 14).

Canada's bilateral relationship with the United States in foreign direct investment assets is even more startling. The growth of U.S. direct investment in Canada was $25.1 billion over the period (row 6) despite a cumulative capital outflow from Canada of $12.5 billion (row 13). Meantime the growth of Canadian direct investment in the United States was slightly greater at $26.5 billion (row 2), of which $16.2 billion was financed by capital outflows from Canada (row 15). This suggests that the typical U.S. direct investment in Canada was by an already established multinational wishing to expand or diversify operations using retained earnings, whereas the typical Canadian direct investment in the United States was by a Canadian firm seeking to establish a presence and secure access to the U.S. market.

According to rows 12-15, Canada has been a net exporter of foreign direct investment capital both bilaterally with the United States and in aggregate every year throughout the period from 1978 to 1985, which stands in sharp contrast to its traditional role as a substantial net importer. However, it does not follow from this that Canada's net liability position in foreign direct investment assets has been steadily declining. In fact, the increase in foreign direct investment assets in Canada has continued to outstrip the increase in Canadian direct investment assets abroad (although on a bilateral basis with the United States, Canada's net liability position has actually declined slightly). The reason for this is the overwhelming contribution of retained earnings to the expansion and diversification of existing multinational enterprises operating in Canada and the fact that retained earnings do not enter Canada's balance of payments accounts even though they should be treated as a debit on current account (an import of capital services) and a credit on capital account (an inflow of foreign direct investment capital).

The experience of the last several years illustrates the need to distinguish carefully between foreign direct investment flows (as recorded in the balance of payments statistics) and the contribution of foreign savings to domestic capital formation, which is much larger. Unless Canada becomes an attractive location for new foreign direct investment, it can look forward to a steady net outflow of direct investment capital while its net international indebtedness position continues to increase.[16] This pattern of net outflows is a predictable phenomenon that is quite independent of trade liberalization. It must eventually happen with or without an FTA because the stock of foreign capital invested in Canada is so much larger than the stock of Canadian capital invested abroad. However, an FTA ought to reduce, if not reverse, the net outflow from Canada at least temporarily as new avenues for inward direct investment are opened up. In addition, the flow of Canadian direct investment abroad that reflects a purely defensive reaction to the growing risk of U.S. protectionism should abate under an FTA.

In sum, an FTA should tend to stimulate foreign direct investment flows in both directions, with no strong presumption that the overall impact will be biased one way or the other. This follows because an FTA will not only promote conventional arm's-length trade but will also promote trade within multinational firms, and intrafirm trade constitutes a substantial proportion of U.S.-Canadian trade. By improving the climate for the internationalization of production within North America, an FTA should stimulate a host of complementary investments within the typical multinational enterprise along the lines of comparative advantage. Assuming that an FTA is comprehensive with respect to the elimination of barriers to trade but conservative with respect to the development of Canada's natural resources and energy for the North

16. Foreign direct investment flows reflect the difference between the earnings on existing assets and the annual increase in the stocks. Thus, if all of the earnings cannot be profitably invested in Canada, there will be a net outflow of foreign direct investment even though the stock continues to grow.

American market, the growth of long-term liabilities to foreigners should decline over time as the increased supply of Canadian savings finances more of Canada's expanded investment opportunities. Finally, the rate of growth of Canada's net international indebtedness position (as recorded in row 10 of table 1) should decline, although whether the level of net indebtedness will cease to grow remains debatable, given the dominant role played by the retained earnings of existing foreign enterprises in financing new investment opportunities in Canada.

Conclusion

In assessing the effect of an FTA on new investment and plant location, it is important to keep in mind the current situation. For several years Canada has been suffering from lagging investment and productivity growth and a deteriorating international competitive position. It has become increasingly apparent that this cannot be reversed without an FTA. Therefore the fundamental objective for Canada should be secure access into the U.S. market for as wide a range of goods and services as possible. The tighter the limits on the use of contingency protection and the more comprehensive the application of the principle of national treatment, the more favorable will be the long-run prospects for investment and plant location in Canada. If an FTA removes or substantially reduces the threat of contingency protection, it will serve to allay fears about locating new plants in Canada to serve the North American market. In the present environment, the risk of contingency protection poses a much greater threat to firms choosing a Canadian location over a U.S. location. The typical firm that locates in Canada to serve the North American market would sell most of its output to the United States, whereas the typical firm that locates in the United States would sell only a minor fraction of its output to Canada. Of course, there will always remain some risk of dislocation if an FTA were to be abrogated, but that kind of risk is currently being faced and has resulted in a great deal of defensive foreign direct investment by Canadians in the United States in recent years.

An FTA is not a zero-sum game for long-run investment in which one country stands to gain investment at the expense of the other. By eliminating trade barriers and reducing the risk that they might be erected under future unspecified conditions, the entire North American market becomes a more attractive location for investment in general from anywhere in the world. Since an FTA will undoubtedly divert some trade between North America and the rest of the world, it will tend to encourage investment from third countries seeking to recapture lost markets.

The impact of an FTA on plant location and investment flows is an empirical question that cannot be resolved by purely theoretical analysis. Whether an FTA would lead to an increase in the number of firms or plants operating in Canada and how it might affect direct investment flows are interesting questions in their own right, but the answers should not compromise the central point that the real incomes of Canadians will be higher under an FTA. If more foreign investment is desirable, it is optimal policy to subsidize it and not to achieve an appropriate level indirectly by manipulating trade barriers. An FTA as envisaged here would be consistent with any conceivable level of foreign ownership and control of the Canadian economy, since Canada could reserve the right to screen new foreign investment as well as to repatriate specific sectors of its economy at fair market value. In fact, reducing the level of foreign ownership and control of any sector would be more feasible under an FTA than under present conditions because it could be financed from the higher real incomes that an FTA would bring.

There is no doubt that an FTA would put greater restraints on Canadian (and U.S.) policy formulation by removing from the politicians' tool kit a variety of instruments that have been used (and abused) in the past. But this would be good for Canada, since it would make credible the government's new posture of promoting the national interest rather than special interests. The quest for economic rents would be discouraged by the government's inability to accommodate special interests, and a climate more conducive to entrepreneurship and wealth creation would be established.

Weak natural resource and energy prices for the rest of this decade and perhaps well into the 1990s may mean that Canadians can no longer hitch a ride on their resource base to raise their real incomes as they have in the past. While a secure energy supply will undoubtedly remain a valuable asset and a powerful inducement to plant location in Canada, the fact remains that large gains in terms of trade are not in prospect. This makes it even more important in Canada to have assured access to a large market for its manufactured goods and processed and semiprocessed raw materials if it wishes to avoid an ever-widening gap in living standards between itself and its neighbor to the south.

Comments by Randall Wigle

Burgess analyzes Canadian fears and concerns about proposed free trade arrangements (FTAs) with the United States, particularly those fears relating to factor flows and plant location. My intention is to briefly summarize Burgess's responses to the concerns, and supply my own comments where I feel they are warranted.

The first Canadian concern discussed is that an FTA will lead to the closing of the Canadian subsidiaries of many U.S.-based enterprises, since it would no longer be necessary to produce those lines behind Canada's tariff wall. Burgess points out that this argument ignores the fact that any *bilateral* FTA will have offsetting locational incentives for firms that previously located in the United States (rather than Canada) for a symmetric reason. On balance, Burgess's argument is undoubtedly valid but it does ignore two important qualifications. First, there are plants that produce the same lines in Canada and the United States, and these lines might well be relocated to the United States, particularly where the Canadian production runs are much shorter. It would be very nice to know how many such product lines there are, but I expect they are few, given the Canadian government's willingness to provide duty remissions, and the level of current protection. The second qualification is that the locational incentives would not be offsetting to the extent that Canadian tariffs on manufactures are higher than those in the United States.

The second concern addressed is that an FTA would deprive Canada of much new investment because it would become more attractive to serve Canada from the United States. My only comment is that if this concern is with the level of new investment, I think Burgess deals with the concern quite effectively. If, however, the relevant concern is with the level of investment in *manufacturing* (which it well might be), I think we need a different line of response altogether than that supplied.

The third concern is that if an FTA succeeds in raising real wages in Canada (as Harris suggests), then Canadian location will lose a large part of its cost advantage. Burgess responds (correctly) that this argument confuses cause and effect.

Finally, Burgess addresses the concern that an FTA will expose many small Canadian firms to takeover by larger U.S.-based companies. He notes there is an associated fear of an FTA being associated with large net capital inflows and excessive foreign ownership.

Harris presents results that suggest that a bilateral free trade arrangement with the United States would be associated with large capital inflows and a dramatic (28 percent) increase in the Canadian real wage.[17] Burgess argues that the large capital inflows are to some extent an aberration, because the Harris model does not allow increases in real income to generate increased savings, which, it would be hoped, would partially displace some of the U.S. investment. On this subject, I have a few things to say.

First, I am highly skeptical that there is any widespread suspicion that a future FTA with the United States will increase the Canadian real wage by over 25 percent. Second, if my simple calculations are correct, the increased savings generated annually by the increased real income of workers would be sufficient to replace only 5 percent of the once-and-for-all capital inflow. Third, and perhaps most important in cases like these, attempting to reinterpret existing results of numerical models does have its limitations. I do believe that using the Harris and Harris-Cox results as a backdrop does reveal the importance of other extraneous but important considerations more clearly than might otherwise be the case. What is not clear to me is that by introducing endogenous savings behavior one necessarily leaves the rest of the Harris results intact.

Having said all of these things, I do believe that the exercise undertaken by Burgess is a useful one, given the uncertain state of the theoretical work concerning plant location and multinational firms.

17. Harris, "Summary of a Project on the General Equilibrium Evaluation of Canadian Trade Policy," p. 173.

MELVYN FUSS and LEONARD WAVERMAN

A Sectoral Perspective: Automobiles

THE 1965 auto pact between Canada and the United States is a carefully designed scheme that uses the incentive of duty remission to encourage designated auto assemblers to rationalize their North American production facilities. Before the auto pact, Canada imposed substantial tariffs on the entry of assembled passenger cars as well as parts. These tariffs were designed to protect the domestic Canadian industry from imports from the United States. Completed vehicles faced a 17.5 percent tariff. Remission of duties was allowed on imported parts (not cars) as long as the Canadian assembler maintained domestic content of 60 percent in passenger cars and 50 percent in commercial vehicles. Because of the tariff barrier, most models were produced in Canada, resulting in inefficient, high-cost production, small scale, short production runs, and higher prices.[1] There was little trade in finished automobiles across the U.S. border and no exports of parts from Canada.

In 1960, in the face of a large and growing deficit in auto trade, the Canadian federal government appointed a one-man royal commission (the Bladen commission) to investigate the automotive industry. The commission's report, issued in April 1961, recommended a duty-free zone for auto trade between Canada and the United States subject to a number of contingency protection clauses for Canada. The cornerstone of the report was the need to increase the scale of production in Canada,

The authors wish to thank the Donner Canadian Foundation for financial support.

1. Carl E. Beigie, *The Canada-U.S. Automotive Agreement: An Evaluation* (Montreal: Canadian-American Committee, 1970).

principally through the production and export of automotive parts.[2] In November 1962 the Canadian government instituted the first of two duty remission schemes. Automotive parts exported from Canada earned a dollar-for-dollar remission of duty on imports into Canada of automatic transmissions or partially assembled engines. The second scheme expanded the allowable imports to all original equipment automotive parts as well as finished vehicles.[3] U.S. parts manufacturers called these plans "unfair subsidies" and lobbied in Washington for countervailing duties.

The 1965 Auto Pact

While the United States was considering action against Canada, a series of meetings between Canadian and U.S. officials led to the negotiation and ratification of an "agreement concerning automotive products" between the two countries—the auto pact—in 1965. It is important to recognize that the auto pact is not a free trade agreement, but an elaborate duty remission scheme open to a limited number of automotive assemblers. It was not a bold initiative, but an extension (with important advantages) of the Canadian duty remission schemes first used in 1962. The pact appears to have been signed with the two participating countries holding different expectations as to the evolution of trade under it. For Canada, Canadian content protection was paramount and was ensured as long as the duty remission provisions remained in place. For the United States, the content provisions were expected to be temporary (perhaps three to five years), after which unrestricted trade would prevail at the manufacturing level.

The auto pact allowed duty-free importation of parts and vehicles into both the United States and Canada if certain conditions were met. Imports of finished vehicles and parts for assembly from Canada would be duty free into the United States if there were a minimum North American content of 50 percent (but not if the imports came from a third country). Parts for assembly and vehicles from anywhere in the world would be duty free into Canada under the following three conditions:

2. V. Bladen, *Report of the Royal Commission on the Automotive Industry* (Ottawa: Queen's Printer, 1961), p. 67.
3. See Henrick O. Helmers, *The United States–Canadian Automobile Agreement: A Study in Industry Adjustment* (University of Michigan, Graduate School of Business Administration, 1967), p. 14.

1. The importer had to be a "qualified Canadian manufacturer." Imported parts could come from independent U.S. parts producers (or European or Asian producers) as long as they were used in assembly of a finished vehicle in Canada.

2. The manufacturer had to maintain the 1964 ratio of Canadian vehicle production to vehicle sales in Canada, or 75 percent, whichever was higher.

3. Canadian content had to be no less than the actual dollar amount achieved in the 1964 model year.

In addition, a letter of undertaking from the four qualified Canadian manufacturers (American Motors, Chrysler, Ford, and General Motors) stated that by 1969 they would increase their value added in Canada by an amount equal to 60 percent of the growth in the sales value of cars relative to 1964 and 50 percent of the growth in the sales value of commercial vehicles sold in Canada, plus an additional $260 million.[4]

Most commentators argued that this agreement, by eliminating U.S. tariffs, allowing the duty-free importation of finished cars into Canada, and allowing North American automobile manufacturers to meet the Canadian content rule by exporting parts, would lead to a rationalization of the Canadian automobile industry.

The auto pact of 1965 is not a symmetric treaty. It allows automotive firms based in Canada duty-free entry into the United States (subject to a minimum North American content); it allows firms based in Canada duty remission in exchange for production requirements in Canada. This asymmetry between the provisions for the two countries has led to periodic controversy over the years.

The "Big Four" assemblers had three alternative strategies open to them to meet the 1965 content rules. First, the Canadian content provisions could be met by assembly of cars principally for the Canadian market and by the purchase in Canada of most of the parts required for those vehicles. Since this was the inefficient pattern of operation before the auto pact, it was unlikely to continue after the pact. A second scenario could have been to rationalize auto assembly, exporting and importing cars and purchasing Canadian-produced parts for an entire model run in Canada or the United States (the scenario envisioned by Bladen). A third scenario was to expand assembly in Canada beyond the point required by rationalization, export vehicles, and earn content credits on

4. For parts, the floor constraint was simply to maintain the same absolute level of value added achieved in 1964.

the Canadian value added embodied in these exported vehicles. In this case, Canadian parts would be purchased only in sufficient quantities to meet the minimum content requirements. Because economies of scale are greater in the production of many parts than in assembly, and there is greater relative protection of assembly than parts in the Canadian portion of the auto pact, this final alternative dominated.[5]

The important element that must be considered in evaluating the auto pact is the realism of the dream for the growth of the Canadian parts industry. It was hoped that the opening up of the U.S. assembly market to Canadian parts producers would increase the scale and efficiency of parts production. However, Canadian parts could not be imported duty free for the U.S. replacement parts market. This forced Canadian parts producers to sell to the four assemblers. In any case, given the virulent opposition of many U.S. parts producers to the duty remission schemes of 1962 and 1963, a substantial use of Canadian parts in U.S. assembly might have been difficult to achieve. The recommendations of the Bladen commission required that Canadian content be calculated on the *sum* of production in Canada and the imports of vehicles and repair or service parts. Such a scheme required increased use of Canadian parts. The auto pact (actually the letters of undertaking) calculates Canadian content based on *sales* in Canada, thus diminishing the need to utilize or export Canadian-made parts.

The Structure of the Canadian Automobile Industry

Table 1 provides some statistics on auto trade between Canada and the United States. The total value of auto vehicle and parts trade was $366.7 million in 1961; in 1966, the year after the auto pact, this trade was valued at $2,354 million. In 1961 Canada imported 16,574 vehicles from the United States and exported a mere 175. In 1966 car exports from Canada to the United States were nearly 147,000, and in 1984 over 1 million.

Auto parts have been a growing source of trade between Canada and the United States, but have been the source of a frequent Canadian deficit in auto trade with the United States under the auto pact. In 1984

5. Bladen, *Report of the Royal Commission;* and Lawrence J. White, *The American Automobile Industry since 1945* (Harvard University Press, 1971).

Table 1. *Canadian-U.S. Auto Trade, Selected Years, 1961–84*
Millions of Canadian dollars

Year	Canadian imports from U.S.		Canadian exports to U.S.	
	Motor vehicles	Parts	Motor vehicles	Parts
1961	65.5	292.0	0.4	8.8
1962	69.4	378.8	0.4	10.1
1965	153.5	797.9	80.6	150.2
1966	384.0	1,093.0	488.0	389.0
1973	2,082.0	3,553.0	3,060.0	2,171.0
1974	2,531.0	3,892.0	3,407.0	1,953.0
1975	3,126.0	4,522.0	3,790.0	2,045.0
1978	4,360.0	8,086.0	7,033.0	4,746.0
1979	5,699.0	8,659.0	6,706.0	4,488.0
1980	4,605.0	7,600.0	6,670.0	3,405.0
1982	3,748.0	9,676.0	11,116.0	4,902.0
1983	5,852.3	10,852.4	13,599.6	6,882.2
1984	7,914.2	14,654.6	18,986.6	9,484.8

Sources: Statistics Canada, *Exports by Countries*, catalog 65-003, various issues; *Exports by Commodities*, catalog 65-004, various issues; *Imports by Countries*, catalog 65-006, various issues; and *Imports by Commodities*, catalog 65-007, various issues.

Canada imported $5.2 billion more in parts from the United States than it exported; half of all the imported parts were the result of transactions within multinational enterprises. In 1984 Canada exported $11.1 billion more in finished vehicles to the United States than it imported. Thus, on balance Canada had a net surplus in auto trade with the United States of $5.9 billion. The auto pact has not provided the incentive for parts production envisioned by Bladen; Canada has become an assembler of cars.

In 1961 five automobile producers assembled some forty-nine nameplates in Canada, totaling 327,000 passenger vehicles. White concluded that minimum efficient scale required assembling 400,000 units of a single car model, with a higher requirement for engines and transmissions.[6] Thus the output of the *entire* Canadian auto industry in 1961 was less than White's estimate of the efficient level for a single plant producing one model.

The auto pact allowed for (but did not mandate) the rationalization of

6. White's analysis was undertaken for the U.S. market. We are assuming that the same underlying technology existed in Canada, a reasonable assumption given that the same firms produced cars on both sides of the border.

North American production facilities. Finished vehicles could be imported and the required import duty not paid if the provisions of the pact were met. Beigie describes how the designated manufacturers rationalized their production in the years immediately following 1965.[7] GM concentrated its Canadian production in Chevrolet; Ford phased out two chassis sizes in Canada; Chrysler by 1965 was producing only two nameplates and one chassis size in Canada. Trade in vehicles and auto parts verifies the impact of the pact, as shown in table 1. Yet Canada continued to run a deficit in auto trade with the United States: $1.8 billion in 1975 and $2.1 billion in 1980. In no year has Canada had a surplus in parts trade with the United States. Overall Canadian auto trade with the United States moved into surplus in 1982 and has remained in surplus (at substantial levels) since that year. This reversal in the trade account has little to do with the rationalization of the auto industry in Canada, which clearly occurred at least a decade before 1982. The current account surplus in auto trade was due to the devaluation of the Canadian dollar, which lowered the relative costs of production in Canada.

In a larger study, we have examined in detail the sources of costs and productivity differentials between automobile manufacturing in Canada and the United States over 1961–80.[8] In the fifteen years between 1962–64 and 1977–79, unit production costs fell in Canada relative to those in the United States, so that in the latter period Canadian unit production costs were well below those in the United States. This overall relative decline in Canadian unit production costs was itself the result of several conflicting movements. First was the substantial improvement in the scale of Canadian automobile production—a result that some would attribute to the auto pact of 1965. However, when scale effects are removed, the efficiency level of Canadian auto production declined relative to U.S. production in the period following the auto pact.[9]

We examined a hypothetical world where net automotive imports

7. Beigie, *The Canada-U.S. Automotive Agreement,* pp. 21–23.
8. See Melvyn A. Fuss and Leonard Waverman, "The Canada-U.S. Auto Pact of 1965: An Experiment in Selective Trade Liberalization" National Bureau of Economic Research Working Paper 1953 (Cambridge, Mass.: NBER, June 1986), and *Costs and Productivity in Automobile Production: Japan, the United States, Canada, and Germany* (Cambridge University Press, forthcoming).
9. Relative price changes between the United States and Canada occurred over the fifteen-year period, some to Canada's advantage and some to the U.S. advantage. Relative changes in product mix (as we measured it) and capacity utilization had no major impact over this period (except in 1980).

(cars and parts) from the United States to Canada remained at the low prepact level and where exports from Canada to the United States above the prepact levels would not have occurred. In this hypothetical world, Canadian auto firms produce for the domestic market rather than being integrated into the North American market. Using these hypothetical data, we calculated that in 1970–72 the auto pact reduced unit production costs in Canada by 3.1 percent over what they would have been without the pact.[10] The data suggest that most the improvements in the scale of operations in the Canadian automobile industry over 1962–64 to 1970–72 would have occurred anyway through the growth of the domestic market. We also estimated that the auto pact lowered Canadian unit production costs by 1.7 percent in 1977–79. These results are in the expected direction but lower than the proponents of the pact would suggest. We attribute the continued efficiency gap mainly to the limited free trade contained in the auto pact. The pact allowed, but did not force, increased efficiency, at the same time as it increased the effective protection of the oligopolistic industry.

The Japanese Presence

Since 1980 several significant events have shaken the auto industry in both Canada and the United States. In 1980 capacity utilization was at a postwar low in both countries (58 percent in the United States, 62 percent in Canada). The rapid rise of gasoline prices in 1979–80 shifted consumer demand to the more fuel-efficient Japanese car imports. The rapid rise in Japanese imports in both Canada and the United States in 1980 (to 20 percent of the U.S. market and 21 percent in Canada) led to import controls. The voluntary restraint agreement imposed by the United States in 1981 maintained Japanese imports at 20 percent of the market. The United States ostensibly dropped the restraints in 1985, and the Japanese government now controls exports to the United States. Canadian authorities imposed their own version of these voluntary restric-

10. Before the pact, some rationalization could have occurred, since parts effectively were importable if a 60 percent domestic-content requirement was met. One might then assume that at least 40 percent of the costs of producing a car in Canada was a minimum level. If the pact lowered unit production costs in Canada by 3 percent relative to U.S. production costs, then it represented a 5 percent reduction (3 percent ÷ 60 percent) in the Canadian costs.

tions, maintaining Japanese imports at 18 percent of the Canadian market. Canada now holds Japanese car imports at 21 percent of sales.

Japanese auto producers had excess demand for their products in North American markets after 1980. Prevented from importing the number of cars that consumers wanted, Japanese producers undertook two strategies: they raised the price and quality of cars imported, and they announced they would establish auto plants for North American assembly. The decision to produce cars in North America probably was intended to remove the voluntary trade restrictions and prevent more permanent constraints.

The entry of Japanese firms as local producers is changing the structure of the North American automobile industry and its labor relations. This entry has created competition among jurisdictions for the plants and has put pressure on the auto pact since these firms are not as yet "designated" manufacturers. Honda was the first entrant into North America, initially producing small sedans in Ohio in 1982. Nissan began assembling light trucks (which faced a 25 percent tariff) in Smyrna, Tennessee; in March 1985 this plant was altered so as to produce small sedans. In the fall of 1983, GM and Toyota announced a joint venture in a closed GM assembly plant in Fremont, California. Chrysler has announced a joint venture in Illinois with Mitsubishi for fall 1988 production; Mazda has begun construction of a facility in Michigan to produce cars for itself and possibly for Ford. Toyota and Fuji/Isuzu have announced plans for assembly facilities in the United States as well. In total, the Japanese U.S.-based plants now in production or announced will add capacity to assemble 1,770,000 cars annually. This volume is 18 percent of the 1986 capacity of U.S. car makers and 77 percent of present Japanese auto exports to the United States.

The Canadian authorities witnessing the Japanese investment induced by the U.S. restraints acted to entice Japanese investments to Canada. Three Japanese passenger vehicle assembly plants have been announced for construction in Canada. GM-Suzuki plan a 200,000-unit assembly plant aimed at the North American market. This plant will probably meet the auto pact's Canadian content provisions because of excess credits available to GM. Honda and Toyota have announced auto assembly plants of 80,000 and 50,000 units respectively; the planned Canadian value added for these two plants is unlikely, at least in the short run, to meet auto pact minimums. Therefore they will be liable for duty on imported components into Canada. Among the enticements that attracted these plants to Canada is one that has attracted special criticism in the United States—duty remission.

Duty Remission, Once Again

In 1975 the Canadian government reintroduced duty remission for foreign auto manufacturers who were not qualified for duty-free entry under the auto pact. This scheme allowed duty remission on finished vehicles to the extent of the Canadian value added in equipment or parts exported from Canada to countries *other* than the United States and physically embodied in the actual vehicles imported into Canada. In 1978 the scheme was changed to allow the remission of duty on imported vehicles to the extent of the Canadian value added in parts exported but not necessarily "reimported" in finished vehicles. The scheme was not easy to implement and was not used by importers.

In the early 1980s the Canadian Financial Administration Act was amended to give the governor-in-council authority to remit duties and taxes. This change made duty remission a subject of cabinet discretion. The additional simplification of the act in 1983 greatly expanded its use. Two levels of benefits became possible. A foreign assembler who does not have significant manufacturing facilities in Canada can export Canadian-made original equipment and parts to any part of the world and receive 70 percent duty remission on imported vehicles if the Canadian value added of the parts exceeds the dutiable value of the vehicles. If the manufacturer is commited to constructing "significant" manufacturing facilities in Canada, 100 percent duty remission is possible. On March 14, 1985 (retroactive to August 1, 1984), these duty remission schemes were expanded to include exports of parts to the United States.

Two firms have received 100 percent remission orders—Volkswagen in 1982 and Honda in 1985. Toyota, which now has a 70 percent remission order, most likely will receive 100 percent. Seven other firms—Jaguar, Mazda, Mercedes-Benz, Nissan, Peugeot, Subaru, and BMW—have received 70 percent duty remission orders.

In 1981 the United States objected in writing to a draft of the Volkswagen remission order. Representative John D. Dingell, chairman of the House Subcommittee on Oversight and Investigations, recently raised the issue of these duty remission schemes (and their applicability to exports to the United States) in letters to the U.S. Trade Representative. The Office of the U.S. Trade Representative concluded on investigation that: "Canada's duty remission program is a subsidy to the export of Canadian-manufactured auto parts. As such it appears to be inconsistent with Article 9 of the [GATT] subsidies code. . . . Duty remission is contrary to the commitments in Article 1 of the Auto Pact . . ."[11] The U.S. Motor and Equipment Manufacturers Association and the Automotive Parts and Accessories Association have lobbied against the duty remission scheme.

Three questions arise: are such duty remission schemes export subsidies; are they likely to cause material injury to U.S. manufacturers and be subject to countervail; and are they inconsistent with the auto pact?

Are Duty Remissions Export Subsidies?

The U.S. Trade Representative cites two reasons for classifying the duty remission scheme as an export subsidy. First, GATT article 9, item 1, cites as an illustrative export subsidy "the remission or drawback of import charges in excess of those levied on goods that are physically incorporated . . . in the export product." Second, article 16 defines as an export subsidy "any subsidy . . . which operates directly or indirectly to increase exports of any product from . . . [the subsidizing country]."

It is unclear whether article 16 does apply to the case of duty remission schemes. No subsidy is paid to the exporter. The price he receives is the same whether the part is exported under the duty remission scheme or not. If the buyer is the assembler-importer, his cost is lower with the scheme than without it, the difference in price being the duty that would have been paid on the import had the part not been purchased and exported from Canada. If the assembler-importer sells the part to a third party, the subsidy element is very indirect, since neither the seller nor the ultimate buyer of the part receives any benefits (or subsidy) from the scheme.

GATT article 9 was addressed, in part, to such duty remission schemes. The Canadian scheme would appear to be in conflict with this article because the exported parts do not have to be reimported in

11. Memorandum, Office of the U.S. Trade Representative, July 22, 1986.

finished vehicles but can be exported to any country for any purpose. The subsidy is small. The Canadian tariff on cars is not exceptionally high at 9.2 percent as of January 1987. An auto assembler with no Canadian manufacturing who imports 30,000 cars at an average whole-sale price of $10,000 Canadian each (total wholesale revenue of $300 million) would pay a duty of $27,600,000. To save this $27,600,000, the importer with a 70 percent duty remission order would have to export Canadian auto parts with a Canadian value added of $428,570,000. For an assembler-importer the duty remission scheme saves 6.4 cents per dollar of Canadian value added exported, not an enormous subsidy.

It would be to the benefit of the assembler-importer to use the duty remission scheme if, at the margin, the exported Canadian part was not more than 6.4 percent more expensive than the foreign-produced part. Given the cost of transport to Japan or Europe, the duty remission scheme does not appear to be a compelling export subsidy. If the assembler-importer builds "significant" manufacturing facilities in Canada, the export subsidy is increased by 43 percent, making the savings 9.2 percent of imports.

Is the Duty Remission Scheme Significant?

The duty remission scheme is unlikely to prove to be of material injury to U.S. producers. First, the subsidy element is small. Second, a parts manufacturer who sells to a "qualified" Canadian assembler under the auto pact does not pay duty on imports in either country. None of the assemblers presently having duty remission orders are "qualified" manufacturers under the pact. However, for duty-free entry of parts into the United States, only 50 percent North American content is required. As a result, exports of Canadian-made parts to the United States by firms who maintain 50 percent North American content (VW, Nissan, Honda, and Toyota) would be duty free. The Canadian duty remission scheme would then involve a net potential cost savings of 6.4 percent from producing parts in Canada and shipping to an auto pact assembler in the United States and a 3.9 percent savings to a nonqualifying assembler, neither terribly significant. The other recipients of the duty remission orders have no U.S. assembly plants, so U.S. parts manufac-turers are not directly threatened. If an assembly plant in a third country was indifferent between auto parts from Canada and similar parts from the United States because they were equal in quality and price, the

Canadian duty remission scheme would tip the decision toward purchasing the Canadian parts.

In 1985 there was minimal use of this duty remission scheme. The total duty remitted under all twelve outstanding duty remission orders was $1.3 million, which therefore must have come from exports of $16 million of auto parts.[12]

Is Duty Remission Contrary to the Auto Pact?

The duty remission scheme is not contrary to the specific provisions or intent of the auto pact for several reasons. First, the auto pact itself is a duty remission scheme. Second, exports to the United States under such a duty remission order are dutiable on entry (as they would be if they came from any third country), unless the U.S. assembler qualifies under the auto pact for duty-free entry of parts. Third, there always has been significant bilateral auto parts trade between Canada and the United States outside the auto pact, specifically in parts designed for the "after purchase" market. Fourth, the designers of the auto pact did not envision either a day when the "Big Four" producers would be threatened by offshore imports, or a voluntary restraint agreement with such importers. In 1965 large-scale investment by foreign assemblers in North America was not foreseen. Canadian authorities have acted to ensure that the Canadian economy was not hurt unduly by these unforeseen developments. Finally, the biases of the auto pact toward assembly in Canada induced corrective action in terms of incentives toward parts exports and production. These actions, in our opinion, do not violate the spirit or the letter of the auto pact.

Free Trade Negotiations and the Auto Pact

The talks now under way between Canada and the United States cast a new focus on the auto pact. The United States appears to view the content provisions of the pact as unnecessary protection for the Canadian automotive industry. Canadians view the contingent protection in the pact as both necessary and as a likely model for the manufacturing sector

12. Half was from VW under a 100 percent duty remission order, and the other half was from BMW and Mercedes-Benz under 70 percent remission orders. *Toronto Globe and Mail*, November 17, 1986.

as a whole. Canadians also appear to view the pact as substantially increasing the efficiency of Canadian auto production. U.S. trade representatives appear to want the auto pact included in the free trade area negotiations, while their Canadian counterparts are reluctant to renegotiate the auto pact.

Where does the situation go from here? We would not use the auto pact as a model of general applicability to all manufacturing industry. The key to long-run survival for the auto industry in either country is long-run efficiency in production, something Canada has yet to achieve in the auto industry. Contingency protection has its cost, as do bureaucratic rules and biases induced by specific codes.

A more generalized free trade pact between Canada and the United States for most commodities would, under article 24 of GATT, probably have to include commodities yielding at least 80 percent of present trade between the two countries. On the surface, then, autos would have to be included in the present negotiations, as the auto sector involves nearly 25 percent of the trade between the two countries. The 1965 auto pact, however, was approved by GATT and thus conceivably could be outside a future free trade pact.[13] On the other hand, the United States or GATT could suggest that both the ancillary letters of undertaking signed in 1965 between the Canadian federal government and the then "Big Four" producers and the Canadian duty remission scheme for parts are contrary to free trade.

Trade is always analyzed in different terms by the two parties. The United States sees the present overall deficit in automotive trade with Canada and "facilitating factors" such as the letters of undertaking with the major North American assemblers and the duty remission schemes of the last ten years. Canada sees the history of fifty years of overall deficit, nine years of overall surplus, and continuing deficits in parts trade. In both countries, as elsewhere, the automotive industry is undergoing profound structural changes. Consolidations and joint ventures signal increased concentration. Manufacturers are adding significant new capacity in North America and elsewhere. The "Big Four" are no longer all North American firms. Japanese and Korean companies are significant players or manufacturers in the North American auto market. Both the United States and Canada want as much domestic content as

13. The Canadian provisions did not have to be approved by GATT since they did not single out for special favor imports from any specific country. The U.S. provisions, allowing duty-free entry only from Canada, did require and receive GATT approval.

is possible from these new domestic assemblers. It is unlikely, therefore, that either country will want to dismantle the auto pact immediately.[14] With satisfactory rules of origin generally agreed upon, however, the American side may well argue for a phased removal of the auto pact's safeguards. (Without effective rules of origin, Canada could be a conduit for low-priced entry into the U.S. market as long as current exchange rates persist.)

Should Canada continue to view provisions of the type in the auto pact and contingent protection as essential? Our deeper analysis, only cursorily described here, suggests that the auto pact was not of great value in terms of improving the efficiency of Canadian automobile production, the sine qua non for long-term growth and wealth. A larger number of qualified manufacturers (as will happen in the medium term) and greater competition in the Canadian market may increase the efficiency of Canadian production. There is a trade-off between the short-term objective of the government—jobs—and the longer-term efficiency of Canadian production. It is only by concentrating on efficiency that long-term jobs will be guaranteed. Domestic-content rules and contingent-protection schemes must be carefully analyzed to determine the exact nature of the trade-off and whether the benefits are worth the cost.

14. For two reasons, the United States could technically ask for a renegotiation of the auto pact. First, the short-term contingency protection clauses inserted by the Canadian government are still in effect, twenty-one years later. Second, a free trade pact between the two countries should, under GATT rules, cover 80 percent of present trade, as noted above.

ROBERT W. CRANDALL

A Sectoral Perspective: Steel

THE PAST DECADE has not been kind to steelmakers in any developed country. In the early 1970s, they had all planned upon reaping substantial rewards from rapid economic growth and the resulting periodic shortages of steel. Many large companies—including some in the United States and Canada—launched ambitious expansion plans that often went sour when demand failed to grow. Unfortunately, steel consumption in the developed world has remained below its 1974 level in the fifth year of an economic expansion, and it is now quite clear that many of these investment programs will never pay for themselves.

Canadian and U.S. steel producers share many of the problems of steelmakers elsewhere in the world, but the Canadian companies appear generally healthier. The U.S. integrated industry is declining rapidly, while two of the three large integrated producers in Canada seem to have weathered the 1970s and early 1980s more successfully. In this paper, I shall attempt to explain this divergence in economic performance and to ask whether it is likely to continue.

The U.S. Steel Industry

Since 1970 U.S. integrated steel producers have found it impossible to build new plants. The last plant—Bethlehem's Burns Harbor facility—was completed in 1969, and even though plans were made for others, none has been built. Part of the reason for this inability to build new facilities has been the slow growth in demand. Steel consumption in the United States has been far below its 1973–74 peak in the 1980s (table 1),

231

Table 1. *The U.S. Steel Industry, 1970–85*
Million tons per year unless otherwise indicated

Indicator	1970	1974	1978	1982	1985
Finished steel consumption	97.1	119.6	116.6	76.4	96.4
Raw steel production	131.5	145.7	137.0	74.6	88.3
Raw steel capacity	153.8	157.0	157.9	154.0	133.6
Integrated raw steel production	124.5	137.7	125.0	60.6	70.7
Integrated raw steel capacity	146.3	148.0	143.9	136.0	111.8
Minimill raw steel production	7.0	8.0	12.0	14.0	17.6
Total compensation per hour for production workers (U.S. dollars)	5.68	9.08	14.30	23.78	22.50
Scrap prices (1967 = 100)	120.0	242.6	139.1	88.0	98.0

Sources: American Iron and Steel Institute, *Annual Statistical Report* (Washington, D.C.: AISI, various years); Donald F. Barnett and Robert W. Crandall, *Up from the Ashes: The Rise of the Steel Minimill in the United States* (Brookings, 1986); and data from U.S. Department of Labor, Bureau of Labor Statistics.

and many industry observers believe that it may not return to its 1973–74 level again in this century.

Impact of Slow Growth

Slow growth has had two related effects upon the big steel companies. First, it has produced low prices and low capacity utilization because they had been planning for much greater demand. The 1975 forecast of the American Iron and Steel Institute for 1983 raw steel production was 170 million tons; the actual figure was 85 million tons.[1]

Second, the slow growth in demand has placed enormous downward pressure upon scrap prices because potential scrap supply has been growing while demand has been falling. These low scrap prices make the melting of scrap in electric furnaces very attractive relative to the production of steel from iron ore, coal, and limestone. Since electric furnace facilities have a minimum efficient scale of only 250,000–500,000 tons rather than the 3 million to 5 million tons required annually in an integrated works, there has been rapid entry of small "minimill" steel companies in the past ten years, substantially eroding the larger integrated companies' market share. Minimills now account for 22 million tons of capacity, a dramatic rise from 10 million tons in 1975. These

1. American Iron and Steel Institute, *Steel Industry Economics and Federal Income Tax Policy* (Washington, D.C.: AISI, June 1975).

Table 2. *The Outlook for U.S. Steel Producers, 1985–2000*
Million tons per year

Indicator	1985	1990	2000
Steel consumption	96.4	98.0	100.0
U.S. raw steel production	88.3	90.0	79.9
Integrated raw steel production	70.7	68.1	49.0
Integrated raw steel capacity	111.8	80.1	57.6
Minimill raw steel production	17.6	21.9	30.8
Minimill raw steel capacity	22.0	25.0	35.2
Imports (finished and semifinished)	24.3	24.5	30.0

Source: Barnett and Crandall, *Up from the Ashes*, p. 98.

minimills now dominate all of the markets for the basic small-diameter products.[2]

Because the large U.S. companies were convinced that demand and inflation would surge periodically and provide them with a very attractive operating environment, they were far from cost conscious. In the early 1970s, they embarked upon an industrywide collective bargaining strategy of granting at least 3 percent annual real wage increases in return for a no-strike provision in the contract. Productivity was not an issue, nor was the very high cost of building new facilities. Labor peace was sought as insurance against surges in imports—the only threat that the industry could foresee. The cost of this strategy was to create a labor cost disadvantage of at least $100 per ton relative to costs in Japan by the late 1970s.

The impact of slow growth is dramatically shown in table 2. In 1985 the industry produced only 88 million tons of crude steel, but the minimills produced almost 18 million of this total. The integrated firms, which had as much as 145 million tons of capacity in the late 1970s, produced only 71 million tons in 1985, the third year of an economic expansion.[3] Based on the forecasts of steel consumption shown in table 2, the integrated firms' raw steel production will fall to less than 60 million tons by 2000— one-third of the 180 million tons of capacity once predicted for the 1980s.

2. For a discussion of U.S. minimills, see Donald F. Barnett and Robert W. Crandall, *Up from the Ashes: The Rise of the Steel Minimill in the United States* (Brookings, 1986).

3. Most of these data may be found in American Iron and Steel Institute, *Annual Statistical Report* (Washington, D.C.: AISI, various years). Included in totals for integrated producers are data for specialty steel companies.

Impact of Exchange Rates

In the midst of the general decline in growth of steel consumption, U.S. producers were battered further by a sharply rising dollar in the 1980s, which created substantial direct and indirect import pressure. The result has been to increase the role of imports of both steel and goods fabricated from steel, further reducing final U.S. steel demand, and to keep U.S. steel prices at their 1981 levels for four years while costs were generally rising. By 1986, these pressures had reached crisis proportions. One firm, Republic, was forced to seek a merger partner, and another, Sharon, was in substantial financial difficulty. Three integrated companies—McLouth, LTV, and Wheeling-Pittsburgh—went through bankruptcy proceedings, while another—Kaiser—simply closed.

The high value of the dollar, however, was far from the industry's only problem. In fact, as the dollar receded in 1985-86, there was little evidence of a recovery in the industry. The average U.S. integrated steel company continued to lose money on its steel operations in a relatively strong general economy.

Modernization and Cost Cutting

It has been almost twenty-five years since ground was broken on a new integrated U.S. steel plant. Moreover, it has been fifteen years since such an investment could have been justified on purely economic grounds. The cost of operating and amortizing a new integrated steel plant today is approximately $47 a ton more than the cost of operating the more efficient existing plants. Since even the latter are not very profitable in the current environment, a new plant would clearly be unprofitable.

If the construction of entirely new plants is uneconomic, replacing individual facilities such as coke ovens, blast furnaces, basic-oxygen steelmaking furnaces, and even rolling mills is also not likely to be remunerative. Obviously, there are instances in which replacing a needed cog in the integrated process can be justified, but large "rounding-out" or modernization expenditures must be viewed as suspect in the United States at recent steel prices, construction costs, and wage rates.

I have calculated the reinvestment rate between the end of the 1974–75 recession and the onset of the devastating 1982 recession for all the major integrated steel companies in the United States and related these rates to the companies' recent performance. Not surprisingly, the companies that have encountered the most difficulty are precisely those that have engaged in the most intensive reinvestment in steel. The logical extension is that the firms that invested little should be relatively more healthy. Indeed, until recently, those with a very low reinvestment rate performed better for their shareholders than those who invested more aggressively in steel.

The Success of Minimills

No discussion of the U.S. steel industry would be complete without a discussion of the steadily growing minimill sector. As recently as ten years ago, these small electric-furnace companies accounted for perhaps 7 percent of U.S. steel output. They are now producing about 20 percent of U.S. output, and they are continuing to grow.[4] These companies are generally privately held; hence, there are few data on their financial performance. Two of the largest publicly traded minimill companies—Nucor and Florida Steel—increased their common share prices by 647 and 164 percent, respectively, during 1976-85 while the large integrated firms were losing between 33 percent and 55 percent of their share value. On the other hand, until recently, Northwestern Steel and Wire has underperformed even the larger U.S. integrated companies, in part because of its older facilities.

The minimills are pressing steadily into new markets. They have virtually driven the integrated companies from the wire rod market. They dominate the market for small carbon bars and shapes and are steadily moving into the medium-sized structurals. The major news, however, is that the minimills are now entering the sheet market, both hot-rolled and cold-rolled.

Within the next fifteen years, the U.S. minimills are likely to double their share of U.S. steel production, producing most of their output at some distance from the declining industrial Midwest, where most of the remaining integrated capacity is now located. This will probably make the congressional representatives from these states even more protectionist.

4. Barnett and Crandall, *Up from the Ashes.*

The Canadian Steel Industry

In many respects, the Canadian steel industry has faced the same problems as the U.S. industry: slow growth in demand, a declining price of scrap relative to hot metal from the blast furnace, import pressures in downstream markets, and low prices. Nevertheless, two of the three major Canadian integrated producers have performed rather well in the past few years, and one of these companies—Dofasco—has been the most consistently profitable integrated steel producer in North America. There are several reasons for the Canadian industry's greater success. Among these are the relatively weaker Canadian dollar, lower wage rates, and apparently a better targeted investment program.

Exchange Rates

The comparatively weak Canadian dollar (relative to the U.S. dollar) has made the United States an attractive source of export sales. Of course, the declining Canadian dollar has increased the cost of importing raw materials, particularly coal, from the United States. But the impact of the Canadian exchange rate cannot be gauged simply from the U.S.-Canadian comparison, for the Canadian dollar generally appreciated against European and Japanese currencies for most of the 1980s. As long as U.S. steel prices remained high by world standards, however, the Canadian producers could export profitably to adjacent markets in the United States.

Wage Rates

High labor costs have been particularly damaging to the U.S. integrated producers since the early 1970s. The Canadian industry has been much more successful in collective bargaining until recently. Throughout the late 1970s and early 1980s, it paid its workers only about 70 percent of the total hourly compensation paid U.S. steelworkers (table 3). This difference has begun to narrow, however, as U.S. producers obtain wage concessions and Canadian wages drift upward. The differences in wage rates between U.S. and Canadian producers have, by themselves, provided the Canadians with a $40–$50 cost advantage on an average ton of steel, or about 10 percent of the value of a ton of steel in 1981–85.

Table 3. *Total Employee Compensation in the U.S. and Canadian Steel Industries, Production Workers, 1975–86*
U.S. dollars per hour

Year	United States	Canada	Canadian-U.S. ratio
1975	10.24	7.47	0.729
1976	11.23	8.95	0.797
1977	12.31	9.49	0.771
1978	13.56	9.99	0.737
1979	15.15	10.58	0.698
1980	17.46	11.40	0.653
1981	19.04	12.78	0.671
1982	22.72	14.58	0.642
1983	21.14	15.46	0.731
1984	20.24	15.49	0.765
1985	21.45	15.17	0.707
1986	22.24	15.57	0.700

Source: Data from U.S. Department of Labor, Bureau of Labor Statistics, Office of Productivity and Technology.

Investment

The U.S. producers, who often cite lack of investment funds for their difficulties, appear to have encountered problems in direct proportion to their investment spending. Since the economic climate for steel production is only marginally better in Canada, have Canadian companies been more successful in modernizing?

The answer of most students of the steel industry is that the two largest Canadian producers, Stelco and Dofasco, have indeed modernized more than their U.S. counterparts and have generally superior facilities. Their rolling mills and raw steel operations are said to be better. They are investing heavily in continuous casting, and the coke rates in their blast furnaces are much lower.

Surprisingly, the Canadian industry has spent less per ton of steel output on new investment than its U.S. rivals. Table 4 compares government estimates of investment spending per reported ton of steel shipments for 1976–84. The U.S. industry's spending was about 20 percent higher: an average of $39 per ton over the period, compared with $33 per ton for Canada. One might argue that these calculations should be based upon capacity, not shipments, but the best measure of the industry's economic size is capacity that is actually in use, not the total amount of unused, inefficient, redundant capacity. Nevertheless, a

Table 4. *Investment Expenditures by Steel Producers in the United States and Canada, 1976–84*
Millions of U.S. dollars unless otherwise indicated

	Canada			United States		
Year	Invest-ment	Shipments (millions of tons)	Dollars per ton	Invest-ment	Shipments (millions of tons)	Dollars per ton
1976	409	10.80	38	3,130	89.45	35
1977	386	11.38	34	2,880	91.15	32
1978	303	12.89	24	2,600	97.94	27
1979	382	13.48	28	3,210	100.26	32
1980	551	13.55	41	3,440	83.85	41
1981	739	13.23	56	3,480	88.45	39
1982	493	10.31	48	3,780	61.57	61
1983	186	11.02	17	3,250	67.58	48
1984	203	12.74	16	3,540	73.74	48

Sources: U.S. Department of Commerce, Bureau of Economic Analysis; Statistics Canada; American Iron and Steel Institute.

calculation based upon capacity would show that the investment rates were about the same, with apparently far better returns in Canada.

Despite Stelco's construction of a new plant, it reinvested at a slower rate than its smaller rival, Dofasco. In 1975–81, Stelco invested 14.5 percent of its 1975 year-end market value per year while Dofasco invested an average of 20.2 percent. Neither company invested as intensively as the most aggressive U.S. companies, but Dofasco has clearly outperformed all other integrated steel producers in the United States or Canada. Its shares increased by 160 percent in 1976–85, while Stelco's shares declined by 1.6 percent. Both outperformed the large U.S. intergrated companies by a wide margin. Thus the Canadian industry's success cannot be said to be the result of greater investment than its U.S. counterparts. It must be the result of better-targeted investment.

Clouds on the Horizon for Sheet Producers

Both the U.S. and Canadian flat-rolled steel (sheet and plate) producers are now facing a dilemma. They are discovering that the new demands for quality, particularly from the automobile industry, are requiring enormous investments in continuous casters, continuous annealing facilities, cold-rolling mills, and galvanizing mills. These investments are by no means guaranteed to yield a satisfactory rate of return, given the low price of high-quality steel in the current world market.

The problems of the flat-rolled producers are being exacerbated by trends in the automobile industry. The North American car industry is under tremendous pressure from Korea and Japan. With protectionist policies in both the United States and Canada, both Japanese and Korean automobile companies are now investing heavily in North American production facilities. Perceiving that their comparative advantage derives from organizing the workplace and designing their vehicles so as to obtain high productivity and reliable cars, these companies are generally avoiding the large urban U.S. midwestern areas as plant locations. Rather, they seem intent upon choosing sites in rural Tennessee, Kentucky, Ohio, and Illinois for assembly facilities. This will only add to the problems of the Great Lakes area and to the pressure for protecting whatever industry—including steel—that remains there.

The foreign assemblers are likely to place very stringent quality demands on their sheet steel suppliers. In many cases, they will purchase much of their supply from joint ventures between Korean or Japanese and U.S. steel producers. U.S. producers with capacity in the Great Lakes area may suffer both a locational disadvantage and a quality problem if they do not upgrade their finishing facilities, but such investments may not prove economic at current or prospective relative prices.

To make matters worse, the minimills will surely take away 10 or 15 percent of the low-quality end of the U.S.-Canadian sheet market within the next fifteen years and perhaps just as much of the higher-quality market. And the automobile companies are eagerly investigating plastics as substitutes for steel in the bodies of their cars. Thus the sheet steel business, already greatly reduced by the downsizing of automobiles and the loss of the beverage can market, will atrophy further in the years ahead.

U.S.-Canadian Trade Issues

At today's U.S.-Canadian exchange rate, the Canadian producers have an extremely attractive market in the United States that is immune to charges of dumping or subsidization. As a result, there have been few steel trade cases filed against Canadian producers. The 1984 decision by

President Reagan to negotiate steel quotas with all U.S. trading partners has been artfully avoided by the Canadians. There is no doubt, however, that the Canadians are under strong political pressure to moderate their exports to the United States despite their large cost advantage in nearby midwestern markets.

The surface tranquility in U.S.-Canadian steel trade relations could easily be upset by events ahead. Both countries could slip into a recession in the next two or three years. With U.S. firms unable to earn positive returns during the 1983–86 expansion, they are likely to find themselves in great difficulty in the next recession unless world steel prices (in U.S. dollars) rise sharply. The sharp depreciation of the dollar should help, but it is interesting that the recent depreciation of the dollar against the European and Japanese currencies had not firmed import prices much by early 1987.

Nor should one expect much from the Reagan administration's misguided attempt to function as U.S. cartel manager for steel exporters. Steel quotas cannot work because there are simply too many potential suppliers and each exporter can simply move up to a slightly more finished steel product for export. Unless the Reagan administration is willing to create a Gosplan-like office of steel restraints and control the importation of all steel fabrications from nails to automobiles and refrigerators, the current quotas will have only a minor effect upon the health of U.S. steel producers. Their success will be measured in terms of shrinkage of the steel market in the United States, not in the growth of U.S. steel company sales and profits.

Free Trade in Steel Products?

Looked at narrowly, the steel sector should not present a major problem in the negotiation of a Canadian-U.S. free trade area. American and Canadian tariffs on most carbon steel products are between 7 and 9 percent *ad valorem*. A free trade agreement undoubtedly would provide that these tariffs would be reduced to zero gradually, perhaps over five to ten years. The effect on trade flows would probably be modest in comparison with the impact of determinants other than customs duties.

In practice, the American industry will see bilateral free trade in steel as threatening to worsen an already hugely unbalanced relationship. In 1985 the volume of U.S. imports of steel products from Canada was nine

Table 5. *U.S.-Canadian Steel Trade Flows, 1985*
Thousands of tons

Product	U.S. imports from Canada	U.S. exports to Canada
Semifinished steel	70	11
Sheet products	891	112
Plates	171	33
Structurals[a]	260	26
Tubular products	429	64
Wire rod	354	2
Bar products	363	51
Wire	265	11
Other	65	4
Total	2,868	314

Source: American Iron and Steel Institute, *Annual Statistical Report, 1985*, tables 18, 23.
a. Larger than three inches in diameter.

times that of exports (table 5). Much of the imbalance was in the flat-rolled items produced by the integrated American companies. Imports of sheet, plates, and semifinished slabs were 1.1 million tons, compared with exports of only 156,000 tons. Imports of structural and tubular products exceeded exports—689,000 tons to 90,000 tons. Thus net imports from Canada of major integrated products were about 1.8 million tons. Wire rod and wire products contributed another 619,000 tons and bar products 363,000 tons.

To aggravate matters further, Canada has been one of the few steel-exporting countries (Sweden and Taiwan are the others) to resist U.S. pressures for an export quota agreement under the U.S. program referred to earlier. Since Canada is the third largest supplier of steel products to the American market (after Japan and the European Community), its unwillingness to participate has left a sizable gap in the coverage of the intended export restraint system or international cartel.

Nevertheless, a free trade agreement that does not extend to iron and steel products is an unlikely outcome. An exception for steel would almost surely have to be matched by a balancing exception for some product or service of interest to another American economic sector. Once begun, the exchange of exceptions could quickly undermine the free trade negotiation in its entirety. The assumption must be, therefore, that ways will be found to include the steel sector in an arrangement that will provide for eventual free trade in steel.

Assuming, then, that tariffs will be declining slowly and that quantitative limits will not be placed on trade flows, what can be expected in bilateral trade in steel products? The most important factors affecting net flows will be, first, relative costs, as determined by wage levels and exchange rates, and, second, the locational decisions of U.S., Japanese, and Korean automobile assemblers. The present outlook is for U.S. automobile capacity to expand substantially as Japanese producers hasten to establish assembly, stamping, and even engine facilities in the United States. Japanese and Korean automobile companies are also beginning to make investments in Canada, but on a much smaller scale.

Canada currently exports roughly 15 percent of its sheet and strip output to the United States. Its capacity to produce these products is expanding, while U.S. capacity has contracted substantially. This suggests greater U.S. sheet imports from Canada in the next few years, at a time when U.S. integrated firms will be continuing to reduce employment. Given that implicit American pressures are probably restraining Canadian sheet exports to some extent at present, an increase in exports under free trade could not fail to be an irritant in the midwestern and northeastern United States. A rising Canadian dollar, however, would make Canadian steel less competitive, possibly diverting trade to suppliers elsewhere.

In bar products and wire rods, the situation is quite different. U.S. minimills will be able to compete quite well with any exporter of these products. Thus one may expect that the Canadian exporters would find it increasingly difficult to penetrate the U.S. market in these products.

A final concern may be the impact of protectionist government procurement rules. In the United States, "Buy America" requirements in state and federal law may affect as much as 3 to 4 percent of steel consumption. Similar laws and practices in Canada obviously have an impact on Canadian steel imports. Given the desperate condition of the U.S. structural steel market and the depressed Canadian market in these products, removal of these nontariff barriers may well have to be deferred to a more auspicious time.

Conclusion

The Canadian integrated steel industry is much healthier than its U.S. counterpart and is even expanding. With a depreciated currency relative to the U.S. dollar, Canadian sheet exports to the United States may expand substantially. Even though the Canadian sheet capacity is less than one-fifth of the U.S. capacity, increased Canadian exports under a free trade arrangement could exacerbate the local problems caused by continued reductions in U.S. capacity and employment. A strong U.S. automotive sector or a stronger Canadian dollar, or both, would help to ease the transition to free trade.

ANDREW SCHMITZ and COLIN CARTER

A Sectoral Perspective: Agriculture

AGRICULTURAL products are an important component of Canadian-U.S. trade. Canada ranks as one of the top five customers for U.S. agricultural exports, and the United States is the largest market for Canadian agricultural products, receiving shipments valued at $1.5 billion (U.S. dollars) in 1984 (see tables 1 and 2). Canada experiences a large agricultural trade imbalance with the United States. The Canadian trade deficit was an average of $1.4 billion a year in 1975–79, increasing to $2.0 billion in 1981 and then declining to $1.4 billion in 1984.

It may be extremely difficult to achieve more liberalized trade in agricultural products, partly because of the nature of Canadian institutions and the subsidized aspect of U.S. agriculture. Many segments of Canadian agriculture are governed by supply-managed marketing boards. These boards control output in Canada, and in certain cases they also regulate the volume of imports from the United States.[1] Marketing boards have not only curtailed the volume of trade but have also distorted resource use within Canada. There are many cases in which comparative advantage within the domestic economy is not realized because several provinces are striving for self-sufficiency in specific commodities. If interprovincial trade barriers were removed in Canada, there would be a greater degree of regional specialization and trade. U.S. agriculture,

We thank Thorald K. Warley, Dale Sigurdson, and Garth Coffin for their comments on an earlier version.

1. For example, the Canadian Wheat Board issues permits on wheat imports into Canada. However, for commodities such as eggs the federal Department of External Affairs sets import quotas.

Table 1. *Canadian Exports of Agricultural Products to the United States, 1975–84*
Thousands of Canadian dollars

Commodity	Average, 1975–79	1980	1981	1982	1983	1984
All agricultural commodities	703,131	1,112,715	1,260,183	1,606,109	1,736,431	2,235,992
Grains	38,575	36,180	38,831	72,991	65,760	73,307
Grain products	49,838	83,508	93,500	108,033	122,272	136,243
Animal feeds	48,868	68,243	77,376	80,573	99,028	117,856
Oilseeds	22,055	27,061	72,638	43,134	58,043	57,445
Oilseed products	5,121	9,380	19,264	14,620	26,743	36,898
Animals, live	128,442	202,683	166,205	264,320	271,056	439,977
Beef and veal	54,527	109,855	126,140	139,015	137,780	177,851
Pork	34,138	136,257	156,379	269,128	232,467	305,962
Other animal products	69,166	93,161	90,909	83,823	85,309	109,951
Dairy products	6,753	7,163	8,880	10,732	12,034	13,893
Poultry and eggs	6,797	12,021	12,060	11,612	18,113	25,527
Fruits and nuts	32,441	40,938	46,766	65,044	65,411	68,657
Vegetables (excluding potatoes)	22,560	39,543	46,460	57,758	81,033	83,982
Potatoes and products	7,053	18,658	42,107	44,186	36,255	48,926
Seeds for sowing	15,781	17,177	18,223	19,571	39,541	18,712
Maple products	8,460	13,021	15,159	17,216	18,324	19,757
Sugar	27,432	1,116	1,862	26,010	36,673	40,145
Tobacco, raw	8,576	12,999	20,896	33,846	25,971	26,710
Vegetable fibers	5,812	7,594	11,924	18,791	20,372	16,376
Plantation crops	11,619	5,199	11,181	21,458	20,165	52,510
Other agricultural products	79,873	139,297	141,955	154,571	206,072	310,407

Source: Agriculture Canada, *Canada's Trade in Agricultural Products 1982, 1983, and 1984.*

as a result of the 1985 farm bill, has become highly subsidized through deficiency payments and the grain export enhancement program. This issue has created extreme financial difficulties for Canadian prairie grain producers and has clearly aggravated the problem of policy harmonization between the two countries.

The Regulation of Canadian Interprovincial Trade

In discussing the costs and benefits of freer agricultural trade between these neighboring countries, it is important to recognize the extent to which agricultural trade is currently restricted among the various provinces in Canada. As an illustration of the extent of government involvement in Canada agriculture, table 3 gives a breakdown of Agriculture Canada expenditures for 1981–82. However, expenditures by Agriculture Canada do not account for all federal spending on agriculture. There are large federal outlays made by Transport Canada, the Department of

Table 2. *Canadian Imports of Agricultural Products from the United States, 1975–84*
Thousands of Canadian dollars

Commodity	Average, 1975–79	1980	1981	1982	1983	1984
All agricultural commodities	2,090,540	2,916,249	3,263,689	3,060,499	3,117,792	3,609,229
Grains	114,969	232,079	260,761	162,508	113,778	156,902
Grain products	45,148	65,940	77,867	87,494	104,896	147,034
Animal feeds	37,828	56,762	61,647	75,598	72,695	76,290
Oilseeds	143,401	191,276	161,261	190,147	161,888	169,223
Oilseed products	180,641	207,756	214,092	195,759	227,264	305,814
Animals, live	52,439	84,586	165,824	96,145	91,802	55,101
Beef and veal	25,486	34,240	52,847	47,777	56,273	109,236
Pork	108,728	30,272	38,732	36,637	36,489	19,882
Other animal products	135,112	201,043	209,543	184,286	205,749	229,529
Dairy products	7,995	10,458	10,308	10,933	10,540	13,678
Poultry and eggs	54,277	55,639	69,442	73,329	76,677	108,157
Fruits and nuts	437,252	648,091	735,242	773,602	741,812	842,460
Vegetables (excluding potatoes)	266,434	354,608	444,686	458,626	483,687	528,078
Potatoes and products	28,035	28,288	48,982	36,312	34,921	53,256
Seeds for sowing	33,213	52,195	56,943	45,947	48,100	51,718
Sugar	20,664	41,767	37,270	15,293	22,598	31,682
Tobacco, raw	5,675	31,477	5,476	10,213	20,261	8,271
Vegetable fibers	70,157	119,504	126,521	74,846	100,460	122,084
Plantation crops	140,083	223,919	175,186	164,769	167,116	200,073
Other agricultural products	163,042	224,346	283,560	291,632	309,646	349,757

Source: Agriculture Canada, *Canada's Trade in Agricultural Products 1982, 1983, and 1984.*

Regional Economic Expansion, Industry Trade and Commerce, and External Affairs. The regulated rates in rail shipment constitute an appreciable subsidy to prairie grain since under the Crow's Nest Pass agreement the federal government in effect makes an annual payment of $650 million.[2]

In contrast to dairy and grains, federal expenditures on beef and hogs are relatively minor. Perhaps this explains why there are several provincial government programs for these sectors. The number of provincial programs supporting the red meat sector has grown significantly, including some form of a red meat stabilization plan, tax credits for feeding cattle, and livestock feeder associations offering low-interest loans.[3]

Government expenditures give only a partial indication of income transfers to agriculture. Producer transfers via supply-managed com-

2. The direct expenditures for grains appear to be larger than for the dairy sector; however, the degree of protection afforded dairying may well exceed that for grains.
3. Ken A. Rosaasen and Andrew Schmitz, *The Saskatchewan Beef Industry: Constraints and Opportunities for Growth,* Technical Bulletin BL:84-02 (University of Saskatchewan, March 1984).

Table 3. *Agriculture Canada Expenditures, 1981–82, by Province*
Millions of Canadian dollars

Type of expenditure	Newfound-land	Prince Edward Island	Nova Scotia	New Brunswick	Quebec	Ontario	Manitoba	Saskatch-ewan	Alberta	British Columbia	National capital region[a]	Total
Administration	…	…	…	0.62	0.63	0.74	0.55	0.42	0.45	0.23	36.54	40.18
Research	1.62	4.49	6.52	6.47	15.18	34.32	10.30	16.44	23.65	8.04	32.50	159.58
Crop insurance	0.01	1.11	0.20	0.51	[b]	15.99	11.23	52.86	31.92	2.13	…	115.86
Advance crop payments	…	0.45	0.19	0.47	2.20	2.54	0.31	…	0.13	1.46	…	7.75
Stabilization[c]	0.27	5.16	2.55	4.51	44.90	42.33	10.03	6.13	13.18	8.68	…	137.74
Dairy program	…	5.38	3.94	3.22	141.22	91.94	10.63	7.18	17.98	9.64	10.38	301.51
Food inspection	1.70	3.29	3.50	6.05	34.51	38.43	10.44	8.94	19.30	13.04	30.81	169.51
Grain inspection	…	…	…	…	2.47	11.23	9.70	0.82	0.98	5.78	…	30.98
Grain embargo	…	0.01	0.02	0.02	0.94	7.13	9.92	39.16	20.88	0.63	0.53	79.24
Feed freight assistance	…	…	…	…	8.79	0.13	0.03	…	…	0.30	…	9.22
Livestock feed board[d]	1.23	2.53	1.73	0.57	4.97	0.65	0.03	…	0.01	5.78	…	17.50
Other expenditures	0.09	0.39	0.64	0.24	4.76	5.34	8.58[e]	1.04	1.31	3.82	29.31	55.52
Total	4.92	22.81	19.29	22.68	260.57	250.77	81.72	132.99	129.69	59.53	139.57	1,124.54

Source: Agriculture Canada, Regional Development Branch, *Selected Agricultural Statistics, Canada and the Provinces* (Ottawa: Supply and Services Canada, 1983), p. 81.
a. Includes expenditures outside Canada and program storage, interest, and other expenditures not allocatable by province.
b. No payment pending signing a federal-provincial agreement.
c. Agricultural Stabilization Act payments, excluding dairy payments.
d. Mainly contributions to feed transport costs.
e. Includes a $6.4 million grant to Canadian Cooperative Investments Ltd.

modities are affected by restrictions on imports and domestic production. Though these transfers do not show up in government expenditures, they are real transfers that affect consumers directly via higher prices. These are, in essence, hidden subsidies. Studies have found them to be substantial. For example, it has been estimated that in the mid- to late 1970s, the consumer costs associated with such transfers for the dairy industry were two to three times the size of the government expenditures reported for the sector in table 3.[4] The consumer costs of egg regulation have been estimated to range from $39 million to $100 million for 1979, compared with farm cash receipts of $340 million for eggs in that year.[5]

Regional patterns of trade have also been directly affected by government intervention in the case of poultry and dairy products. The national supply control programs for these products involve the determination of national quotas and the division of these quotas among provinces. Although a number of economic features are listed as guides to the allocation of quotas among provinces, reallocations reflect provincial negotiating power rather than economic criteria. These features have probably impeded the transfer of quotas toward low-cost producing areas, as Michelle Veeman has indicated:

> The tendency for political pressure towards self-sufficiency on a provincial level may be expected to lead to higher cost levels of the producing sector with consequent loss of the benefits of regional specialization in trade. The result has been a general tendency for supply deficient provinces to become more self-sufficient since the supply controlling programs for poultry products have been introduced. There is evident pressure also for reallocation of quota to provinces where there has been more rapid population and income growth and consequently more rapid increase in consumption levels. These pressures are in the interests of local producers but are not necessarily consistent with comparative advantage.[6]

These observations indicate that the regional nature of Canadian domestic farm policy is potentially a major constraint to the establishment of freer trade between Canada and the United States. Not only is

4. Timothy Josling, *Intervention and Regulation in Canadian Agriculture: A Comparison of Costs and Benefits among Sectors* (Ottawa: Economic Council of Canada and Institute for Research on Public Policy, 1981).

5. Michelle Veeman, "The Regulation of Interprovincial Trade in Agricultural Products," in Barry Sadler, ed., *Transforming Western Canada's Food Industry in the 80s and 90s* (Banff Center, 1984), pp. 55–70; and Andrew Schmitz, "Supply Management in Canadian Agriculture: An Assessment of the Economic Effects," *Canadian Journal of Agricultural Economics*, vol. 31 (July 1983), pp. 135–52.

6. Veeman, "Regulation of Interprovincial Trade," p. 66.

the Canadian government perceived as favoring agricultural development in central Canada and the Maritimes, but also several provincial governments are subsidizing agricultural production in order to achieve self-sufficiency. Provinces freely construct nontariff barriers to protect their own industries. The net effect is the balkanization of Canadian agriculture. The swine industry perhaps best illustrates this problem. Government programs contributed to the decline in western Canada's share of national hog production from 46 percent in 1971 to 30 percent in 1984. During the same period, eastern Canada's share increased from 54 percent to 70 percent.[7] However, basic economics also played a role: western Canada capitalized on a prosperous grain economy in the 1970s, but eastern Canada could not do the same.

Institutions and Government Policy

Canada has a set of institutions that have a significant effect on the Canada-U.S. free trade initiative in agricultural products. For instance, the major agricultural commodity exported from Canada is grain, and the Canadian Wheat Board is the sole exporter of wheat and feed grains. There is very little movement of grains between the United States and Canada under the current system. This is partly due to the low number of import licenses granted by the Canadian Wheat Board. However, there is a sizable export trade of malt barley from Canada to the United States. Corn is allowed into Canada under a small tariff, and most of the corn has been imported into eastern Canada. Likewise, under section 22 of the Agricultural Adjustment Act, the United States limits grain imports from Canada. The free movement of grain between the United States and Canada could bring into question the effective marketing of grain by the Canadian Wheat Board and thus the entire grain marketing system in Canada. In a free trade area, the Canadian Wheat Board could have difficulties in carrying out its current marketing programs, which use producer marketing quotas.

In addition, under a free trade arrangement in grains, a portion of Canadian grain might be shipped to export markets via the U.S. rail and barge system. This would certainly cause concern to the Canadian

7. Colin Carter and others, "Canadian-U.S. Trade Relations: Issues and Policy Options," paper prepared for International Agricultural Trade Research Consortium, December 1984.

National and Canadian Pacific railroads, and it would also result in a lower volume of traffic on the St. Lawrence Seaway. However, the outcome would depend on the subsidies given Canadian railways. If subsidies were high enough, a certain volume of U.S. grain would move via Canadian railways under freer trade.

In dealing with international trade between the United States and Canada, one cannot underestimate the role and political strength of domestic institutions. It is not simply a matter of removing or reducing tariffs on imported goods into Canada in order to achieve more liberalized trade. Many of the commodities imported into Canada are regulated through these institutions via quotas. If these quotas are substantially reduced, the entire institutional structure comes under serious challenge. It would be extremely difficult for marketing boards to operate since they achieve part of their strength through quotas imposed by the External Affairs Department. They also regulate interprovincial trade. Therefore, if these bodies were removed, not only would the pattern of trade change between the United States and Canada, but there would be a significant change in the pattern of interprovincial trade and regional specialization within Canada.

In addition, one can be reasonably sure that freer trade in grains would not happen if it necessitated the elimination of the Canadian Wheat Board. The Canadian Wheat Board is a very popular institution among the majority of grain farmers in Canada. It is possible, but not probable, that an arrangement could be worked out to modify the Canada Wheat Board's authority, for example, expanding its scope by making it the marketing agency for both U.S. and Canadian spring wheat.

Questions have been raised as to whether provincial red meat stabilization policies are also producer subsidy schemes. In the case of hogs, in 1985 the United States levied countervailing duties on the importation of live hogs from Canada into the United States after the U.S. Commerce Department had ruled that there were significant production subsidies in Canada and the International Trade Commission had ruled that injury was being done to U.S. hog producers.[8] The Canadian cattle industry

8. The issue of what constitutes a subsidy is important as is the effect of subsidies. Schmitz and Sigurdson contend that stabilization policies do not necessarily generate producer subsidies. In the case of hogs, the actual subsidy was far less than calculated by the Commerce Department, and the injury to U.S. producers was insignificant. See Andrew Schmitz and Dale Sigurdson, "Stabilization Programs and Countervailing Duties: Canadian Hog Exports to the U.S.," working paper (University of Saskatchewan, Department of Agricultural Economics, 1985).

Table 4. *Government Outlays for Grain Producers, 1985–86 and 1986–87*
Canadian dollars per bushel

Commodity and exporter	Government outlays	
	1985–86	1986–87
Wheat		
European Economic Community	2.60	3.13
United States	1.49	2.63
Canada	0.75	0.85
Barley		
European Economic Community	2.41	3.11
United States	0.41	1.06
Canada	0.36	0.33

Source: Canadian Wheat Board, Planning Directorate, Winnipeg, May 1986.

has expressed concern that further stabilization programs for beef in Canada could well lead to similar countervailing action on the part of the United States.

The U.S. government also has numerous agricultural subsidy programs and trade restrictions. The most obvious examples of U.S. regulation of imports to support domestic industry are in sugar, tobacco, and dairy products. Transportation subsidies are less direct than the Canadian freight assistance programs, but there are significant federal subsidies associated with the construction and maintenance of internal waterways in the United States. Heavily subsidized irrigation programs are used to expand agricultural production of grains, livestock, fruits, and vegetables that compete with Canadian production. Another major issue is the size of the deficiency payments that U.S. wheat, corn, soybean, and cotton farmers receive from the U.S. Department of Agriculture when market prices are low. In this regard, a complaint by Ontario corn growers led to a countervailing duty action against U.S. corn exports in late 1986, on the basis that the United States is able to sell into the Canadian market well below the cost of production because U.S. deficiency payment schemes (that is, the difference between the loan rate and the target price) are production subsidies.

Perhaps the biggest stumbling block to a Canadian-U.S. free trade agreement is the size of U.S. treasury outlays for its grain producers. The resulting impact is not on Canadian-U.S. trade flows, but in export markets where the United States and Canada compete. As shown in table 4, U.S. government support to wheat producers is presently two to three times the level supplied by the Canadian government. In addition, the U.S. grain export enhancement program will provide $1 billion to $1.5 billion in export subsidies for grain sales over 1985–88. These programs give the U.S. farmer a sizable economic advantage over Canadian producers in competition in world grain markets. The 1985 U.S. farm bill heightens protectionism and thus goes against the spirit of free trade discussions.

Market Size, Economies of Scale, and Costs of Production

The discrepancy in the sizes of the U.S. and Canadian markets has important implications for freer trade between the two countries. Red meat, a major product shipped from Canada to the United States, offers an illustration. Until recently, pork and live hogs entered the United States essentially duty free, although nontariff barriers existed. For beef, there are no restrictions on the exportation of live animals from Canada except nontariff barriers. However, there is a quota on the amount of processed beef Canada can export to the U.S. market. Recently this quota has not been binding because Canada's exports of beef products have not reached the quota limit.[9]

Canada is essentially a price taker in the North American beef and pork industry: it can increase output without significantly affecting the North American price, because U.S. imports of pork and beef from Canada represent a very small percentage of U.S. consumption. Thus under freer trade in these products it is unlikely that the U.S. producers would suffer greatly from Canada's greater access to their markets.

9. Andrew Schmitz, "Prospects for Change in Livestock Production and Trade," in G. E. Lee, ed., *World Agricultural Policies and Trade* (University of Saskatchewan, 1984). The fact that Canada does not fill its export quotas on beef shipments into the U.S. market implies that under present prices beef is not a highly profitable industry. Otherwise, the Canadian beef industry clearly would expand in order to increase exports into the U.S. market. The profitability of the North American red meat industry has been under serious pressure for the last several years. This has very little to do with U.S.-Canadian trade relations, however, and more to do with Japanese import quotas and European Economic Community subsidies, along with decreasing per capita consumption of red meats. See W. A. Kerr and S. M. Ulmer, *The Importance of the Livestock, Meat and Processing Industries to Western Growth* (Ottawa: Economic Council of Canada, 1984).

However, products that could be exported from the United States to Canada in a freer trade regime present a different picture. For example, it is likely that the egg and broiler industry in Canada would come under significant short-term pressure. Unless Canadian producers become more efficient through larger-scale operations, the size of the Canadian industry would probably be reduced significantly.[10] This would have a significant impact on the Canadian producers since a small increase in U.S. production, and hence a large increase in exports from the United States to Canada, represents a large percentage of total Canadian production. As with beef and pork, in a truly free trade arena Canada would be a price taker in eggs and broilers. In other words, the United States would have market power because of its relative size, whereas Canada has no real market power.

In the large U.S. markets there are opportunities to exploit economies of scale. For example, there are now several producers in California that have over 2 million laying hens. It would be relatively easy for these organizations to increase output in order to meet the Canadian demand. Costs of production are influenced by economies of scale, and therefore the Canadian industry would have to increase the size of its operations significantly to compete. However, if it does so in order to meet U.S. competition, it will end up with fewer producers.

In the U.S. dairy industry there is a significant difference between the structure in California and Arizona and that in the Midwest. Many of the herds in California are twenty times the size of those in the Midwest. This can be explained partly by geography and partly by other factors, including heavy regulation of the U.S. milk trade. Because of marketing orders, the interstate flow of milk is as highly regulated in the United States as the interprovincial flow is in Canada.

What would happen to the U.S. dairy industry if U.S.-Canadian barriers to milk trade and related products were removed? If interprovincial and interstate barriers were also removed, a significant structural change would occur. It is our hypothesis that unless the Midwest industry drastically changed its structure and thus lowered its costs, production

10. As Barichello and Warley point out, rationalization of the industry may well occur. Hence the size of the industry measured in terms of output need not be affected. However, there will be a reduction in the number of producers and a loss in quota value rent. See Richard Barichello and Thorald K. Warley, "Agriculture and Negotiation of a Free-Trade Area: Issues in Policy Harmonization" (Toronto: C. D. Howe Institute, December 1985).

would shift to the western United States in spite of the increased transportation charges that would accompany such a restructuring. Under the same circumstances, the Canadian dairy industry would become more concentrated and more efficient. It is doubtful that the average-sized dairy in Canada could survive against competition from California. Many of the California dairies are at least ten times the size of those in Canada. However, as is the case with eggs and broilers, once rationalization occurred and the average size of a firm increased, relatively few dairy producers would be needed to satisfy the Canadian milk market.

Canada's Comparative Advantage

When discussing free trade between the United States and Canada in agricultural products, one must ask in which products Canada has a comparative advantage. This is extremely difficult to determine, especially if one gives serious consideration to the role played by institutions, subsidies, and trade restrictions. Unless Canada has an advantage over the United States in producing some agricultural products, there will not be a significant expansion of exports to the United States under a free trade initiative. To examine this in detail is beyond the scope of this paper. However, a few examples will suffice to illustrate the complexity of this issue. Several studies have concluded that there is a significant potential for increased beef exports into the California market.[11] As already indicated, if this is true, why hasn't the current U.S. quota been filled? In addition, even though California has over 25 million people, it has a vast area suitable for livestock production. In addition, some of the largest feedlots in the world operate in the United States. Given its relatively small feeding operations, Canada may be unable to expand its trade into the U.S. market. If red meat prices were to increase significantly, a major improvement would take place in pasture management of public lands in the United States. This is not occurring now because of the low profitability of the North American beef industry.

One factor that could give an advantage to Canada is the existing exchange rate, which has enhanced Canadian agricultural exports to the

11. Dawson, Dan and Associates, "An Overview of Beef Market Opportunities in California, Washington, Oregon and Idaho," working paper, March 1982.

U.S. market. However, if the exchange rate should once again approach par, this would have a serious negative effect on beef exports to the United States. Another possible area of advantage for Canada may be in relative opportunity costs. Given the opportunities that exist for nonagricultural employment in such states as California, the level of profitability in beef production would have to be relatively high or producers will seek other employment and deemphasize the livestock industry. In many regions in Canada, nonagricultural employment does not offer as great an opportunity as in the United States and therefore Canadian production costs may well be lower.

Much of the current trade between the United States and Canada (excluding red meats) is in commodities that Canada cannot produce because of its climate. Fresh fruits and vegetables enter Canada from the United States in large volumes and will continue to do so in all likely circumstances.

A country's comparative advantage is determined not only by improved access to market. In addition, a "secure" access is needed.[12] This is what Canada desires in a Canadian-U.S. free trade agreement. However, in view of pressures for countervailing duty actions, the achievement of this security is certainly a challenge to negotiators.

Gains from Liberalized Agricultural Trade

Estimates of the effects of greater liberalized agricultural trade between the United States and Canada are provided in table 5. Positive effects are predicted for the Canadian beef and pork sector, canola, flax, rye, and mustard, pulses, and specialty crops. The chicken and turkey industry and the feed grain sector will lose, and there will be no effect on sheep raising or the wheat economy. The net gain from trade approximates $60 million a year by 1995. As pointed out, this figure includes anticipated increases in sales in the current trade environment plus the incremental impact of free trade. Sales increases in the current trade environment should have been netted out. In any case, the $60 million is an underestimate of the true gains, because consumer welfare changes were not calculated.

We question some of these results. As pointed out earlier, wheat will

12. Thorald K. Warley, "What Would Free Trade Mean to Agriculture," Ridgetown College of Agricultural Technology, January 1986.

Table 5. *Estimated Effects of Free Trade between Canada and the United States in 1995, Selected Agricultural Commodities in Prairie Provinces*
Receipts in millions of 1983 Canadian dollars

Commodity	Direction of effect[a]	Change in production by 1995 (percent)	1983 prairie farm cash receipts	Change in receipts by 1995
Beef[b]	+	12	1,690	200
Pork[b]	+	2	433	9
Sheep	0	0	9	0
Chicken and turkey	−	− 80	150	− 120
Wheat	0	0	4,118	0
Feed grains	−	− 6	906	− 53
Canola[b]	+	3	712	21
Flax	+	1	151	1
Rye	+	1	60	1
Mustard, pulses, and specialty crops	+	1	99	1
Total	+	1	8,328	60

Sources: Deloitte, Haskins, Sells and Associates, *Canadian Agricultural Trade Issues*, July 1985; Canada Grains Council, *Statistical Handbook '84;* and Alberta Agriculture.

a. From point of view of Canadian producers. Excludes impact on input and value-added (processing and distribution) industries.

b. Includes anticipated increase in sales in the current trade environment of 5 percent for beef, 2 percent for pork, and 2 percent for canola. The incremental impact of free trade is therefore 7 percent for beef, no change for pork, and 1 percent for canola.

be unaffected if controls remain on the importation of wheat from the United States and grain is not allowed to be shipped to foreign countries through the United States. In addition, if the Canadian Wheat Board remains intact in its present form, wheat would be unaffected. However, if wheat was allowed to flow freely between the United States and Canada, then the wheat sector would certainly be affected. In addition, we believe that there may be gains in the trade of feed grains and question whether the poultry industry would be negatively affected. It certainly would be in the short run, but because of economies of scale in production, in the long run the Canadian industry may well become rationalized enough to allow Canadian producers to compete with those in the United States. This would require increased concentration and regional specialization within Canada.

The U.S. Agricultural Economy

As a result of the 1985 farm bill, the U.S. grain sector currently receives substantially greater subsidies than does the Canadian grain sector. Because the United States lowered the loan rate in 1986, Canadian wheat prices will have to drop to allow Canada to compete in the world market. This raises the important question as to what role U.S. subsidies will play in a U.S.-Canadian free trade arrangement. For example, if these subsidies remain or are increased, Canadian grain producers are at a disadvantage because of the relative sizes of the government treasuries involved. It is conceivable that millers in Canada could purchase relatively cheap wheat from the United States, where production is highly subsidized. The current two-price system for Canadian wheat could not function under a U.S.-Canadian free trade agreement.

The U.S. dairy industry, like Canada's, is also highly subsidized, and so is U.S. livestock production, because a large percentage of ranching is done on public lands where grazing fees are extremely low. However, the U.S. egg and broiler industries' subsidies are relatively small.

In discussing the bilateral free trade issue, one should not lose sight of the potential gains to be had through cooperation in the international market, where the United States and Canada are now in competition. Perhaps the greatest payoff from freer agricultural trade in North America will come about through harmonized policies and increased cooperation in third-country markets. However, the 1985 U.S. farm bill has created an unprofitable situation for Canadian sales in world markets and has exacerbated the problem of policy harmonization. It appears that the costs to Canadian farmers of the farm bill exceed $1 billion a year, far outweighing any potential gains from freer Canadian-U.S. agricultural trade.

Conclusions

The foregoing should suggest that free trade in agricultural products between Canada and the United States will be extraordinarily difficult to negotiate. Both countries manage their agricultural industries through various forms of subsidies. In Canada, and to a lesser extent in the United States, the provincial and state authorities do some of the managing. To undo completely the numerous resulting impediments to the free flow of farm products across the Canadian-American border is not a realistic short-term objective. Beginnings may be possible in some sectors—perhaps in red meats and eggs and broilers—on the basis of carefully planned phase-in periods. Otherwise, the better part of wisdom would be to agree to keep agriculture on the negotiating table, after agreement on other matters, seeking to find openings for modifying and eventually eliminating the national or local policies that now hamper or prevent the bilateral exchange of agricultural goods.

Contributors

with their affiliation at the time of the conference

Margaret Biggs *North-South Institute, Ottawa*
Drusilla K. Brown *Tufts University*
David F. Burgess *University of Western Ontario*
Larry G. Butcher *U.S. Department of State*
Colin Carter *University of California–Berkeley*
Robert W. Crandall *Brookings Institution*
Melvyn Fuss *University of Toronto*
Richard Harris *Queen's University*
Michael M. Hart *Canadian Department of External Affairs*
Harold Hongju Koh *Yale University Law School*
Sperry Lea *National Planning Association*
Peter A. Petri *Brandeis University*
J. David Richardson *University of Wisconsin*
Andrew Schmitz *University of California–Berkeley*
Murray G. Smith *C. D. Howe Institute, Toronto*
Robert M. Stern *University of Michigan*
Philip H. Trezise *Brookings Institution*
Leonard Waverman *University of Toronto*
John Whalley *University of Western Ontario*
Randall Wigle *University of Western Ontario*
Martin Wolf *Trade Policy Research Centre, London*

Index

Agricultural Adjustment Act, 250
Agricultural sector, 33–34, 51; Canadian comparative advantage, 255–56; economies of scale, 254–55; free trade effects, 7, 256–57; governmental structure differences, 250–52; interprovincial trade regulation, 246–47, 249–51; market size, 252–54; United States, 257–58
Agriculture Canada, 246
Aho, C. Michael, 41n, 143
Alejandro, Carlos F. Diaz, 168n
Antidumping duties, 24, 36, 39, 41–45, 62, 63. *See also* Trade remedy laws
Armington model, 159–61, 169, 189
Armington, Paul S., 159–60
Aronson, Jonathan David, 143
ASEAN countries, 146
Automobile industry: Japanese, 223–25, 239; production in Canada, 22, 217, 221–22; U.S.-Canadian trade, 220–21
Automotive Products Trade Act of *1965,* 91
Automotive Products Trade Agreement of *1965,* 2, 8, 21–22; Canadian approval, 103–04; duty remission, 35–36, 218–19, 225–28; and free trade negotiations, 228–30; GATT compliance, 108, 110, 229; production effects, 221–22; provisions of, 218–20; trade effects, 220–21; U.S. approval, 90–91; value-added requirements, 35–36
Auto pact. *See* Automotive Products Trade Agreement of *1965*

Baldwin, John R., 204n
Baldwin, Robert E., 46n, 185
Bale, Harvey E., 46n
Barcelo, John J., 44n
Barichello, Richard, 254n

Barnett, Donald F., 233n, 235n
Batchelor, Roy, 66n
Beigie, Carl E., 217n, 222
Berglas, Eitan, 159n
Bernier, Ivan, 105n
Bilateral negotiations: agricultural issues, 7, 33–34, 51, 250–58; and automobile industry, 228–30; dispute settlement, 53–54; exchange rate issues, 37–38, 194; and foreign investment, 46–48; GATT compliance, 107–10, 142–43; history of, 1–5, 75; implementation of, 51–53, 95–98, 101–07; modeling of effects, 173–79; and multilateral system, 54–59, 141–44, 148–54; objectives of, 32, 59–60, 130–34; and steel industry, 240; termination procedure, 54; and third countries, 34–37, 43–44, 57–59, 134–35, 138–40, 145–48; trade effects, 134–35, 138; trade remedy laws, 38–45, 123–24, 192–95; trade in services, 48–50, 145, 194; transition arrangements, 50–51. *See also* Free trade areas
Bladen commission, 217–20
Bladen, V., 218n, 220n, 221
Boadway, Robin, 160n
Boothe, Paul, 37n
Brean, Donald J. S., 203
Breecher, Richard A., 168n
Broadcasting Act of *1934,* 47
Brown, Drusilla K., 169n

Camps, Miriam, 141, 144n
Canadian-American Committee (CAC), 11–21
Canadian Wheat Board, 250, 251, 257
Carbonneau, Thomas E., 54n
Carter, Colin, 250n
Cassidy, Robert C., Jr., 102n